UNDOING THE SOCIAL

UNDOING THE SOCIAL

TOWARDS A
DECONSTRUCTIVE SOCIOLOGY

Ann Game

UNIVERSITY OF TORONTO PRESS
Toronto   Buffalo

First published in North America in 1991 by
University of Toronto Press
Toronto and Buffalo

ISBN 0–8020–5970–8 (cloth)
ISBN 0–8020–6897–9 (paper)

Canadian Cataloguing in Publication Data

Game, Ann
Undoing the social
Includes bibliographical references and index.
ISBN 0–8020–5970–8 (bound)   ISBN 0–8020–6897–9 (pbk.)

1. Sociology – Philosophy.   2. Deconstruction.
I. Title.

HM24.G35   1991   301′.01   C91–093872–5

Printed in Great Britain

CONTENTS

LIST OF ILLUSTRATIONS

Front cover photograph: A. Zahalka, 'The Sunbather 1a', 1990

PREFACE

Deconstruction and sociology sit oddly together. That is the common perception, and with some justification. My project over the last few years, in both teaching and research, has been to engage, as a sociologist, with the tradition of thought that is referred to as 'contemporary French theory'. This has not been an altogether easy task. On the one hand, there is considerable hostility to and suspicion of French theory in sociology. On the other hand, I have been greeted by a certain puzzlement on the part of people in the humanities: Why bother with sociology? One answer to this question is that one cannot simply be free of disciplinary location. While the significance of this should not be underestimated, there is a more important issue at stake – that of disciplinary property. The central ideas in contemporary French theory – those of reading, writing and text – defy disciplinary appropriation. In this tradition of thought any object can be constituted as a text. By reconstituting what might be understood as sociological objects as texts, one of my concerns has been to contest the view, held on both sides of the social sciences – humanities divide, that deconstruction is appropriate to some objects of analysis (for example, philosophy, film and fiction) and not others. In this regard this project is one of interdisciplinarity. This is not a question of combining sociology and deconstruction, but rather of contributing to a dispersion of disciplinary boundaries. In short, the aim is to unsettle.

Sociology, as it is currently defined, is indeed incompatible with intellectual traditions informed by structural linguistics and psychoanalysis. It is a discipline that claims to know the whole of society, the extra-textual real, and deals in abstractions, the 'aim' of which are a combination of welfare and reform (helping others) and total change in the future. So, my question has been: What are the possibilities of a different sociology, a sociology concerned with the immediate, the lived of everyday life and experience, and with transformations in the now? Concerned, then, with a sociology of

human possibilities now, or moments of redemption in a world of commodification, this book takes up themes that have been excluded from the
discipline – desire, memory and time, and the body.

Contemporary French theory allows us to address these issues and rethink
the rather problematic question of experience. One of my principal concerns
has been to develop a materialist semiotics, that is, an understanding of
meaning processes as both temporal and embodied. This approach to
meaning breaks with distinctions between representation and the real, text
and context, theory and practice. Furthermore, the deconstructive 'concept'
of writing as transformation provides the opportunity to reformulate the
question of social change. Reading a text is a writing practice, and in this lies
the possibility of a rewriting of texts of the culture, in the now. A
deconstructive strategy is a positive strategy of transformation: undoing is
simultaneously an unmaking and a making, a process without end.

There is a connection between the interdisciplinary aspect of this project
and the question of experience. Sociologists claim to be concerned with the
empirical, but they rarely address the experience or practices of everyday life.
When they do, experience becomes the unmediated inversion of sociological
abstractions. Semioticians have tended to be wary of experience, emphasising
meaning in a critique of any notion of unmediated experience. Once
signification processes are understood in terms of practice, and any everyday
practice as a reading-writing or textual practice, it is possible to 'dissolve' the
distinction between meaning and experience. Hence the interest in a
materialist semiotics.

So, let me introduce this book through my own experience – by addressing
the image on the front cover. This photograph by Zahalka produces a chain
of associations that relate to the central themes in this book, but perhaps,
more pertinently, to my pleasures. For writing this book has been about
pleasures – disturbing pleasures.

This image combines two of my major pleasures: Bondi and photography.
Both of these have been central to the process of puzzling over meaning; in my
attempts to formulate a materialist semiotics I have constantly returned to the
experiences of looking at photographs and/or being on Bondi beach. If
photography is regarded as a proper object of semiotic analysis, Bondi, for all
that it is central in Australian popular culture, has received remarkably little
academic attention from any discipline. It would seem to have no place in the
disciplinary demarcation of objects.

So what are some of the associations of this photograph? Most obvious is
the experience of being on the beach, the pleasure of letting oneself drift,
immersed in sand, sea and sun. And, the colours, particularly the changing
blues of the sea, in relation to the sky. I have found the experience of being in
the sea – the fluidity and movement in the relation between the body and
the sea – very suggestive for ways of thinking about meaning processes,
and the connections between meaning and the senses. Furthermore, this
raises the question of our relation to nature and provokes a rethinking of the

oppositional relation between culture and nature. What is this desire to be immersed in, to give over to, nature? This is to ask the question posed by French feminists: Is this a desire to return to origins, or might we discern something of another desire, a desire that gives the prerogative to the other, a desire without end or goal – in short, a desire not structured around binary opposition?

The subject of this photograph is also drifting in and out of reading. Are there ways of reading and writing that are akin to being in the water? What, then, might we understand by the idea of 'writing the body' and how does this differ from Western conceptions of knowledge processes?

And, what is it that is being read? Proust, *Remembrance of Things Past*: possibly the most famous text of memory and experience, or the remembering body. The beach and photography are both 'about' memory. Some of the strongest childhood memories are of the beach (freedom from school, summer holidays), and every new experience at the beach invokes these memories. In this photograph there is an association with my childhood with references to the 1950s: the bathing costume, and particularly the bathing cap with flowers on it – the sort of cap worn by my mother when I was a child. But as with looking at personal photographs, there is an 'almost' in the desire to relive the past of beach experiences. The sound or the smell of the sea produces an affect, but also makes us aware that the past cannot be relived as a presence in the present. It 'lives', however, through memory embodied: the affect. This photograph allows for nostalgic desire, but it also opens up the possibility of thinking about memory and the past in other ways. Might it be the case that memory does not take us back so much as move us forward?

The subject of this photograph is both solitary and a subject of memory. This bears on one of the central themes of this book – that of sociality, or the 'always' relational of the subject and meaning. That there is no originary wholeness or singularity of the subject is constantly attested to by the effects of memory – the workings of the unconscious. Memory 'reminds' us that the so-called 'present' self is defined in relation to the past of the self, and that the present is marked by the traces of the past – past and present (and future) cannot be held apart. If memory is personal and particular, it is also necessarily cultural, constituted in and through sociality – in relation to an other.

One of the most significant issues to have emerged out of French feminism is that of different structures of desire, or relations between self and other. To think of sociality, and knowledge, as a matter of desire is in itself a departure from traditional sociological conceptions of the social. As part of a project of undoing the social I take up the idea that the social world might be thought of as comprised of a multiplicity of orders, different ways of meaning that inscribe and are inscribed in different structures of desire.

A methodology of multiplicity is applied in analyses of social texts. This involves the idea that any 'object' can be understood as meaning in different ways: if there is a singular order of quantification and sameness, is there not also a multiple order of qualitative difference? This in turn bears directly on the issue of transformation in the now.

The texts I have chosen for analysis are close to me, have moved me. This strikes me as preferable to any hierarchisation in worthiness of objects; and it guards against the dangers of representing others. Furthermore, it provokes the self-critical question: What desire is implicated in our research-writing?

Zahalka's photograph invites a rewriting: I can tell my story, other people would tell different stories. In every reading practice the photograph is also rewritten. This is to raise one of the central questions in contemporary French and cultural theory, that of the openness of texts. I come from a discipline which is characteristically closed in form of address; it defines itself as a science. Coming from a background in Marxist feminism, one of my major obstacles has been overcoming this form of address. It is not simply a matter of presenting a critique of science and knowledge, but rather of practising such a critique, in the writing. The following quotation from Barnes's *A History Of The World in 10½ Chapters* encapsulates something of the principle of writing that I aspire to:

> All novelists know their art proceeds by indirection. When tempted by didacticism, the writer should imagine a spruce sea-captain eyeing the storm ahead, bustling from instrument to instrument in a catherine wheel of gold braid, expelling crisp orders down the speaking tube. But there is nobody below decks; the engine-room was never installed, and the rudder broke off centuries ago. The captain may put on a very good act, convincing not just himself but even some of the passengers; though whether their floating world will come through depends not on him but on the mad winds and the sullen tides, the icebergs and the sudden crusts of reef. (Barnes 1989: 227)

This could be applied to any writing practice; to constitute 'objects' as texts is to break with a distinction between fact and fiction. Metaphor is real, and the real is metaphor; and living by the sea – so prevalent as a metaphor for writing the body – has brought this 'home' to me. There is no deep real (or engine-room) below the surface; there is no extra-textual ground for social analysis to cling on to. We, like writers of 'fiction', are at sea.

ACKNOWLEDGEMENTS

I would like to acknowledge the following people for discussion of ideas, comments on my work and parts of this book in draft, and for providing a convivial intellectual environment: David Frisby, Annette Hamilton, Vicki Kirby, Ian Lennie, Paul Patton, Ross Poole and Lesley Stern. I am particularly indebted to Genevieve Lloyd and John von Sturmer for their enthusiasm and encouragement throughout the project, and for their critical readings of drafts of the book. And I would like to thank Annette Kuhn for her support, for an exchange of ideas on photography, and for the research jointly undertaken with her on English heritage. The section in Chapter 7 on English heritage draws on this joint research.

Many friends and colleagues have been supportive over the last few years. Those who have offered various forms of assistance and support for this project include: Ann Daniel, Tim Game, Anna Gibbs, Reg Graycar, Jennifer Kitchener, John Milfull, Lesley Ruda and Bernice Ryan. I would especially like to thank Anne Zahalka for inviting me to write an essay in the catalogue of her Bondi exhibition 'Playground of the Pacific' (December 1989), and for her reworking of one of the images from the exhibition for the front cover of this book.

The section in Chapter 6 on bosses and secretaries comes out of a research project jointly undertaken with Rosemary Pringle, conducted over a three-year period, and funded by the Australian Research Grant Scheme. See R. Pringle, *Secretaries Talk: Sexuality, Power and Work*, Sydney, Allen & Unwin (1988). Research on Bondi, photography and English heritage was supported by the Special Research Grant, University of New South Wales. I also received some funding assistance from the Faculty of Arts, University of New South Wales, in order to write this book during a six-month period of leave without pay in 1989. During the autumn term of 1989, I was a visiting fellow in the Department of Sociology at Glasgow University. I am grateful for the opportunity of presenting work in progress papers at the following universities: Bradford, Edinburgh, Essex, Exeter, Glasgow, London (Centre for Australian Studies), New South Wales, and Strathclyde. And I would like to thank the students of 'Power and Desire' at the University of New South Wales, for their engagement with many of the ideas in this book.

Earlier versions of sections of Chapters 6 and 7 have been published as 'Research and Writing: "Secretaries and Bosses" ', *Journal of Pragmatics*, vol. 13 (1989); 'Death and Desire in *Camera Lucida*', *Photofile*, vol. 6, no. 2 (1988); 'Sense of Place: Bondi' in A. Zahalka, *Bondi: Playground of the Pacific*, Bondi Pavilion Community Centre, Sydney (1989); 'Nation and Identity: Bondi', *New Formations*, no. 11 (1990).

Permission to reproduce images has been granted by the following: the Mitchell Library, State Library of New South Wales, for all old photographs of Bondi; Max Dupain for 'Sunbaker'; Oliver Strewe/Wildlight for 'front cover, *Bondi*'; and the estate of Percy Trompf for 'Trompf: travel poster'.

PART 1

DECONSTRUCTING SOCIOLOGY?

1

SOCIOLOGICAL
FICTIONS

Why does it disturb us that the map be included in the map and the
thousand and one nights in the book of the *Thousand and One Nights*?
Why does it disturb us that Don Quixote be a reader of the *Quixote* and
Hamlet a spectator of *Hamlet*? I believe I have found a reason: these
inversions suggest that if the characters of a fictional work can be readers or spectators, we, its readers or spectators, can be fictitious. In 1833,
Carlyle observed that the history of the universe is an infinite sacred
book that all men write and read and try to understand, and in which
they are also written.

(Borges 1970: 231)

The idea that reality is fictitious and that fiction is real does not find favour
with sociologists. A quotation from Borges would be dismissed unless it
could be demonstrated to be theory, not fiction. For sociologists deal with
facts – social reality, the empirical – and theory, and the correspondence
between these. Sociological practice is conceived of as representation of the
real, which for this discipline is constituted as the social. And there is
nothing fictitious about the social or the sociological representation of it.
Thus, the discipline is defined through the oppositions, fact–fiction and
theory–fiction; and, with the negation of fiction, the dualism, fact and
theory, remains. Social reality is taken as determinant; theory is a reflection.
But, this reflection is privileged as adequate correspondence to social reality,
as opposed to fictional reflection. When the latter is taken as an object (in
the sociology of literature, for example), the concern is with reflection. The
sociology of literature, which in general favours social realism, represents
the relation between social reality and fictional reflection. This book is concerned with the possibility of a different sociology. It argues for a form of
analysis understood as a reading and writing of texts, that breaks with the
reality–fiction opposition.

There is, in this, an implicit critique of sociology as it is currently
constituted, but the project is not a negative one of argument against the
discipline so much as a demonstration of what the ideas of reading, writing
and text might contribute to social and cultural analysis. My concern is to

identify themes that have been neglected in sociology as a consequence of the prevailing disciplinary models; themes such as desire, subjectivity, the senses, time and the body. This is understood as a positive project of developing a different approach to social analysis, one informed by contemporary French theory. If anything of sociological discourse is being 'rejected', it is the notion of refutation: a mode of argument that is negative, and is based on an understanding of theory as correspondence.

To take up ideas associated with contemporary French philosophy and theory is, for a sociologist, an interdisciplinary move. In the humanities, an encounter with 'French theory' and French feminism has had considerable impact – in literary theory, cultural and film theory, and philosophy – and has produced both disciplinary shifts and radical reformulations in feminist questions. But despite a rhetoric of interdisciplinarity, particularly among feminists, the social sciences have remained impervious, if not hostile (Giddens, 1987: 73–108); and feminist sociologists have continued to work within the discursive constraints of the discipline. The concern here is with the implications of a critical practice informed by French theory for the social sciences; or, to put this another way, a *deconstructive sociology* which implies also a *deconstruction* of sociology. Interdisciplinarity is not understood, then, as a matter of taking insights from other areas in order to produce a better or more complete sociology – a colonising and appropriating activity to which sociologists have been all too prone. The issue is rather one of dispersion of disciplines through a questioning of the rules and closures that provide the basis of claims to the status of truth or science. In short, this is an exercise of 'opening up', of putting new questions on the agenda. As Barthes (1986: 73) puts it, interdisciplinarity is not a matter of arranging several sciences around a theme; it consists in creating a new object which 'belongs to no one'. The 'Text' is such an object.

The distinction between the social sciences and the humanities assumes a distinction between social reality and representation. One of the central contentions of this book is that 'writing' and 'text' open up the possibility of dissolving this distinction. It is frequently assumed that deconstructive strategies are applicable specifically to literary and philosophical texts. This reinvents the real–representation distinction, albeit reformulated as a context–text distinction. Texts and language are somehow less real than social reality which remains as extra-discursive context, and properly the object of a different analytic approach (Jameson 1981: 35).[1] As a means of moving beyond the impasse of these distinctions this book starts with the basic semiotic assumption that culture or the social is written, that there is no extra-discursive real outside cultural systems. In this view the social world does not consist of ready-made objects that are put into representation. And the converse of this claim is that texts are real. As Weber (1987: 152) has said of the possibility of a transgressive redefinition of interdisciplinarity, this will depend on the capacity 'to admit and accept the fictionality of what it assumes to be real, as well as the reality of its fictions'. Weber's remarks are addressed to the humanities, the study of literature, 'fiction'; they could just as well be addressed to the social sciences, the study of the 'real'.

In a paper to a different literary audience from Weber's, a Marxist one, Frow (1983: 230) made the suggestion that

> a *semiotic* understanding of history and of the social formation opens up precisely the opportunity that marxist literary theory needs: . . . to be able to extend its practices to other forms of discourse and to the 'extra-literary' realm itself.

His proposal was that forms of analysis that had been developed in literary theory be extended to an analysis of 'discourses in which the "real" is constructed' (Frow 1983: 230). To constitute objects of analysis as discourses of the real, or as social texts, is to 'change the object' (Barthes 1977: 165–9). This involves a dispersion of the reified object 'social reality', the givenness of the social and/or history, and a dislodging of their status as referent or, as Frow (1983: 229) put it so nicely, 'the safety rail' that contemporary Marxists cling to with a 'misapplication of materialism'. This approach eschews attempts to fix an object or find the signified, thus displacing the sociological question: 'What is the social?' (Runciman 1983: 19–20).

Once the social is thought in terms of textual production the question becomes: 'How does this particular social text mean?' Analysis is concerned with 'the how' of meaning rather than 'what is' questions that demand *a* meaning or signified. It is not that the social is in a different register from the literary (for example, the material) or that it is the context of the text. Both 'the social' and 'the literary' are practices with specific principles of meaning. Furthermore, textual analysis is not understood as representation, but as itself a writing or discursive practice. This radically departs from the conception of knowledge as correspondence, in this case correspondence between sociology and the social. And, most importantly, it draws critical attention to sociology as a discursive practice in which 'the real' or 'the social' is produced: sociological fictions.

The ideas that the social is written and that sociology is a writing, present a disturbance to the discursive rules of the discipline of sociology. They cannot be accommodated within the frame of sociological self-definition. Thus a common charge is that semiotics is idealist as opposed to the materialism of Marxist sociology: an argument that is made with reference to 'the safety rail' of the real – history, mode of production, class society, and so on. The discursive production of such concepts themselves is thus not addressed. Reflexive issues invited by intellectual traditions concerned with productions of meaning are all too easily closed off by rejections of those traditions as not sociological. Giddens (1987: 73), for example, has no qualms about pronouncing, in an opening sentence, that 'Structuralism, and post-structuralism also, are dead traditions of thought.' This claim is based on an argument that structuralist assumptions are incompatible with *his* sociological theory and account of what the discipline is. While this is indeed the case, what is of particular interest is the strategy of closure and boundary defining, rather than any openness to the possibility of a different sociology through a sympathetic engagement with these theories. What is at stake here, what threatens to disturb, what impels sociologists to reject French theory when they address it at all?[2] This is a question that has motivated this book. Here, some propositions will be put forward about what is disturbing in the idea that cultural processes, including knowledge processes, be understood as textual productions. In a sense, this is to ask Borges's question: What is disturbing about the inclusion of the map in the map?

Looking for a clue in Borges, here is an imagined sociological response to the above quotation: the proposition that history is a text is to be rejected because the implication that we are written by texts is not acceptable. That 'all men write and read' the text of history would be elided. It might be presumed that the idea that 'all men write and read' would not be perceived as incompatible with that of agency, a favourite term among sociologists. But, it is precisely on these grounds that Giddens (1987: 94–5) argues against 'post-structuralist' conceptions of writing and text: they do not take adequate account of 'human agency'. As Giddens (1987: 89) acknowledges, the issue here is how the subject is conceptualised; he prefers to understand the subject as characterised by consciousness, rejecting a notion of a split between the conscious and the unconscious. The idea that we write and read culture *is* incompatible with the sociological conception of human agency; they are based on fundamentally different assumptions about the subject and meaning. One of the concerns of this book is to argue for the significance of the concept of the unconscious to an understanding of cultural processes. And, indeed, I will argue for the importance of questions of subjectivity, sociality, and the particular – all of which, if somewhat paradoxically, I would suggest are evaded with an emphasis on consciousness. But let me pursue this question of agency for a moment. Why does it have such prominence in sociology, and what is so objectionable about the idea that we are written?

When sociologists speak of agency they usually refer to the agency of 'oppressed groups' – the working class, women, and so on. But what I want to propose here is that the agency in question is *their* agency, the status of the subject of sociological knowledge. By focusing on the agency of the oppressed, critical reflection on the desire for agency is evaded. Giddens's emphasis on consciousness hints at this desire, for consciousness is above all about the knowing subject. In the course of this book I will argue that 'oppressed groups' are the other which are constituted as objects of knowledge, in order to effect a return to self, the subject of sociological knowledge. However, the operations of this knowledge process are hidden, or repressed, in the claim to be concerned with the real of the social. For what is indeed at stake is 'our' writing culture or the social. Thus I want to propose that the question of agency be reformulated as a question of mastery: that sociologists hang on to a will to knowledge which is a 'symptom of the desire to have a self and a world' (Spivak 1988: 105). The fantasy of mastery is directly related to the fantasy of the possibility of representation; it is to presuppose that it is possible for a subject of knowledge, a consciousness, to have direct access to a world which is given, to know and to represent an object. And, in this knowing, the self is constituted. The inclusion of the map within the map unsettles this approach to knowledge, raising as it does critical questions about self-representation – issues of reflexivity.

The idea that culture is written shifts the ground of representation: there is no pre-cultural real to be represented in knowledge. If this dislodges the object of knowledge as that which can be known, or the truth of which can be found, it also displaces the subject of knowledge. Thus, my project of undoing 'the social', the object of sociological knowledge, is simultaneously one of undoing the subject of sociological knowledge. This is a reflexive move: whereas the identity, sociology and the social, forecloses on the question of reflexivity, textual production provokes the question of the ways in which 'we' are implicated in knowledge processes, in the writing of culture. It is to be argued that this turns on the issue of desire in knowledge. The reference here is to Hegel, whose story of power and desire in knowledge informs much of this project.

In making this reference to Hegel it is clear that issues being addressed are by no means peculiar to sociology – they relate to Western conceptions of knowledge. But it is important to specify the particular forms these take in different disciplines; and, sociology is my institutional location. This is not simply 'context' that I could be free of; it defines where I write from, and the point of departure of an interdisciplinary strategy (Weber 1987: 19). But the critical strategy to be employed here differs fundamentally from what is generally understood as critique in the discipline of sociology. In sociological discourse critique is framed in terms of adequation: 'this is a better theory'. Theory and the real are regarded as distinct; theoretical disputes turn on correspondence. To quote Giddens (1987: 31) again as representative of this approach: 'theories can always be in some degree evaluated in terms of observations generated by empirical research'. Theories, understood as models, are modified or refuted in the light of the empirical; there is a demand for a coherence with respect to the real of the social world.

To break with the fact–theory opposition has important implications for an understanding of theorising. If we take theorising to be a writing practice, theory cannot be seen to operate as a model to be tested for adequacy to the real, and there can be no appeal to the real in refutations of theories. Thus one of the principal concerns of a critical strategy is to bring to light the discursive operations through which a knowledge or discipline maintains its claims to coherence and the status of knowledge; in the case of sociology, a privileged representation of social reality. Some of these have been hinted at: the repression of fiction, and the materialism–idealism, real–representation dualisms. In bringing the repressed of discourse, and discursive exclusions, to light, the concern is not to refute sociological theory. Rather, this is a project of shifting the rules, a move in the spirit of deconstruction which is taken to be a strategy of transformation.

More will soon be said about critical strategy; here I want to indicate how theoretical texts figure in this book, and what this contributes to interdisciplinarity. My analytic strategy will consist in reading theoretical or philosophical texts with social texts. This is understood as a knowledge practice that consists in putting texts into dialogue. To constitute both 'theory' and 'the social' as text implies a practice of transformation which radically differs from an understanding of theorising as translation. In a textual production that aspires to neither translation nor representation, both philosophical and social texts are rewritten. Analyses of specific social texts make no claims to being the best or correct reading; on the contrary, one of the central concerns here is to develop a form of analysis that invites further rewritings. Addressing texts that would be classified as philosophy, not social theory, is in itself an interdisciplinary move, raising as it does questions about disciplinary definitions. But, coming from sociology, I do not read philosophy as philosophers do, that is, primarily in relation to other philosophical texts. Thus, the concern is not only with how the object 'the social' might be changed, but also with a rereading of philosophy in relation to texts of the social.

It seems appropriate, then, to say something about philosophers who inform this project. Here I shall give brief accounts of the ways in which three of these – Hegel, Bergson and Irigaray – are relevant to my concerns. Why Hegel? The short answer is that this project is concerned with questions of knowledge. Hegel's master–slave story tells us a lot about power and desire in knowledge processes and, importantly, the failure of the will to knowledge, the undoing of mastery. Furthermore, he provides an account of the operations of power in knowledge by which we can understand the effects of *his* philosophy in both philosophical discourse and, I will argue, other discursive practices.

There are four Hegelian assumptions that are relevant here. The first is that knowledge is necessarily inter-subjective, involving self–other relations. The second is that knowledge is a matter of desire rather than disinterested cognition. Both of these assumptions stand in opposition to the Cartesian approach to knowledge as a speculative activity on the part of a unitary subject. For Hegel, knowledge is dependent on sociality and thus is neither pre-social nor outside the social. The third relevant assumption is that the inter-subjective of knowledge is a relation of power; desire is structured around power. In Hegel, power and knowledge are inextricably linked through desire. The fourth is that knowledge is dialectical: in a process of negation and supersession mastery fails, only to reproduce again endlessly the desire for mastery. This is crucial to an understanding of knowledge processes: the acknowledgement of both the desire for mastery and resolution, and the impossibility of any such resolution. The simultaneous fantasy and failure of mastery, which is the very movement of the dialectic, has important implications for a project of undoing.

This is related to the feminist question asked of Hegel: What is the connection between mastery and masculinity, and where is the feminine in all this? What is at issue for feminists working in the tradition of contemporary French philosophy is the Hegelian structure of desire and the self–other relation constituted in, and constitutive of, this desire. Different conceptions of knowledge and meaning are based on a radically different structure of desire and relation to the other. These issues are central to this book, and, it will be argued, provide not only a starting point for critiques of knowledge but also a basis for opening up terms of thinking 'the social'. The key idea that I 'take' from Hegel is the concept of desire, a concept that has been neglected in social analysis.

Theorists such as Bataille, Derrida and Cixous have made the claim quite forcefully that 'Hegel is right', 'Hegel is real'. This idea will be taken up as part of a project of shifting the boundary between sociology and philosophy and questioning the real–representation distinction. These two aspects of the project are directly connected, as, from a sociological point of view at least, sociology deals with the real, while philosophy deals with representations. To claim that 'Hegel is real' presents a challenge to these divisions and the implied status of theory or philosophy as representation. Discourse *is* practice; it is not in a relation of exteriority with respect to the material. Philosophy, then, is no more or less real than 'the real' with which it has been contrasted. This is to make a stronger claim than to say that the influence of Hegel is apparent in contemporary philosophy, which is, none the less, also the case. Philosophy is not simply commentary on, or a mirror of, the real world; it is constitutive of it. This is to reiterate the Foucaultian argument that knowledge is discursive *practice*, and that all practices are productive of and produced in networks of power and knowledge.[3]

As a sociologist I have been struck by Cixous' (1986: 78) statement that Hegel 'is commonly at work in our everyday banality'. Hegel is not only at work in philosophical discourse but also in the domains of social life that sociologists might take as their object. In this book the workings of Hegel will be considered both in knowledge practices, specifically sociological discourse, and in texts and discourses of the everyday. Cixous' statement suggests that the same principles can be discerned in both domains of practice. This bears on my concern to demonstrate that knowledge is not something distinct from or qualitatively different from 'the real world'.

Hegel is excluded from sociology which commonly defines itself against him; the origins of the discipline are located after Hegel. Sociologists tend to dismiss Hegel as idealist and, unlike Marx, not adequate to an account of modern society. The issue of sociology's self-definition will be addressed elsewhere. Here, I wish to raise the question of how this exclusion relates to 'the disturbing'. It might seem surprising that sociologists do not pick up on Hegel's accounts of either the sociality of knowledge or power relations. But I suspect that the clue to this is desire; the omission of Hegel points to a reluctance to acknowledge the significance of desire in knowledge. For if indeed, as Hegel claims, knowledge is a matter of desire, the question can be asked: What is the itinerary of desire in my knowledge, and in the choice of my objects of study? Who is the other to whom desire is addressed, and how is this other constituted in relation to (one)self?

In this regard Derrida's (1978: 251–77) comments on those who dismiss Hegel seem pertinent. Emphasising that deconstruction is not destruction, that systems of thought cannot be abolished or simply replaced with others, he claims that projects that pronounce the end of the dialectic are themselves caught in a Hegelian mode of negation and supersession. Of those who shrug their shoulders at Hegel, and bear his self-evidence lightly, perhaps because it would be 'too heavy to bear', Derrida (1978: 251) says 'this puts one, without seeing or knowing it, within the very self-evidence of Hegel one often thinks oneself unburdened of'. This could be said, for example, of sociologists' rejections of Hegel for his idealism – based, perhaps, on the very same assumptions about knowledge that they/we imagine themselves/ourselves free of.

The French philosopher, Bergson, writing around the turn of the century, provided a basis for moving beyond the dualisms of idealism and material-ism, representation and the real. In connection with my project, it is the critique of the idea of representation, running through all of Bergson's writings, that is of particular significance. This critique is most fully developed in his theory of time – for which Bergson is best known. The chapter on 'Time' in this book focuses on Bergson; here I will introduce some of the basic premises in his philosophy that relate to the question of representation. This turns on his conception of image, which is to be distinguished from representation: while representation is an epiphenomenal correspondence to the real (sameness), image is embodied, and the principle of relations between and within body-images is one of differentiation.

One of Bergson's principal concerns is to 'dissolve' the philosophical question of spirit and matter, mind and body. In his view both realists and idealists pose badly stated questions that are insoluble. An impasse comes of an assumption they hold in common, namely that there is a qualitative difference between consciousness and the world or spirit and matter. Both end up privileging consciousness as that which knows matter; the debate is over determination, or what comes first: mind or matter. The problem for both sides is one of correspondence, getting the different substances to correspond in knowledge. Realists hypothesise an epiphenomenal conscious-ness which they simultaneously privilege and 'pretend to attach no import-ance to', making 'perception an accident'. Idealists 'begin by excluding the order of nature', but then have to 'assume some pre-established harmony between things and mind' (Bergson 1950b: 15–16); 'To ask whether the universe exists only in our thought or outside of our thought is to put the problem in terms that are insoluble' (Bergson 1950b: 13). Bergson (1950b: 13) proposes a common ground: since it would be agreed that 'we can only grasp things in the form of images, we must state the problem in terms of images, and of images alone'. For Bergson what is 'given' is that the world is comprised of bodies, and that these bodies are in motion, that they are centres of action. (This idea of centres of action should not be read as a conception of the subject as centred; in fact, Bergson presents a disarming critique of such a notion.) As we only grasp the world in images, however, we must think of the material world in terms of images acting on each other: 'to say that the body is matter or that it is image is of no importance' (Bergson 1950b: 5). And, 'I call matter the aggregate of images and perception of matter these same images referred to the eventual action of one particular image, my body' (Bergson 1950b: 8). It is important to note that perception is about action as opposed to speculative activity, and, furthermore, that in the aggregate of the material world, 'my body' is an 'image which acts like other images, receiving and giving back movement' (Bergson 1950b: 4). This suggests the possibility of changing one's bodily image through practice and action, and indeed that it can be changed only through such processes, rather than changes of consciousness.

All objects have a bodily form, and, contrary to the usual privileging of consciousness, bodies – the human body included – are sites of action, influencing each other in movement. Perception is not qualitatively different from image-body; it is these images, *referred*. Action rather than consciousness characterises bodies: 'my body is a centre of action, it cannot give birth to representation' (Bergson 1950b: 5). The subject lives the material world; it is of that world and produced by it. We are not the source of meaning or representation, but in the movement of relations between bodies change is always possible.

This stands as a radical critique of the philosophy of consciousness. And, in claiming that bodies are both matter and image, Bergson 'dissolves', as he constantly puts it, the distinction between representation and the real. Spirit and matter are both real. Bergson (1913: 261) claims that to start with a conception of the world as comprised of body-images acting on each other in movement is a radical departure from the common conception of the world as comprised of ready made things and a thing which creates: 'There are no things, there are only actions'. At a later point I shall draw out the significance of this for an understanding of the subject and of meaning processes, and point to a convergence with Foucault's account of power and the subject. Here it should be noted that the idea of moving bodies acting on bodies informs all of Bergson's arguments. It will be argued that his philosophy of the body contributes to the development of a materialist semiotics, that is, an understanding of meaning processes as embodied.

What are the implications of Bergson for questions that have been raised about sociological discourse? Marxist sociologists are adamant about materialism, and on this issue I agree with Frow that it is a misapplication of materialism. The material referent functions to establish a truth and certainty in the face of alternative accounts of the social (Frow 1983: 229). A particular consciousness is privileged – that which has access to the truth of materiality, the real. Thus materialist sociologists are caught in the contradiction referred to by Bergson: the determination by the material and the privileging of consciousness. This in turn presents insoluble epistemological problems: How do we know that this consciousness has the truth of the matter? Bergson's philosophy moves beyond such problems, and, as he says, has implications for a theory of knowledge in general. 'The material world' is made up of body-images which act and react on each other by movements, and the '*actuality* of our perception . . . lies in its *activity*' (Bergson 1950b: 74). He is counterposing this conception of perception to theories of knowledge which regard perception as a kind of contemplation, a speculative activity, and claim to 'seek some strange disinterested knowledge' (Bergson 1950b: 74). While most sociologists would not claim that their knowledge is disinterested, none the less they make truth claims about it (indeed for Marxist sociologists, truth is partisan), and they assume that it is a contemplative process. Bergson (1950b: 74) argues that to separate perception from action is to render it inexplicable and useless.

The emphasis on knowledge processes as actions, as part of 'the real' (Bergson 1950b: 74, 17–21) is precisely the point that Cixous makes about the 'reality' of Hegel. And it suggests the possibility of reformulating the sociological problem of agency/structure. Agency figures prominently in sociological accounts of change; it is the other side to structure, the materiality of the social world that is to be changed by the human subject. In this approach agency is a characteristic of a consciousness adequate to the social world, and which thus puts change into motion. Sociologists spend a good deal of time arguing their way out of the dualisms involved in this: consciousness–action, theory–practice and the subject and the social. These stem from a conception of knowledge as correspondence between consciousness and the real. In refusing a distinction between speculative contemplation and the world, Bergson breaks with these dualisms. For him there is no opposition between theory and practice; knowledge is action, like other actions; perception is not qualitatively different from image-matter. And the converse of this is that movement and action are properties of bodies, they do not result from perception. His understanding of theory as practice is based on the assumption that the world is comprised of bodies. In sociological accounts of the material and practice, the body is curiously absent (Corrigan 1988). Perhaps this suppression is necessitated in order to maintain a conception of agency as consciousness. If the body of the knowing subject is acknowledged the status of sociological consciousness is unsettled.

Bergson's philosophy can be read as a critique of what Derrida calls the metaphysics of presence, the idea that an element can have a meaning in and of itself, and can be present to a knowing subject. But his work has a significance beyond this for developing an understanding of signifying processes as transformation. In particular, it will be argued that his theory of time and the body contributes to the development of what is possibly the central concern in cultural and feminist theory – an understanding of textual transformation as writing the body.

I shall now return to the question of a critical strategy, with particular reference to the French feminist, Irigaray. The strategy, employed by French feminists, of rereading and rewriting discourses of Western culture, also breaks with a distinction between theory and practice. This strategy implies a very different conception of 'theory' from that which informs much Anglo-American feminism. In the latter tradition, which includes feminist sociology, theory is understood in terms of adequation and explanation of the extra-discursive real, of 'women', gender relations or patriarchy. The feminist project is one of developing a feminist theory which has an end, a purpose; an adequate theory can be put into practice to change gender relations. Theory informs practice, which is in the real. When Irigaray (1985a: 170–98) addresses discourses of the social order she is starting from the assumption that there is nothing outside cultural systems; thus, these discourses *are* the social order. A critical strategy of rewriting such discourses is potentially disruptive of the order; critical practice consists in constituting the social order differently, changing it. Irigaray (1985a: 78) claims that her project is one of 'jamming the theoretical machinery'; Cixous (1986: 96) says the issue is one of 'jamming sociality', which is a reference to Hegel's subject–object relation. They are making the same point: 'sociality' and 'theoretical machinery' are not two sides of a dualism; both refer to the discursive which is real.

French feminism has been the major influence in the development of feminist critical strategy, a strategy, however, that has been taken up predominantly in the area of literary theory (Sheridan 1988: 5–6; Jacobus 1986). I will give an account here of Irigaray's deconstructive strategy, with reference to an essay in which she provides just such an account – 'The Power of Discourse and the Subordination of the Feminine' (Irigaray 1985a: 68–85).

As the title of the essay suggests, Irigaray is concerned with the connection between power and knowledge, 'the power of discourse', and with how this is dependent upon and produces 'the subordination of the feminine'. Her project is one of disrupting the philosophical order of discourse and conceptions of knowledge in the Western philosophical tradition by demonstrating how this order is dependent on the subordination of the feminine. It is in this sense that her deconstructive strategy is feminist: what accounts for 'the power' of the 'systematicity' of philosophical discourse, 'the force of its cohesion', is the repression of the feminine (Irigaray 1985a: 74). She speaks (Irigaray 1985a: 74) of

the necessity of 'reopening' the figures of philosophical discourse – idea, substance, subject, transcendental subjectivity, absolute knowledge – in order to pry out of them what they borrowed that is feminine, from the feminine, to make them 'render up' and give back what they owe the feminine.

The power of systematicity, which she also refers to as a 'position of mastery', is a power to 'reduce all others to the economy of the Same'. This reduction of the other and difference to sameness, which is characteristic of the 'philosophic logos', stems from the 'power to eradicate the difference between the sexes in systems that are self-representative of a "masculine subject" ' (Irigaray 1985a: 74). It is important to note the connection that French feminists have made between logocentrism (dominance of the word in a conception of knowledge that involves truth based on presence), and phallocentrism (self-sameness and presence of a masculine subject or privileging the phallus). Hence the term 'phallologocentric', which refers to conceptions of truth as consisting in self-presence, or the unmediated knowledge of self, of a masculine subject. The connections between truth and the masculine are by no means self-evident, as formulations such as 'all knowledge is male' suggest. It is also important to emphasise this in the light of a tendency to appropriate the term 'phallologocentrism' as a feminist given. Irigaray is insistent on rigorous readings of specific texts to bring to light the ways in which the repression of the feminine is effected in particular discourses, and how the conditions of systematicity are concealed.

Irigaray (1985a: 68) claims that what is important is to 'disconcert the staging of representation according to exclusively "masculine" parameters, that is according to a phallocratic order.' She says: 'It is not a matter of top-pling that order so as to replace it – that amounts to the same thing in the end – but of disrupting and modifying it.' This is an argument against a simple reversal that would leave the structure intact, but can also be read more generally as a statement of an approach that differs radically from Anglo-American feminism and feminist social science. The latter can be seen as concerned to free truth from power. The assumptions in this are, first, that such a separation is possible; second, that the production of a feminist knowledge is desirable; and third, that the conditions of production are freedom from patriarchal power and knowledge. For Irigaray any project involving a feminist knowledge or theory amounts to the same, it would consist in a reversal, putting the feminine in the structural position of the masculine. This would change neither the structure of knowledge nor the sexual underpinnings of knowledge: the dependence of the positive valu-ation of the dominant term on the negation of the subordinate term, the feminine.

In other words, the issue is not one of elaborating a new theory of which woman would be the *subject* or the *object*, but of jamming the theoretical machinery itself, of suspending its pretensions to the

production of a truth and of a meaning that are excessively univocal
(Irigaray 1985a: 78)

Thus it is not a matter of women's aspiring to be men's equals in knowledge:
to take up the position of subject of knowledge.

The other side of this is a refusal of the question: 'What is woman?' Rather
the issue is one of interpreting 'the way in which, within discourse, the
feminine finds itself defined as lack, deficiency' (Irigaray 1985a: 78). When
Irigaray (1985a: 68) speaks of disruption from an 'outside', she does so in the
context of the assumption that we are constituted in language, and hence that
we have to work on language. The outside is so by virtue of repressions, and
thus not outside the operations of discourse, even if not 'in discourse'. The
'outside' implicit in the idea of being free of power comes from a failure to
recognise the significance of the constitution of the subject in meaning
systems. Proposals for a new subject, 'woman', are based on the assumption
that a self, woman, might be liberated if free of the constraints of patriarchal
power. For Irigaray masculine and feminine are discursive; knowledge is
based on a sexual hierarchisation and supposed sameness which in fact
privileges the masculine. Thus the project is to disrupt this structure of
masculine–feminine. Questions of meaning, or knowledge, and the subject
are inextricably tied together.

Irigaray contends that a critical rereading of Freud is of particular
importance. Her argument is that Freud brought to light what had been
operative, but hidden, in discourse: 'the sexual indifference that underlies the
truth of any science' (Irigaray 1985a: 69). And he did so through elaborating
a theory of sexuality; his object was male and female sexuality. But Freud
defines female sexuality with respect to the masculine; the 'feminine' is
always described as a deficiency, 'as a negative image that provides male
sexuality with an unfailingly phallic self-representation' (Irigaray 1985a: 70).
This is to deny any specificity to the female sex. In Freud, then, something is
made explicit that is implicit in all philosophical discourse: 'the mirror, most
often hidden, that allows the logos, the subject, to reduplicate itself, to reflect
itself by itself' (Irigaray 1985a: 75); that is, makes possible the fantasy of
self-presence. But, Irigaray (1985a: 75) claims that the significance of Freud
goes beyond this: interpretive rereading or deconstruction is in some
important respects a psychoanalytic undertaking. It consists in, for example,
paying 'attention to the way the unconscious works in each philosophy'
(Irigaray 1985a: 75), the procedures of repression. So Freudian theory both
contributes to a disruption of the order of discourse, and remains subject to it
(Irigaray 1985a: 72).

This argument about Freud encapsulates something of what is distinctive
to a deconstructive approach, and relates to Derrida's comments on Hegel
cited above. The concern is with the specificity of discourses and how they
might undo themselves. An argument against a theory is not presented from a
position 'outside'. A deconstructive strategy consists in an undoing of

knowledge that makes claims to truth and coherence by bringing to light the repressions on which pretensions to truth are dependent; and, following Freud, a negation in discourse is taken as indicative of a repression. Feminists make the claim that the repressed is the feminine. But they also insist that the how of this repression needs to be specified in any particular discourse.

It is clear from the use of the term 'repression' that deconstruction owes a lot to Freud. This is a debt acknowledged by Derrida and Irigaray, among others. At a later point I will address in detail the Freudian concepts that have been taken up by deconstructive theorists. But in general terms the claim is that Freud contributes to an undermining of the possibility of presence, of any element; and, in particular, the self-presence of the subject. Most important here is the concept of the unconscious. In asking what is disturbing to sociology, what is repressed, I have been asking a psychoanalytic question. This is a form of question that sociology would refuse. Giddens's (1987: 89) rejection of any concept of the unconscious as incompatible with his concept of conscious agency would find wide acceptance in the discipline, and indeed among feminists who lay stress on consciousness-raising as the precondition of social change. My argument is that such notions are themselves dependent on repressions, repressions that are hinted at in the exclusion of desire, the mediations of knowledge through a relation to the other, and the exclusion of the body. But the way I want to approach this issue is by starting with an assumption of the unconscious and demonstrating the implications for cultural and social analysis.

The tradition of thought that informs this project does, of course, make this assumption: for Freud the unconscious is the precondition of culture; for Lévi-Strauss cultural processes are unconscious; for Derrida the unconscious is an alterity that marks the impossibility of self-presence. Despite different 'conceptions' of the unconscious, in all these approaches it is regarded as important for an understanding of the principles of meaning of cultural systems. In turn this means that culture (knowledge) can be read symptomatically. Irigaray's reading of Freud is a symptomatic or psychoanalytic reading. The significance of Derrida's understanding of the unconscious as radical other is that as such it is not a potential presence, and thus points to the impossibility of knowledge. His argument is that as no 'object', least of all the subject, can be finally known, meaning should instead be understood as a process of infinite referral. This argument is based on Freud's account of the principles of meaning of the unconscious – most importantly, referral and deferral (Derrida 1982: 18–21). However, theorists such as Derrida insist that the desire for knowledge cannot simply be refused: it is important simultaneously to acknowledge it and to find strategies that might undo this desire. This is the point that he is making in relation to Hegel. Weber makes the same point in connection with Freud and the significance of the unconscious to Freud's own knowledge: 'Interpretation partakes of a process of conflict that no totalisation can ever comprehend', but 'If the psychic conflict that structures the subject of desire precludes any enduring resolution, any kind of totalisation, the process of interpretation cannot simply renounce such aspirations either' (Weber 1987: 57–8).

Weber's claim is that the unconscious undermines the desire for resolution in knowledge; it is the undoing of consciousness. Irigaray's argument is that the unconscious is subversive: if the feminine is the repressed that underpins culture there is something in the feminine that escapes, that might disrupt the cultural order. Thus, quite contrary to the sociological view of social change, the 'source' of change is the unconscious. Perhaps the pertinent question to be asked here is how we ever come to the view that change has anything to do with consciousness. What is this desire all about? As the issue of social change is a central concern in sociology, this question will be addressed in some detail in this book. Cultural processes will be considered in terms of a tension between the conscious and the unconscious. And it will be argued, in connection with specific objects of analysis, that while the unconscious is the precondition of culture, and in important respects 'creates' culture, unconscious processes are also subversive of the social or the cultural order. 'The order' is taken here to include discourses that make claims to knowing the whole or the totality of the social.

If the idea of the unconscious informs this project, another central idea is that of system. Most closely associated with the linguistics of Saussure, system is crucial to the ideas of reading, writing and text. For structural linguistics any element only has meaning in a system, in relation to other elements; it has no meaning in and of itself – hence the basic principle that meaning is relational, and that no element has a positive (linguistic) value of itself. An element means in relation to what it is not: systems are characterised by differentiation. The major analytic task is one of identifying the rules of relations or the code of a system – most importantly, the rules of combination and substitution. This bears on what has been said previously about a focus on 'the how' of meaning rather than 'the what'. Systematic thinking is to be contrasted with an approach that pretends to take an element or event in isolation and look for its meaning, or ask what it is, in its essence. This form of thought is concerned with explanation, causal determination, and a search for meaning in origins or source (which does imply a relation between elements, a relation of sameness). As semioticians would point out, any answer to 'what' questions will in fact refer to other signs. This is what is to be understood by the oft-repeated quotation from Derrida (1976: 158): 'there is nothing outside the text'. The real is constituted in and by cultural systems. Given the process of referring of elements in any system, and indeed between systems, contemporary cultural theorists emphasise the signifier and chains of signification or, in Freudian terms, chains of association (Derrida 1987: 20; Barthes 1977: 158). A signified (meaning, or concept) is itself a signifier in such a chain.

In practice, systems are complex and composite: any cultural product or text is comprised of different systems in a specific combination. Crucially, this includes the system of observation: an analyst is not a privileged observer,

standing outside (Barthes 1977: 164). Observation itself changes or transforms the text; no text exists in a pure state. The idea of intertextuality
(Barthes 1977: 160) provides a way out of the problems posed by the
distinction that is frequently made between the text and reception, or
between text and context, which assumes that the text has a meaning which
changes depending on the context. Furthermore, the notion of context-
dependence presumes the possibility of an observation which is context-free
(Lawson 1985: 20). What is being proposed here is that texts be thought of as
embodied in practice, rather than as separate from reception or practice. In
this view, reading is understood as a writing, and analysis or observation as
textual activity, a practice of writing.

Again, this draws attention to the codes of analysis within which we work.
If sociology is understood as discursive production, sociological language
cannot be regarded as a transparent medium for representing the social or the
real. Rather, we must ask: What are the sociological codes of writing? What
can be said, and how? What is not sayable?

Let me return to my opening remarks about fiction. Sociology's typical
self-representation is that its distinctive concern is with the representation of
the social: it is a social *science* (and a *social* science). I want to suggest that the
sociological *fiction* is that it is not fiction. To put this another way, the
sociological fiction is that it is possible for the subject of sociological
knowledge to know the object, the social. Definition as a science avoids the
issue of how meaning is produced in the discipline. In so far as it is necessarily
in language, sociology is fiction; but the implications of this, that neither the
subject nor the object of sociology are outside meaning, are repressed. As an
initial move in shifting the codes of sociology I will propose a reversal: that we
think of sociological writing as fiction and fiction as social analysis. But as a
reversal, this needs qualification. On the one hand, the concern is to dissolve
the fiction–non-fiction distinction through a focus on writing. On the other
hand, it is crucial that different forms of writing and signification be specified.

If none of the key texts addressed in this book are sociological it is because I
find contemporary sociology as a form of writing particularly closed, and, at
its worst, authoritarian in form of address (Giddens comes to mind here). I
have looked elsewhere for texts that are suggestive for social and cultural
analysis, frequently to fiction. The criterion of choice of 'theoretical' texts has
not been 'scientific', whether a theory is a good representation of the social or
not. But rather, following Barthes (1975: 14) I have chosen texts of
disturbing pleasure, texts that move me, where 'reading is a conductor of the
desire to write' (Barthes 1986: 40). And Barthes is indeed one such 'author'
who has had that effect (see Gallop 1988: 11–20). This is perhaps to suggest
that the central issue in the evaluation of a text – theoretical or otherwise – is
its capacity to provoke disturbing pleasure: not a refusal of knowledge, but a
reformulation of what the desire for knowledge might be about. The question
addressed is then: Does this text produce a closure, does it attempt to fix a
signified, or does it invite a further writing and a rewriting?

For Barthes (1986: 36), reading is a writing which is a 'gesture of the body'. The feminists, Irigaray and Cixous, also understand writing and reading as embodied, as productions which inscribe (or write) the body and through which the body is inscribed. I have chosen texts that have a certain bodily effect in the reading. If we follow Bergson, all texts have a bodily effect, but it is also the case that some elicit from the reader a response that is intellectual, while others invite a bodily response. It is a matter of identifying the nature of the effect. Some texts provoke movement and life, albeit in the pain–pleasure series; others kill desire for knowledge.

The question asked of social texts is much the same as that asked of theoretical texts: How open or closed are they and what are the possibilities of rewriting? The texts chosen for analysis in Part 3 of this book are texts of (ambiguous) pleasure – in one way or another they have touched me. As a sociologist, one of my interests is the imperative of the immediacy of the empirical. Through the analyses in Part 3 I hope to reformulate the question of the desire for immediacy. Texts of everyday life, the ordinary, are taken to be every bit as puzzling and difficult to read as, say, literary texts. From the choice of 'objects' it will be clear that I prefer not to make distinctions and hierarchisations of texts in terms of 'worthiness' of analysis. In these analyses I am engaging in a writing of my own desires. But I hope that these fictions will be sufficiently open to invite further writings.

One of the central concerns of this book is to develop an understanding of meaning as embodied, what Barthes (1977: 182) speaks of as 'the grain': 'the materiality of the body speaking'. The principal concern here is to engage with debates in contemporary cultural theory and to move towards a methodology that might be understood as a *materialist semiotics*. Central to this is the development of an argument that signification processes should be thought of as both temporal and embodied. This is implicit in the conception of signification as transformation which is to be distinguished from representation. Thus this project could be understood as one of rewriting Borges's quotation of Carlyle: history is an infinite book that all [men] write and read *with their bodies*.

2

THE SOCIOLOGICAL
MIRROR

Sociological discourse claims to be a knowledge of modern society, the mirror of modern society or the social. 'The mirror' refers to a conception of knowledge as correspondence or as adequate reflection. It also implies a certain sort of desire in knowledge processes: the desire for a relation of correspondence between the subject and object of knowledge. In *Philosophy and the Mirror of Nature*, Rorty (1979: 170) presents a critique of knowledge understood as representation and philosophy's claim to be a general theory of representation. This chapter addresses sociological representation, the specific nature of the sociological mirror and the assumptions about knowledge that inform sociological self-representation. It asks: What are the mechanisms by which sociological discourse produces a mirroring relation between itself and the social? And what is repressed in attempts to stabilise the double, sociology and the social? I claim that the double is inherently unstable. This prefigures an argument about identity. By invoking the double I am suggesting that there is a desire for self-identity in sociological discourse, a desire for identity of the subject of knowledge. The double also implies the self-identity, or givenness, of objects. In a mutual mirroring, the object of knowledge must reflect the subject. But, if, as was argued in Chapter 1, we think of objects as discursively produced, as products of sociological practice or labour, we must ask the question: How are they produced as a mirror to sociology? My contention is that the discipline assumes the self-identity of the objects that it discursively presupposes (Weber 1987: 44). A project of undoing consists, then, in destabilising the givenness of objects; and an initial move in this is to demonstrate the ways in which objects or 'the social' are constituted in order to effect a return to the subject of sociology.

These issues will be addressed with reference to the themes of the following three chapters – the subject, power and time. Through an analysis of assumptions about the subject and power, which are central issues in sociology, we might discern something of the hidden in sociological discourse – the operations of power in this knowledge and how this is connected with the constitution of the subject of knowledge. With 'time' my principal concern is temporal assumptions in forms of theorising and conceptions of knowledge. It is to be argued, at a later point, that representation requires a suppression of time; mirroring necessitates a standing still. At least, this is the fantasy of the mirror, for there is indeed a necessary temporal component, a movement in oscillation. In this chapter I will draw out temporal assumptions in sociology. One of the main arguments to be developed in this book is that the difference between meaning understood as representation and meaning understood as transformation turns on the question of time. And that the time of meaning processes undoes the mirror, the double.

In speaking of the discipline of sociology I am well aware of the problems associated with typifications, particularly the danger of producing a unity, the very thing that I would undo. The sociology referred to is that of my own institutional location and practice: a Marxist feminist sociology practised in Australian universities where British sociology has been the predominant influence. While it is fair to say that this tradition is the major tradition in both Britain and Australia, the rather more important point here is that it is a sociology that claims to speak for sociology, and indeed to have the whole of society as its object. Giddens (1987: 29–32) quite explicitly says that his project is one of unifying sociology, and that the proper concerns of social theory must remain the macro level of the social and social change (Giddens 1982a: 66). My critical remarks about sociology are addressed to these kinds of totalising claim. This is not to deny the presence of, say, phenomenology or ethnomethodology in the discipline – traditions of thought that are far from totalising.

This sociology that speaks for sociology claims to be radical and theoretical, and designates Marx and Weber, and to a lesser extent Durkheim, as 'founding fathers'. Given a distinction, in the discipline, between theory and research, 'model builders' do not necessarily engage in research. When research is undertaken, although there is no uniformity in this, the favoured approach is qualitative, which is regarded as a counter to the positivism of quantitative methods.

An important influence in experiential research has been the Birmingham Centre for Cultural Studies. Critical of the abstractions of Marxism, this school has been concerned with the lived experiences of the working class, women and subcultures. It has had a considerable impact on Marxist sociology in Australia. The shift to experience has tended, none the less, to be accompanied by a retention of Marxist feminist categories and the concept ideology (with all the attendant problems of surface-deep, representation-real distinctions).[1]

Reflexivity

In 'Partial Magic in the *Quixote*', quoted at the opening of Chapter 1 (and classified, incidentally, as 'essay' rather than 'fiction'), Borges (1970) tells a story about a map which is perfect. Every minute detail of England has its correspondence in the map; in which case, as Borges (1970: 231) points out, 'the map should contain a map of the map . . . and so on to infinity'. If sociology is substituted for the map it could be asked if and how it is located in the map of the social? The short answer is that under the heading 'sociology of sociology' sociologists are indeed concerned with a sociological representation of sociology, but this is effected in such a way as to close on the process of endless mirroring (Runciman 1983: 52). An attempt to hold the mirror still is an avoidance of the disturbing implications of the Borges story: there is no original of which the map is a copy; with each repeated representation there is a difference, and thus the whole can never be represented.[2]

I shall now turn to sociological self-representation and the associated question of reflexivity. One of the central issues here is how sociological forms of authorisation are related to what, in effect, is a closure on reflexivity. While there is nothing new about the problem of reflexivity, the current concern with this is connected with the recognition that any theorising or interpretation is a textual production, is in language. Of the 'new impact of reflexivity', Lawson (1985: 9) claims:

> Our concepts are no longer regarded as transparent – either in reflecting the world or conveying ideas. As a result all our claims about language and the world – and implicitly all our claims in general – are reflexive in a manner which cannot be avoided. For to recognize the importance of language is to do so within language. To argue that the character of the world is in part due to the concepts employed, is to employ those concepts.

In general terms this is an argument against the possibility of a meta-theoretical level providing an absolute, or a certainty outside the text providing a ground (Lawson 1985: 14, 20). Recourse to a meta level is a move in order to avoid reflexivity, to deny the map within the map to infinity. The sociology of knowledge, for example in claiming to present a theory of the social determination of knowledge, makes an exception of itself. However, while Mannheim, for example, explicitly excludes his own theory, it is more commonly the case that sociologists include self-reference. And sociology does claim to be a reflexive discipline.

Introductions to sociology and lists of 'aims of the discipline' invariably include the words 'critical' and 'reflexive'. Such lists also include something like: sociology is the study of modern society, industrial society, or capitalist society. That these substitutions are a matter of dispute might alert one to the fact that they are not the same thing. However, sociologists commonly take the view that it is simply a matter of different accounts of the same thing.

Given this assumption, all of these objects function in the same way with respect to the status of sociological knowledge. An understanding of the object as an extra-textual referent is an attempt to hold the mirror still. And yet sociology claims to acknowledge reflexivity precisely because it is the study of modern society. Sociology is the product of that which it theorises; it is the self-consciousness of modernity. (Undergraduate sociology students are introduced to the idea that sociology is the product of modernity and that it is modernity's attempt to interrogate and understand itself.) Thus it accounts for itself in sociological terms, as socially produced, and simultaneously claims a privileged status 'by arguing that this theory is the theory which accompanies the culminating historical form' (Lawson 1985: 21). This is particularly true of Marxist sociology but it applies to any sociology that has as its object the whole of society. And a common claim is that what makes sociology distinctive *is* the concern with the whole of society (Giddens 1987: 25). The same assumptions are held by feminist sociologists who argue that Marxism has not given the whole picture of the development of capitalism – the sexual division of labour at work and home must be included for a more complete account (Barrett 1988). Sociology then is coextensive with its object, the dynamic of society, the movement of history; in interrogating that dynamic, however it is conceived, it interrogates itself. In taking the social as object, it takes itself as object: the mirror.

This is the basis of claims about reflexivity, claims which are contradicted by the move to a meta level, and the reference to a ground which is extra-textual. As reflection of the whole, sociology is a whole, a truth. What is not acknowledged is the significance of the fact that sociological concepts are necessarily used to account for sociology. 'The development of modern society', 'class struggle', 'rationalisation' are discursively produced by the discipline. When sociologists speak of 'critically locating' their theory, they do so with reference to, for example, class location or specific location in history, that is, 'the real'. As Weber (1987: 48) has said in connection with Jameson's defence of Marxism and the oft-quoted statement that 'History is not a text': 'it can be criticised in *its own name*, . . . because its own "place" is coextensive with *another* space that bears another name, that of History'.

Not only is Marxism the place of the imperative to totalise, but by virtue of that place it is self-critical. As Weber (1987: 48) so nicely puts it, this is 'the attractive self-critical gift-wrap'.

This critical place, for Marxist and radical sociology, is 'inside'; partisanship is acknowledged. But, it is on the basis of the particular nature of this inside that a meta level, a position 'outside', is justified. The insistence on historical specificity consists in locating theory with reference to historical epoch and/or class configuration. This is particularly clear in discourses on the origins of the discipline: the origins of the discipline coincide with the origins of modern society; and introductory lectures and textbooks generally start with this (Giddens 1982b: 11). The unfolding of modern society is also the unfolding of the knowledge of that society: sociology's narrative coincides with that of society. Hence, it is the only discipline that can reflexively locate itself in the social or in history. It is this capacity of reflexive mirroring that is the basis of sociology's differentiation of itself from the discipline of history. While it would be agreed that both have the real as their object, the view is that history, unlike sociology, is not critically aware of its own theorising, it has not *theoretically* located itself in history, and consequently remains immersed in it and undifferentiated from it. Sociology, on the other hand, rises above history to a level of sustained self-consciousness. The social dynamic, be it the class struggle or rationalisation, moves society through historical stages, and sociology is the consciousness of where we have got to now, an end point. This end is found in the origins: the origins or source of modern society and social theory.

The relationship between sociology and its object forms the basis of authorisation. This relates to the issue of partisanship, the connection between a political position and truth. In Marxist and feminist sociology the determining dynamics are characterised by conflict; and, conflict as source of change is a basic premise in this sociology. Theories are not simply theories of conflict, they are theories constituted in and by conflict (Weber 1987: 45). Marxism, for example, is not just a theory of class struggle and conflict, it is a class theory – the theory of the subject of history. Thus Marxist sociologists authorise themselves by putting themselves in the movement of history, in the class narrative; and they are the voice of this narrative. Feminist sociologists have been critical of 'male' sociologists who speak on behalf of the working class, but their authorisation is based on similar assumptions. While it is problematic for sociologists to speak for the working class, feminist sociologists, as women, *can* speak on behalf of women. There is no difference between the subject and object: 'We are it.' Thus, stronger claims to authority are made on the basis of a sameness of the subject and object of knowledge. This assumes a unity, 'women', and fails to acknowledge questions of difference and the production of the other to the subject of feminist knowledge.

In both Marxist and feminist sociology there is a conflation of a moral-political system with a knowledge system which renders the relation between these relatively unproblematic. This is what leads to the charge, on the part of Marxists, that to abandon aspirations to truth is to take up an amoral position, or one that allows for political relativism – anything goes. While there is indeed a connection between conceptions of knowledge and politics and morality, these relations need to be specified, and troubled over. Truth, and a reduction of political position to the dynamic of history, is an avoidance of responsibility – to 'self' and 'the other'.

I am obviously suggesting that, by and large, sociological strategies of coherence have been successful. Even notions of conflict function in a unifying manner. This is so in two respects. First, conflict, class and/or gender, accounts for the whole; or, the contradictions of capitalism are the basis of the unity of the social formation. And second, conflict operates as a means of neutralising difference. It is claimed that the discipline, like the social, is characterised by conflict, we come from different social positions. But to account for differences in approach with reference to the social or what is given, is precisely to repress difference. An accommodation of difference within a reductionist sociological frame amounts to pluralism. However, there are cracks in the discipline, and I want to make reference to work in a tradition which contributes to an undoing of the sociological narrative.

In particular, I have in mind here Benjamin's analyses of the experience of modern society. While his writings have been taken up with some enthusiasm in recent years in areas in the humanities, this has not been the case in sociology. An exception is Frisby, whose work on Simmel, Kracauer and Benjamin (Frisby 1985) makes a considerable contribution to the disruption of the sociological narrative. In choosing these theorists as founders of sociology, Frisby's project can be understood as a rewriting of the origins of the discipline. Not only are these 'forgotten' writers in the sociological tradition, but as Frisby has demonstrated, their approaches refuse historicism and totalisation. Their conceptions of knowledge in fact run against a teleological notion of origins; and it would be difficult to appropriate them in sociological self-representation, in the production of an identity and a whole. This in part accounts for their absence: they do not fit the definition of sociology.[3]

Frisby (1985) addresses the work of social theorists who, in different ways, were concerned with grasping in the fragments of modernity something of the eternal forms of modern social life. They were 'modernist' in the sense that, as both Frisby and Foucault point out, Baudelaire took to be modern: to have a capacity to recapture something eternal within the present moment, and to *transform* it 'by grasping it in what it is' (Foucault 1984: 39, 41; see also Frisby 1985: 32–3). Baudelaire and his figures of modernity are central to Benjamin's account of the forms of modern life. In his essay on 'Modernism' he quotes Baudelaire: 'Everywhere he sought the transitory, fleeting beauty of our present life . . . ' (Benjamin 1973: 82). Commentators on modernity invariably quote Baudelaire on 'the ephemeral, the fleeting, the contingent' (Foucault 1984: 39–40; Frisby 1985: 14, 16). Modernity is characterised by a concern with the transitoriness of the present moment, a consciousness of time as discontinuous, and a break with the continuity of traditional time (Foucault 1984: 39; Frisby 1985: 13). Thus an obsession with history might be understood as a nostalgic response to the experience of modernity as fleeting moments: an attempted totalisation in the face of fragmentation, and the search for an end in an origin. A methodology of grasping the eternal in the moment is a counter to such historicism (Frisby 1985: 32–3).

The significance of this tradition of social thought lies both in the choice of objects of analysis and in forms of theorising. It is the latter that is most pertinent to this discussion, but these issues are, of course, interconnected. In focusing on the 'trivial' of everyday life experiences, and heterogeneous objects, such theorists made no claims to be identifying the determinant objects. This contrasts sharply with most sociology, which designates certain objects as more worthy of attention than others: the workplace, the family, the state, and more recently, the media as the means of ideological production. What underpins this selection is a conception of the workings of a singular logic of society as a whole, a logic that underlies, lies beneath, the surface.

Sociologists ask 'why'-type questions, and both forms of answer, functional and historical, assume causal determination: change is a continuity. Historical explanation, for example, consists in a periodisation: where we are now is an end point, each period or stage being an inevitable move in this direction, orchestrated by whatever the dynamic is in the particular theory. There is a linearity and narrativity in this. (Giddens (1987: 97) takes Foucault's genealogical method to task for its abandonment of chronological time.) Each moment is understood as an identity in a causal relation to other moments; each moment or element, past, present or future, is understood as a presence, on a line marked by cause-effect relations. This can be understood as a desire for the fullness of the present in its extra-textual determination. Derrida (1987: 80) has made the claim that this conception of history represses difference (see also Frow 1983: 230). What is to be emphasised here is Derrida's view that this repression of difference consists in a suppression of time. As Borges (1974: 26) says, a cause, particularly a 'first cause', is necessary 'to avoid proceeding to infinity'; it is a demand for certainty. Infinity – an endless process of referral of traces of elements – is temporal; a causal mode of thinking, which perhaps comes of anxiety, would hold this process still in fixing upon a signified.

It is this conception of causal determination that is refused by theorists such as Benjamin (see Wolin 1982: 79–106). In his 'Theses on the Philosophy of History', Benjamin (1969: 263) is devastatingly critical of historicism which 'contents itself with establishing a causal connection between various moments of history'. Furthermore, he makes a direct connection between this form of theorising and temporal assumptions. Historicism has an atemporal sense of history – the progression of the continuum of homogeneous empty time (Benjamin 1969: 263); the disruptive or shock effect of time proper, which is heterogeneous in character, is repressed. For him, the task is one of grasping the constellation which this era 'has formed with a definite earlier one', establishing a 'conception of the present as the "time of the now"' (Benjamin 1969: 263; see also Foucault 1984: 76–100, 340–72). In his critique of the seamless history of historicism, Benjamin (1969: 264, 257) argued for a blasting open of 'the continuum of history', and 'brushing history against the grain' (see also Nietzsche 1982: 75).

A conception of time as homogeneous and empty, or abstract, is associated with a desire for identity and a whole, a desire to know what the social is in its totality. It is only time understood as abstract or homogeneous that can be held still in order that the whole might be seen by an observer. If observers locate themselves in the line of history, they nevertheless presuppose a position of observation outside. In contesting such an approach to social analysis, Benjamin's work, and Frisby's rereading of it as 'sociology', disrupt sociological identity.

Mention should be made here of Bourdieu, a sociologist who argues for a temporalised theory. This is connected with his concern with theory understood as human activity or practice. There are interesting parallels with Bergson's argument for a temporalised philosophy which is in 'life' (for a detailed discussion see Chapter 5). Bourdieu argues that science has a time which is not that of practice, consisting as it does in a standing outside, with the effect of reifying practices. It is 'detemporalised' in so far as it has 'the time' to totalise; it must predict with certainty. This is to presume the possibility of a repetition of the same; the irreversibility of time and the interval – difference in repetition – must be excluded (Bourdieu 1977: 5–9). By totalising practices which are 'inscribed in the current of time' and hence necessarily detotalised, science forgets 'the transformation it imposes' on these practices. This is particularly pernicious when imposed on practices in which time and rhythm are '*constitutive* of their meaning' (Bourdieu 1977: 9). The central point here is that science disavows the time of practices of observation and theorising, and thus the process of transformation involved in such practices.

Research

Turning now to research discourses in sociology, the critical issue is how these are connected with a desire for a mirroring relation between the subject and object of knowledge.

Barthes (1986: 70) has made the claim that it is 'fiction that research is reported not written'. The idea that there is an end to research – a result – and that this is reported, prevails in the social sciences. Assumptions about science inform this approach: research investigates social facts; it should aim for an objectivity with respect to these facts, and the reporting of findings should use a transparent language which makes for a direct translation. It is method which produces results; in sociology there is an imperative to be representative and use a method that will produce evidence for generalisations. This has the effect of an obsession with method (Crapanzano 1977; Barthes 1977: 200–1). Most sociology departments, for example, have separate courses on research methods, distinct from 'theory' courses. The distinction between theory and research methods in course structures reflects the distinction between representation and the real: research in this discipline is understood as empirical research; theory operates as a model, or as hypotheses, to be tested through research. Theoretical writing is thought of as not quite research; a good sociologist is one who can produce a correspondence between a theoretical model and the real. This is particularly evident in the rules of thesis writing. The structure of a sociology thesis will typically take the form of a refutation of various theoretical approaches, proposing a better approach, giving an account of the research methodology that will be applied in testing the hypotheses, presenting research results, and, in the light of these, modifying, but more usually confirming, the theory that has been adopted.

'Radical sociology', such as that of the Birmingham School, is critical of notions of science, and takes the view that facts are theory-dependent. None the less, experiential research assumes an 'authentic' domain which can be represented: experiences are reported sociologically.

If research is understood as writing, critical attention is drawn to the process of textual production which *is* research, as opposed to a final writing up of research results. To quote Barthes (1977: 198) again: 'from the moment a piece of research concerns the text . . . the research itself becomes text, production: to it, any result is literally *im-pertinent*'. This means, Barthes (1977: 201) says, that method is to be treated not as 'founding privilege', but as a 'spectacle mounted in the text'. The indispensable component of 'method' is responsibility: critique, self-critique of the research discourse (Barthes 1977: 201; see also Luke and McHoul 1989; White 1978: 4). Thus, method becomes part of the writing, rather than the occasion for putting off writing until a result has been found. For Barthes (1986: 71), this implies an acknowledgement of the reflexivity of research, the possibility 'at every moment of its trajectory', of a turning back on itself, thus overcoming 'the scholar's bad faith'. In this process, author and reader are displaced.

The idea that research is writing has been taken up in recent critiques of anthropology. In an introduction to what has become an influential and controversial collection of essays, Clifford (1986: 26) claims that what the contributors have in common is their insistence that ethnography 'is always writing'. Critical of the conception of ethnography as representation, these anthropologists are concerned to draw attention to the artifice in cultural accounts. This is to question the notion that the ethnographer translates the reality of others, which is the basis of ethnographic authority (Clifford 1986: 7; see also Taussig 1988). Whether the voice of the author is manifest or not, depending on the ethnographic tradition, all traditional ethnographies are characterised 'by giving to one voice a pervasive authorial function and to others the role of informants' (Clifford 1986: 15). The singular voice of the author is connected with the production of the other as object. Thus, the critical anthropologists are concerned with developing an approach to ethnography – a writing strategy – that recognises otherness and difference (Clifford 1983: 132–9; 1986: 15). That these critiques have been developed in anthropology rather than sociology might in part be accounted for by the centrality of 'the ethnographic experience' to the profession, and also the visibility of 'the other'. I want to suggest that in researching 'our society', sociologists evade questions about otherness, how 'our' is constituted in relation to the other. This bears on the issue of sociological authorisation, the authority to speak on behalf of, to represent.

In one important respect sociologists are explicit about the other: 'our' society or modern society is defined in relation to pre-modern or traditional society (Giddens 1982b: 9–27). 'Cross-cultural' and 'historical' examples, frequently based on the same periodisations, are cited to make sense of modern society. This differentiation can be understood as an attempt to make modern society a presence via the absent 'pre-modern'. Crucially, it avoids the issue of the otherness within 'modern society'. To say that otherness or difference is repressed might seem like a strong claim in the light of Marxist and feminist concerns with the working class, women, and 'race' (see von Sturmer 1989). But it is precisely this tradition of sociology that is being addressed here. For all that we have been aware of issues about the position of the researcher and the ethical problems associated with researching 'the oppressed', the question of the constitution of the object as other and the other as object has been evaded. In some ways it is precisely through a process of identification with 'objects' of research that this has been possible. Crapanzano (1977) is making an important point when he says that accounts of the other are about an 'affirmation of identity', a sense of self. This might seem obvious, but through an identification with the objects of research, the autobiographical is not fully acknowledged.[4]

Qualitative and experiential research is the research approach in sociology that comes closest to anthropology; it is understood as ethnography of Western culture. A major concern in work influenced by the Birmingham School has been to counter the dominant ideology thesis and the idea that people are passive victims of oppression. As the title of one of the earlier Birmingham Centre publications, *Resistance through Rituals* (Hall and Jefferson 1976), suggests, a central idea informing research has been that of resistance. Through analyses of experiences of subcultures and 'oppressed groups', the concern is to demonstrate that dominant representations are not just passively accepted, that 'ordinary' people produce different, counter-meanings. Cultural studies research has come to be principally concerned with evidence of resistance in lived experience (see Fiske *et al.* 1987). As Morris (1988a: 214) has pointed out, there is something of a slide going on here from cultural 'production' to political resistance. I would suggest that this sociological concept of resistance, which is not to be confused with Foucault's concept of resistance, involves fantasies and projections on the part of the researcher that go unacknowledged. The question that needs to be addressed is: How is the object produced as resistant other in relation to a self (sameness) of the researcher?[5]

The inversion from oppression to resistance is effected through a particular approach to research: lived experience has become the object, with the assumption that experience is more authentic than either the abstractions of Marxist theorising or the numbers of quantitative sociology. And 'the interview' is the privileged method for getting at experience and subjectivity. With the interview you hear it from the horse's mouth; this is the real thing. Although observation and participant observation are included they are not given the same status as they are in anthropological ethnography. And this privileging of speech by sociologists might well be connected with proximity to 'our' culture. The speech of the interview is regarded as a transparent medium of experience.

Politically, experiential sociology has been informed by the idea of letting people speak, speak their oppression: we sociologists can give *them* a voice. Interviews are used as evidence of, for example, working-class culture and resistance. In the genre of experiences at work, extensive direct quotations were used to demonstrate that workers really did find capitalist relations oppressive (Beynon 1975). In a double sense, 'experience' has provided sociological authority: the real of the experience of the oppressed, and the researcher's experience of hearing it. And in this there is an assumption of the possibility of representation – in the sense of both correspondence and political representation. It is the immediacy of such research that holds out the attraction and constitutes its justification: the immediacy of speech and the 'presence' of the object as another subject. However, immediacy is also the illusion of this research. If mediation is not as obvious as in some other forms of research – film and media studies, for example – it is none the less there. The interview itself as mediation is constitutive of the research text; relations between subjects are constituted in and through language. At each point in the research-writing process different meanings are produced; there is no one-to-one correspondence between texts. A transcript, for example, does not simply reflect the interview; any 'final' research text is not a representation or translation of experience. In short, it is not a question of stripping away the mediations to get to the real; which, in turn, means giving up on any notion of a final point of research.

Some brief comments about authorisation in feminist social science research should be made here. Claims to being able to represent women have been based on a moral-political stance and a conception of the particular nature of the relation between research subject and object. Concerned with the objectification of those researched, feminist social scientists claim that the researcher-researched dichotomy should be rejected; feminist research is research 'on, by, and for women' (Stanley and Wise 1983: 17). There are variations on this, but a common assumption is that of the supposed shared experiences of women, which makes a rejection of the subject–object dichotomy possible. In feminist research the position of the interviewer is acknowledged, but it is precisely the researcher's subjectivity that makes for a better, less partial or masculine, knowledge (Oakley 1981: 30–61). It is the combination of 'being a woman' and having a feminist consciousness (Stanley and Wise 1983: 33) that authorises. Not only does this presume a unified category, 'women', but a certain consciousness is privileged as that which knows what it is to be a woman. Having a feminist consciousness authorises a representation of those who do not as yet have this, but might become one of 'us'. This is apparently strengthened by the claim that feminist research is *for* women, 'they' are the audience (Oakley 1981: 48–9). Why should it be assumed that the desire in feminist knowledge processes is structured differently from that of other knowledge processes? Or, to put this another way, can the subject-object opposition simply be annulled? The very idea of representing women, even if in the form of 'letting them speak', is to constitute women as object. To claim that 'they' are subjects is to avert the question of authorship and the constitution of a 'feminist self' via an other.

This form of authorisation sits rather oddly with certain feminist principles: the rejection of totalising truth, and an insistence on difference and different feminisms. Similar problems are evident in more sophisticated feminist writings that take differences among and within women seriously. De Lauretis, for example, is concerned with how feminist film theorists and film makers might produce a 'subject of feminism' through practices of self-consciousness. Although she is careful to emphasise differences and multiplicity in connection with forms of address, it is still a matter of a feminist consciousness that might be produced (de Lauretis 1987: 127–46). I do not mean to suggest that there is an easy way out of these problems. The main point here is that the self-other relation of knowledge will not simply go away; nor will the author function. As Foucault has argued, the critical task is one of analysing how this operates in any discourse (Foucault 1984: 101–20). Hence the importance of self-critique in feminist research texts, and an acknowledgement of the power effects of feminist knowledges: the production of 'women' in feminist discourse.

Critical questions about authorship have been raised in relation to the 'post-modern' anthropologists (Strathern 1987; Kirby 1989a; 1989b). These anthropologists are concerned with the specification of discourses in ethnography, and the power of discourse. Having rejected the idea of speaking for, the issue becomes one of voices in the text, or ways of writing that are dialogical or polyphonic: developing a 'cultural poetics that is an interplay of voices, of positioned utterances' (Clifford 1986: 12). But the critical question here is: Has the singular voice of the ethnographer been too easily denied in claims about multiple voices? (Strathern 1987: 264). Despite the concern with language and mediations there are hints that the new ethnographic writing might represent a dialogic situation, and thus be more authentic, make for a better translation. In this work the fascination with the immediacy of ethnography is evident, and thus the mediations of the 'encounter' are underplayed, or, at least, they are regarded as merely mediation, the implication being that there is something that pre-exists mediation. The power of the self–other relation is not sufficiently taken into account (Kirby 1989a). As Strathern (1987: 269) puts it: 'There is no evidence, after all, that "we" have stopped attributing our problems to "others".' But it could be posed more strongly: that knowledge processes are structured around self-other relations, or a desire for mastery (even if not the only desire in knowledge), and to think ourselves free of this might be illusory. To have research subjects as 'authors' does not avoid these problems: How do they come to be authors; 'Under what institutional and historical constraints' (Clifford 1986: 13) is this speaking, writing taking place?

These anthropologists address issues which are close to Foucault's concern with the 'modes of existence' of discourses, the 'manner in which they are articulated according to social relationships'. But the question is: Does the concern with the discursive relation of the ethnographic encounter end up reinventing the question 'Who really spoke? Is it he or someone else? With what authority or originality?' (Foucault 1984: 119). Nonetheless, this is the most significant critical work on research in a discipline close to sociology. In addressing a form of research that involves the 'immediacy' of sociality it brings into focus the questions of the mediations of the self–other relation and the constitution of the other in research practices. By taking up the idea that research is writing, this anthropology contests notions of representation and research as reported. And it puts on the agenda the issue of how research texts might be written in an open and reflexive way.

The subject and power

Sociologists make a distinction between the subject and the social; they are separate, pre-given entities. This assumption is implicit in two formulations that are basic to the sociological approach to the subject: the individual and society, and agency and structure. The individual–society distinction is prominent in definitions of the discipline: what differentiates sociology from psychology is that its object is society rather than the individual. One of the main aims of introductory courses is to get students to offer social explanations, that is, to account for individual behaviour in terms of processes that structure the whole of society; and there is an insistence that individual psychic processes are not the proper concern of sociology. The sociological question is how these two initially separate entities come together; how the individual becomes socialised or constructed by the institutions of the family, education, work, the state, the media, and in the process, a member of a group or class. Thus, the question that most interests students, that of the individual, and with some justification in a society where the subject *is* constituted as 'individual', is excluded. But, if society and social determinations of class, gender, race, are the objects of sociology, the individual still remains: the structure of the individual–society distinction remains intact as a means of defining sociology. The individual is not sufficiently problematised by simply shifting to the level of the group or society. In more sophisticated approaches to the relation between the social and the subject, socialisation theory has been rejected in favour of a notion of construction: the subject is constructed by, but is also an agent in, the construction of class and gender relations (Connell *et al.* 1982; Game and Pringle 1983). This is still to presume a pre-existing subject that constructs and is socially constructed.

It is in the sociological notion of agency that this assumption is most apparent. The basic sociological premise is that social determination constitutes explanation, and yet sociologists also want to claim that 'human agency' is the source of change: thus the impasse of the dualism of structure and agency. The idea of construction attempts to resolve this by having it both ways: social determination and human agency. By virtue of their structural location, particular social groups are understood to be subjects of history, sources of social change. What is required is a consciousness of their social location, and one of the main aims of sociology is to facilitate the acquisition of such a consciousness. The subject, in this sociological tradition, is an identity, endowed with a consciousness and frequently with rationality. In short, it has much the same conceptual status as the individual of liberal humanism.

In Chapter 1 it was suggested that the insistence on agency, and the understanding of agency in terms of consciousness, could be understood as the desire to privilege sociological knowledge or consciousness. (The concern to 'help' the oppressed in a project of liberation is a significant aspect of this.) The structure-agency formulation is particularly associated with Giddens, whose work has been a major influence in the Australian and British tradition that I am addressing. He is regarded as a contemporary grand social theorist. Current debates about the subject, informed by the work of Foucault and psychoanalysis, have barely touched the discipline of sociology, and Giddens's 'refutations' of these traditions of thought have undoubtedly contributed to these exclusions. *He* conducts the surveys of theories, and advises on what should be read and how; indeed, his books are frequently set as texts in courses on 'classical sociological theory'. There are, of course, exceptions to this; for example, the work of Hall, whose influence in sociology is considerable; the Birmingham School; and, coming out of social psychology, *Changing the Subject*, a book widely read across disciplines (Henriques *et al.* 1984) (see also Beechey and Donald 1985). But mainstream sociology is informed by the individual-society and agency-structure distinctions.

There is an apparent paradox in the combination of these distinctions, as the individual is dismissed but appears in another guise, that of agency. Both distinctions, however, presume a distinction between the subject and the social: How does the individual become social? How does the subject change the social? Sociological self-definition in part turns on a capacity to identify sources of social change. As consciousness of the social, sociology locates itself with the source or subject of social change.

Another opposition that figures in sociological understandings of the subject warrants mention here: the opposition between nature and culture. In sociology it is the social, rather than culture, and the social is defined as that which is not nature. I want to suggest that this opposition provides a certainty for social scientists: the presence of the social through a negation of nature. An important example of this is the sex–gender distinction: sex denotes biology and hence nature, gender denotes the social. 'Nature' is thus used as a means of demarcating the social, which is the proper object of sociology. As Gatens (1983) has pointed out, this erases the body – it is left on the side of nature. From a semiotic perspective, the sex–gender distinction makes little sense as the body is necessarily *in* culture, as indeed 'nature' is in culture. This approach draws attention to the ways in which nature means, the significance of nature to definitions of culture. To take social woman rather than natural woman as object is to neglect the crucial issue of the discursive production of the latter, and indeed the production, in sociological discourse, of the former.

For sociology, nature is outside the social, and constitutes the limit to it. Thus little attention is paid to the ways in which the nature–culture opposition operates in both social processes and knowledges of these. As Derrida (1978: 283) argues, what was a scandal for Lévi-Strauss, namely the convergence of nature and culture in the incest taboo, is only a scandal from the perspective of oppositions, 'a system of concepts which accredits the difference between nature and culture'. But we cannot simply discredit systems of thought either. Thus, 'Lévi-Strauss simultaneously has experienced the necessity of utilising this opposition and the impossibility of accepting it' (Derrida 1978: 283). In Chapter 7 I will address nature and culture in specific analyses, and argue that one way of unsettling this opposition is through a positive relation to nature as other, rather than a negation of nature which leaves the oppositional structure intact.

Assumptions about power are closely connected with assumptions about the subject. Power is a central theme in sociology; it is one of the first concepts that students are introduced to, along with that of social inequality. A connection is made between power and social inequality: power is a dimension or one of the sources of inequality, some groups have more of it than others. The very notion of inequality is premised on assumptions of quantification and sameness: equality would consist in groups not only having the same amount of power, but the same sort of power. Marxist sociologists claim that the Weberian model does not account for where power comes from, and they demand an explanation in economic and class terms. There are, however, important assumptions in common: power is something that is held by some groups, and wielded over others. Furthermore, it has a total form, most notably in the state: it is to be understood at the level of 'the social'. These assumptions are also evident in feminist sociology: patriarchy refers to the power held by men and wielded over women; the disagreement with Marxists is over the source of power.

Thus, there is a reification of power, just as there is a reification of the social in the structure–agency formulation. The problem becomes: How can this all too solid thing – power, the social – be changed? Power stands over and against subjects; having come under its sway, how might they, as agents, be free of it? Power and the subject, as with the social and the subject, are in a relation of exteriority with respect to each other. Furthermore, this is to assume that a knowledge appropriate to social change might be free of power. For example, the idea of a feminist knowledge assumes a position outside patriarchal power. As Irigaray suggests in 'The Power of Discourse', this conception of knowledge reinvents the very structure of knowledge–power that feminists would be free of. Importantly, it fails to acknowledge the power of feminist discourse.

In the following chapter Foucault's account of power and the subject will be addressed. His work has called into question the kinds of assumption about power that prevail in the sociological tradition. His conception of power–knowledge configurations as constitutive of the subject suggests a way out of the dualisms that inform sociological approaches to these questions: the subject and the social, and the subject and power, are not understood to be in a relation of separation. Not only is power – along with other systems – constitutive of subjects, but it has no existence outside or above acting subjects. Foucault (1982: 217) is insistent that 'how' questions rather than 'why' and 'what' questions be asked in connection with power. To ask 'how' is to refuse reified and total conceptions of power, and any notion that power has a source, an origin. With reference to those who insist on 'the why' and 'the what' of power, he suggests that this involves an avoidance of the issue of the how of power in which 'the bearer of knowledge' is implicated. For sociologists to ask 'how' would require an acknowledgement of the power effects of the abstractions discursively produced by the discipline, and a critical questioning of the status of sociological knowledge as science. How does this knowledge produce subjects as objects? In turn, this would require us to address the question: 'How are we constituted as subjects of our own knowledge?' (Foucault 1984: 49). In Chapter 4 I shall return to the operations of power in a mirroring relation between the subject and object of knowledge.

In conclusion, I should like to make some remarks about the politics of social theorising, again with reference to Foucault who is very much concerned with making clear the connections between politics and his approach to social analysis. My principal concern in this chapter has been to question the idea of a privileged knowledge (representation of the social), which is not to deny the 'fact' of different sociological approaches. The critique is directed at any sociology that makes claims to being *the* sociological approach or the most adequate theory, and to know the social in its totality. And these kinds of claim are quite pronounced in this discipline. A demand for a coherent account of the whole can be understood as a desire for identity or completion and coherence on the part of the subject of knowledge. Radical sociologists are critical of society as it is; they are disaffected. But conceptualising the social as a whole implies that real change must be total transformation, which is necessarily in the future. This is the other side to a strategy of 'rejection' of theories as inadequate, as not providing a scientific account of the social. In arguing for 'a practical critique that takes the form of a possible transgression' and the importance of 'partial transformations', Foucault (1984: 45–7) says that we must turn away 'from all projects that claim to be global or radical'. He makes this argument with reference to precisely the sort of 'evidence' that sociologists claim to be interested in – the historical era in which we live:

> In fact we know from experience that the claim to escape from the system of contemporary reality so as to produce the overall programs of another society, of another way of thinking, another culture, another vision of the world, has led only to the return of the most dangerous traditions (Foucault 1984: 46).

In the following chapter I will say more about Foucault's understanding of the politics of the present era, and the partial transformations he has in mind. But his concern is with a positive strategy of permanent critique of the present era and of ourselves, such that we might be engaged in practices of transformation in the now. What are the limits imposed on us and what are the possibilities of 'going beyond them'? (Foucault 1984: 50). As for Barthes, the critical task is one of calling into crisis, particularly calling into crisis the certitudes of *our* knowledge. To put this another way, it is to ask: How are we constituted now and how might we be otherwise, *now*? This bears on the general concern of this book with the question of transformation.

In Part 3 the issue of transformations in everyday practices will be addressed. The argument to be developed there is that transformation does not come of truth or privileged knowledge, nor is it a matter of consciousness. In fact, it is in practices that run counter to these conceptions of knowledge that it is possible to discern a 'redemptive' moment that is disruptive to the cultural order. As we will see in Chapter 3, Foucault argues that power works in and through bodies, and that it has productive effects. My argument is that the body potentially exceeds the power of discourse, makes representation impossible – it is the site of transformation.

In this chapter the concern has been to unsettle a conception of sociology as representation. At the very least, we need to acknowledge the ways in which we are implicated in representations, even if the desire for such cannot simply be dispelled. I am, however, suggesting that we give up on a desire for a mirroring relation, and take on board the idea of the map of the map to infinity, which, it is to be argued, is based on a very different structure of desire. The following section outlines the basis of an alternative approach to social analysis, informed by different traditions of social thought from those which prevail in the social sciences. This is a positive project (rather than a negative one of refutation), concerned with identifying the possibilities opened up for social and cultural analysis by a materialist semiotics.

PART 2

TOWARDS
A MATERIALIST
SEMIOTICS

3

THE SUBJECT

Freud and Foucault are both 'theorists' of the subject. Their approaches, probably more than any others, have informed contemporary debates about this question. And the subject is one of the central issues in contemporary cultural theory where the main concern has been to undo the centred subject – a subject that would be the source of meaning. In both Foucault and Freud, the subject does not pre-exist culture; rather, it is constituted in systems; and, in this respect there is no distinction between the subject and 'the social' in their approaches. (The social is thus not the social of sociology.) However, if necessarily in culture, the subject, in both accounts, in some ways eludes cultural definition or fixing. If meaning cannot be pinned down, nor can the subject. In Foucault, the body is the site of potential transgression; in Freud, the unconscious undoes the coherent conscious subject. It will be suggested here that, despite considerable differences in approach, Freud and Foucault might fruitfully be read together, and that 'the body' and 'the unconscious' provide a starting point for a materialist semiotics. This turns on the idea that the subject is an effect of systems working through the body, unconsciously. And importantly, the very effectivity of systems provokes the possibility of transformation.

Feminists working in the tradition of French theory have made major contributions to contemporary debates about the relation between the subject and meaning. The central issue has been the connection between knowledge and the masculine subject. Such feminists make the claim that the subject that would be whole and know the truth is a masculine subject; the fantasy of coherence and truth is dependent on the repression of the feminine. The discussion of the subject in this chapter is informed by feminist work in this area. My principal concern, however, is with approaches to the subject that might contribute to the development of a materialist semiotics. And the focus is on Freud and Foucault.

Foucault and Freud address 'the individual'. One of my interests is the status of the individual in their respective writings; what in the previous chapter was identified as a neglected object in sociological discourse. Foucault is interested in the discursive production of 'the individual'; Freud is concerned with the particularity of individuals' psychic processes. For both, the individual is necessarily a cultural being. It will be suggested that the individual is a crucial 'object' of analysis, but, more importantly, the concern is to argue for a methodology that addresses particularity, which needs to be distinguished from individuality. Freud and Foucault provide starting points for making this distinction. 'Particularity' is another means of reformulating the sociological question of the relation between the subject and the social. If cultural systems are practices in so far as they can be played through the body, any particular practice can be understood as a repetition which is different. This avoids any notion of a reified social that stands over and above the subject, and suggests that change is internal to the operations of systems.

It is worth noting that Freud and Foucault are frequently regarded as incompatible, or, at least that they have different concerns: the internal and the external of the subject, respectively (Grosz 1987: 9–10; de Lauretis 1987: 1–30). This distinction is, in part, imposed on their writings; they need not be read in this way. And reading them together can contribute to an understanding of the connections between the unconscious and the body. In addition to this task I shall take up Bergson's account of the subject and his critique of the common assumption that there is a qualitative difference between the internal of the self and the external world. Thus, his approach also implicitly breaks with a distinction between the subject and the social. In some important respects Bergson's philosophy prefigures contemporary feminist concerns: the significance of the body, a refusal to privilege consciousness, and a disruption to the external–internal opposition. And, as was suggested in Chapter 1, his notion of body-image provides a good starting point for thinking about meaning processes as material. In the final section of this chapter, as part of a project of undoing the social and the subject, the issue of commodification and the subject will be addressed with particular reference to Irigaray.

Foucault: the subject and power

I will focus here on an essay in which Foucault provides an account of his work on the subject and in which he specifically addresses the question of the discursive production of the individual: 'The Subject and Power' (1982). The basic assumption in Foucault's work is that the subject is an effect of power-knowledge configurations; the subject, in this view, is not the source of meaning, power or action. It is not endowed with a consciousness that power seizes on (Foucault 1980: 58). At the outset of this discussion it is important to distinguish three concepts: those of human being, subject position, and the individual. Human beings are discursively produced as subjects. One specific, but crucial, subject position is that of 'the individual', produced, for example, by liberal discourse.

The subject is a social or discursive effect; power does not work negatively over and against an already free subject ('the individual' of liberal discourse); rather it is productive of the subject.[1] Furthermore, power operates in and through the body; its productive effects are bodily. Unlike Lacan, who gives primacy to language, Foucault is concerned with the relations between different types of system, including language, that constitute the subject. Foucault took up an analysis of the system of power as it had received less attention than other systems. While 'instruments of analysis' have been developed for the economic and signifying relations which place the subject, there has been a lack of such 'instruments' with respect to power relations (Foucault 1982: 209). His primary concern has not been power *per se* but the development of an analytic approach to the subject; thus, to the principal semiotic concern with language he links an analytics of power. He begins 'The Subject and Power' by stating that the goal of his work has not been 'to analyze the phenomena of power', but rather 'to create a history of the different modes by which, in our culture, human beings are made subjects' (Foucault 1982: 208).

In the first part of this essay, 'Why Study Power: The Question of the Subject', Foucault (1982: 208) claims that his work has dealt with 'three modes of objectification which transform human beings into subjects': the modes of inquiry that try to give themselves the status of science, that is, the discourses of life, labour and language; 'dividing practices', that is, the disciplinary powers and techniques of normalisation by which the subject is divided internally or from others; and techniques of self, 'the way a human being turns him- or herself into a subject'. Although these modes can be analytically distinguished, in practice they may well coexist in a complexity of interconnections; this is a matter of specific analysis. In Volume 1 of *The History of Sexuality* Foucault (1981) provides an analysis of the intersection of the three modes; but in his later work (to which Volume 1 of *Sexuality* marks something of a transition), particularly on the subject of sexuality, techniques of self become the focus. This reflects, in part, what he sees as a shift in forms of power from the (external) disciplinary regime of the seventeenth and eighteenth centuries to the (internal) exercise of power over self. However, as is clear from Volume 2 of *The History of Sexuality* (Foucault 1985) there is no neat historical periodisation in this. His genealogical method runs against any notion of causality, historical or otherwise, and is not dissimilar to that of Benjamin discussed in the previous chapter (Foucault 1984: 76–100).

Modes of objectification can be understood, then, as practices of power-knowledge. What are the techniques involved and what are the effects on the subject? Disciplinary powers work by means of surveillance, 'the eye of power', 'eyes that must see without being seen' (Foucault 1984: 189). These powers are exercised through the body of the individual: 'certain bodies,

certain gestures, certain discourses, certain desires, come to be identified and
constituted as individuals'; individuals are not points of application of
power, but 'vehicles' of power (Foucault 1980: 98). Panopticism is a form
of power that has not disappeared. However, there has been a shift to the
interiorisation of the gaze: the subject takes him- or herself as the object of
the gaze, exercising surveillance over self. Foucault's conception of the gaze
as the 'instrument' of objectification and sight as the sense of knowledge-
power bears on issues that are addressed in this book. This was one of the
main themes in the previous chapter, in the discussion of knowledge as
mirror and the production of objects as mirror to self. And, as we will see,
there are parallels in the structure of knowledge-power in Hegel's master–
slave story, and in the significance of the gaze in Sartre's version of Hegel's
story.

The emphasis on the material, bodily forms of power is also pertinent to
my general concerns. As Foucault (1980: 58–9) says in an interview, Marxists would be more materialist if they studied the body rather than ideology
and consciousness in connection with the operations of power. To give an
example: his account of techniques of self suggests a different way of reading one of the classic texts of sociology, Weber's *Protestant Ethic*. This is
usually read as an account of ideas, or ideology, that provided the precon-
ditions of capitalism, and as such, is frequently regarded as idealist. But it
could be read as an account of an ethos with material effects on the body, as
an example of techniques of self-discipline productive of a particular subject
and a body predisposed to work through a certain working on the soul. (In
Freudian terms, this could be understood as a form of self-management in
the face of anxiety.) Foucault (1982: 213–15) does in fact cite the Refor-
mation as a historical instance of a struggle for a new form of subjectivity.
What the account of this struggle suggests, in both Weber and Foucault, is
that it has a form of a subject–object relation: consciousness works on the
body. However, Foucault's insistence on discourse working through the
body should be understood in terms of a concern to unsettle this very
opposition.

Some general points about knowledge might usefully be drawn out at this
stage. First, the eye and sight are central to knowledge processes and the
subject–object relation of knowledge. Metaphors of sight are prevalent in
self-representations of knowledges (Clifford 1986: 11), although the powers
of objectification that go with 'being objective' are rarely acknowledged.
Sight facilitates a distancing of the subject and object, and indeed consciousness and the body, and invites the illusion of correspondence – being objective. Second, knowledge has bodily effects; but the notion of objectivity
allows a certain 'blindness' to this. 'Eyes that see without being seen' involves a distancing between the subject of the gaze and the object – the
body; the bodily effects of the gaze are hidden. This, as we will see, is
Irigaray's argument about 'phallocentric' knowledge: it consists in a distancing from the masculine body through a process of displacement onto and

objectification of the female body. The subject–object relation of knowledge not only privileges sight and consists in a disavowal of the body, but has a masculine–feminine structure.

Foucault, as many commentators have pointed out, does not explicitly address the sexual structure of knowledge (de Lauretis 1987: 14–15). However, his entire project was concerned with the binary opposition that for deconstructive feminists is the 'basis' of all such oppositions: that between 'Same and Other' (Foucault 1970: xv–xxiv; White 1979: 103–4). This is another way of formulating the subject–object distinction, and, as it relates directly to Hegel's account of knowledge, I will be saying a good deal more about it in Chapter 4. However, Foucault's concerns are similar to those of feminists: How is difference (the Other) discursively produced in relation to sameness? And what is the possibility of a difference that escapes the order of the Same? His analyses of the differentiations between the sane and the mad, the healthy and the sick, the good and the criminal, the sexually normal and the sexually deviant – discursive practices of normalisation that function through the opposition between normal and abnormal – need to be understood in the context of a critical questioning of this opposition of Western knowledge between Same and Other. As for feminists, in Foucault's work, the body of the 'Other' is the site of potential disruption to the order of the 'Same'.

In 'The Subject and Power' Foucault takes up the question of objectification in the context of a discussion about the importance of a constant critical checking in any process of conceptualisation. Rather than 'theory' which assumes a 'prior objectification', he argues for a conceptualisation accompanied by a critical checking which must include an awareness of the present circumstances which 'motivate our conceptualisations' (Foucault 1982: 209). He warns against identifying a singular logic to modern culture or to the dynamics of power. Foucault says (with implicit reference to Weberian schools of thought), 'it may be wise not to take as a whole the rationalization of society or of culture', but rather to analyse specific rationalities in a range of fields with 'reference to a fundamental experience'.[2] As examples of the latter he cites such things as illness, madness, sexuality, death and crime. This approach, 'more empirical, more directly related to our present situation', consists in taking as a starting point struggles around a series of oppositions that have developed in recent years: 'opposition to the power of men over women, of parents over children, of psychiatry over the mentally ill, of medicine over the population, of administration over the ways people live' (Foucault 1982: 210–11). This is the historical condition that motivates research.

Why are these struggles significant? Their aim is power effects. For example, medicine is criticised not because it is profit-motivated but because of its power over bodies, life and death. These struggles are immediate, both in the sense that they concern what is closest to people, and in that they are struggles in the now, they do not look for a future solution in revolution.

However, the most important point that Foucault makes about these struggles is that they question the status of the individual. He claims that they assert the right to be different. They also attack that which separates the individual, forces him back on himself, tying him to an identity. (Perhaps what is at stake here is what it means to be human.) Neither for nor against the individual, these struggles question 'the government of individualization' (Foucault 1982: 211–12). They are an 'opposition to the effects of power which are linked with knowledge', struggles against the privileges of knowledge, the mystique and secrecy imposed on people. And they 'revolve around the question: Who are we?' That is, they are a refusal of abstractions.

These struggles are against a form of power in everyday life, a form of power 'which makes individuals subjects'. 'Subject' has the double sense of subject to someone else, and tied to self, to identity or self-knowledge (Foucault 1982: 212). The structure of power, of subjugation, implies that to be subject is to be objectified – which is the case also with the subject taking self as object.

Foucault claims that the prevalence of struggles against forms of submission and subjectivity relates to the development of the modern state. The power of the state is both totalising and individualising, which also accounts for the strength of the state. It is worth pausing on this question of the double moment of totalisation and individualisation, particularly as it relates to issues in both Hegel and Bergson. Totalisation can be taken to refer both to notions of a whole or complete subject, and also to a whole 'people', a homogeneity of the people, particularly where the state is concerned. In liberal democratic discourse the people, as one, is comprised of individual units that are formally equal – that is, without qualitative distinction. As we will see with Hegel, a whole or a unity requires a negation of otherness in a quest for self-sameness. And it is possible to read Foucault in these terms: the production of 'the individual', and 'the people', entails the negative differentiation between normal and abnormal. Bergson claims that 'a whole' presumes a composite of discrete entities (individuals, we might say), that are necessarily the same. It is reasonable to presume that Foucault is implicitly referring to both of these traditions of philosophy. Despite the differences between Hegel and Bergson, in each case the accounts are similar: totalisation is the other side to individualisation, both sides implying a sameness.

Foucault says that with the new form of pastoral power, the state does not stand over and above individuals, but integrates individuals, shaping new forms of individuality. However, the issue is not one of liberating the individual from the state, but imagining what we could be, in order to 'get rid of' the totalisation and individualisation of the state. It means refusing this kind of individuality through the promotion of different forms of subjectivity; the 'target nowadays is not to discover what we are, but to refuse what we are' (Foucault 1982: 216), which could be reformulated as 'what we are made'.

This is a very clear statement of motivations in conceptualisation. It also suggests an extremely useful approach to thinking about questions of subjectivity and change. Foucault's starting point is how we are constituted *now*: it is the very form of power that subjugates that also produces the possibility of refusal, reversal. Strategies of individualisation provoke demands for diversity, difference and particularity: a reversal of the totalisation of individualisation. A challenge to power does not come from outside, but from calling into question the mechanisms of the constitution of subjectivity (Foucault 1982: 216–17).

Power operates through bodies, in a positive way, and thus the body is the site of a possible transgression or refusal. This is elaborated in the second part of the essay, called 'How power is exercised'.[3] What constitutes the specific nature of power, in Foucault's account, is that it consists in actions, the modification of actions by actions. There is no such *thing* as power. Power *relations* are 'rooted in' social networks, the social nexus of lived relations between individuals or groups. And the possibility of change is part of the very play of power. Foucault (1982: 220–1) defines power as a mode of actions upon other actions; it has no existence external to the acting subject.

This conception of power might usefully be compared with Bergson's notion of bodies in movement acting on each other. Bergson does not specifically address power, but Foucault understands power as mobile and bodily. Both Foucault and Bergson borrow from physics the idea of forces and the body as a site of forces (Patton 1989: 272–3). As soon as a subject is immobilised, to use a Bergsonian term, there is, for Foucault, no play of power, but violence, slavery. One of the conditions of power is in fact that subjects be free. In a formulation of the conditions of a power relationship remarkably like Hegel's account of the master-slave relation, a relation between two free subjects, Foucault (1982: 220) says:

> a power relationship can only be articulated on the basis of two elements which are each indispensible if it is really to be a power relationship: that 'the other' (the one over whom power is exercised) be thoroughly recognised and maintained to the very end as a person who acts . . .

Thus, in a relationship of power, a field of possibilities opens up. And if to govern is to structure the field of possibilities, there is nevertheless such a field, more or less open to the subject. Much as in Hegel's scenario of power there are moments of stabilisation, but the power relation is inherently unstable; every 'power relationship implies, at least *in potentia*, a strategy of struggle', and the possibility of reversal (Foucault 1982: 224). When power is fixed, no longer a struggle to the death, it is no longer a power relationship. With instability and mobility there is always the possibility of a reversal. It might be noted that Foucault's account of slavery – a fixity of the position of object, with no possibility of subject position – is remarkably like de Beauvoir's modification of Sartre and Hegel on the master–slave relation in the light of the relation between masculine and feminine, although, of course, Foucault does not specify slavery as sexed.

This tension in the system of power between fixing and instability, is true of systems more generally. And as with systems of signification, despite tendencies to fix, there is a movement in the relational nature of power: a movement of the elements, the acting subjects. Foucault emphasises that any particular human being is positioned in and by a complexity of networks of systems, which in turn opens up strategic possibilities. For Foucault, this multiplicity of determination also undermines systematic attempts at fixing. It is on this point that feminists take issue with him (de Lauretis 1987: 38). While there is no disagreement about the significance of multiple determinations and the refusal of any form of reductionism, feminists claim that Foucault underestimates fixing operations and, in particular, the hierarchisation involved in the production of the sexed subject. Indeed, feminists might argue that the 'free subject' is a masculine position; and if this is the case there is perhaps a repression of the feminine in Foucault's account. In anticipation of a discussion about feminist concerns with multiplicity, a distinction might be made between two sorts of multiplicity. Foucault's concern is with a multiplicity or combination of subject positions; feminists are interested in multiplicity as that which escapes the fixing of systems.

What is important in Foucault's account of the subject is his conception of the complexity of systems and their interrelations, and the particularity in combination of these for any human being. Systems necessarily pre-exist the subject, but only have effects in and through the body. In this regard Foucault's approach to the subject is materialist: systems only have an existence in a material form, as they are lived (see also Eco 1977: 22, 314–17). Foucault is concerned to make analytic distinctions between types of system. However, there is perhaps a problem in distinguishing between, say, production and signification systems as it implies that activities can be understood separately from how they mean.[4] Foucault emphasises that in practice this is not the case, but he does make an analytic distinction. Counter to this, of course, is his insistence that power is necessarily discursive, that power and knowledge cannot be thought externally to each other; economic relations are also necessarily discursive.

One of the critical questions asked of Foucault is whether he takes sufficient account of the 'inner' of subjectivity (de Lauretis 1987: 16–17; Hollway 1984). What motivates or moves the body? In questioning 'the law of desire' (Foucault 1981: 81–3), does Foucault fail to give any account of motivation in the realm of psychic processes? In answer to this it could be said that his positive and productive conception of power is about effects *within* the body. Power 'incites, it induces, it seduces'; it also constrains or forbids (Foucault 1982: 220). In both its negative and positive moments it is productive of subjectivity. Furthermore, it is not as if Foucault (1970: 373–85; 1985: 6–7) ignores the question of desire. Nevertheless, it is true to say that if Foucault *is* concerned with the internal of subjectivity, his concern is not with the psyche as a system – the 'object' of psychoanalysis. It is, of course, in Freud's work that an account of the operations of psychic systems is to be found; the dynamic nature of these systems, psychical energy and the drives, is part of the psychoanalytic account of the internal movement of the subject. Foucault (1984: 114) acknowledges the importance of Freud, claiming that he and Marx are 'founders of discursivity', an 'endless possibility of discourse'.[5] They made possible differences and divergences, something 'other than their discourse, yet something belonging to what they founded'. Freud's texts can be reread in psychoanalytic terms (Foucault 1984: 114–15).

Foucault's work on the subject is particularly important for its emphasis on the bodily effects of systems, the materiality of the operations of systems in and through the body. As the site of subjugation, the body is also the site of potential transgression of the order. For example, the discursive constitution of the individual (the Same) provokes struggles that put difference on the agenda. In Foucault's account, the multiple determinations of 'the subject' provide leverage points for reversal and resistance to an order of the Same. In several respects, then, Foucault contributes to an understanding of the distinction between the individual and the particular: a fixing of the body of the individual, and a body of difference which implies a body in movement. However, it is to be argued that the concepts of the unconscious and memory are crucial to an understanding of the production of the body in movement. Hence the importance of Freud.

Freud: fictions of the subject

At this point one of the central features of the methodology that I am proposing needs to be introduced: the idea of *story*. Theorists and philosophers frequently present 'arguments' in the form of stories; of those that are to be addressed in this book, Hegel, Freud, and Cixous (who rereads the stories of Hegel and Freud among others) are exemplary cases. My argument is that stories and narratives not only tell us something about the culture in which we live, but that they are constitutive of it. In this view, fiction is not understood as mere 'fictional representation'. No more or less true than scientific representation, fictions and stories serve to highlight the discursive production of social orders. Furthermore, as a form of writing, storytelling is a good deal more open than 'science': we are invited to ask 'Is this our story?' and indeed to rewrite stories. It is not surprising that, given the structure of narrative, stories tend to be stories of origins or of an originary experience. My contention is that the temporal structure of this form needs to be distinguished from how we understand the effectivity of narratives, namely that they have a constant effect in the now. 'Origins' is to be understood, then, not as a moment in the past, but as a continuous generative 'source'; different moments in the drama are always there. And, if this idea is accepted, there is always the possibility of rewriting 'origins', in short, the possibility of transformation. One of the key mechanisms of this is a reading of stories across and against each other – a practice of intertextuality. But now to Freud.

Some introductory remarks about Freud need to be made before addressing the specific issue of stories. Freud's most important 'discovery' was that of the unconscious. It is this concept that provides the basis of psychoanalytic understandings of meaning and the subject. The unconscious is the contradictory mark of the cultural constitution of the subject; it is the precondition of culture. The common social scientific view of Freud as a theorist of the individual, and thus not a social theorist, can only come of a rejection of the unconscious and a commitment to an understanding of the individual as a separate entity characterised by consciousness. In a Freudian account the unconscious 'links' the subject with culture, makes it impossible to think the social and the subject as separate.

While Saussure is generally credited as the founding father of contemporary semiotics, Lacan's reading of Saussure and Freud together has had an enormous impact on readings of Freud. In the light of Lacan's emphasis on the principles of meaning in the system of the unconscious (Freud's Usc. system), Freud is now read as both an analyst of individual psychic processes and for the theory of meaning that is most fully developed in his *Interpretation of Dreams* (Lacan 1977: 146–78). His analysis of individual cases is dependent upon a conception of the cultural order and, most importantly, the principles of operation of the system of the unconscious. If in an obvious sense Freud's object was 'the individual' this needs to be understood as the *particularity* of the inscription of the individual in cultural systems; his interpretations would not have been possible without a conception of system. I want to suggest that his approach to the particular has a good deal to offer for cultural analysis and an understanding of meaning in terms of practice, which in turn has important implications for questions of social transformation. Here, I will focus on the issues of the narratives or myths of the subject of Western culture and the particularity of repetitions of these narratives. What do Freud's analyses of particular instances suggest about the possibilities of disturbance to the cultural order?

The unconscious is crucial to an understanding of disturbance. In Freud's account, repression is the condition of 'entry' of the subject into culture. Importantly, the unconscious, a part of which is the repressed (Freud 1984: 167), is simultaneously the basis of culture and potentially subversive of it: as Freud's analyses demonstrate, the return of the repressed is always on the cards. Indeed, this is one of the defining features of the unconscious; the 'representatives' of which it is comprised are 'strongly cathected by instinctual energy', and thus seek to resume activity (Laplanche and Pontalis 1973: 474; Freud 1984 [1915]: 183, 190). In Freud's (1976 [1900]: 774) view, not only does the unconscious constantly undermine consciousness, but it is the most important part of the psyche: 'we are probably inclined to greatly overestimate the conscious character of intellectual and artistic production'. He held the view that the unconscious 'influenced' the conscious to a much greater extent than the reverse (Freud 1984 [1915]: 199).

In contemporary cultural theory, Freud's analysis of the workings of the unconscious in dreams is extended to all cultural phenomena. It is not a matter of either/or, sometimes consciousness, sometimes the unconscious: consciousness is marked by traces of the unconscious. Freud's account of dream-work provides the basis of this view; unconscious elements are 'present' in a distorted form, distortion being the achievement of the principles of condensation and displacement. As Freud (1973a [1916]: 156, 207–8; 1976 [1900]: 414–19) constantly points out in his analyses of symptoms and dreams, a translation of elements is impossible; dream-work, or the principles of meaning of the unconscious, can, then, be understood as transformation. The unconscious has thus come to be understood as that which cannot be known, makes representation impossible. For Derrida, the unconscious, as an absence that is simultaneously 'present', is decisive for breaking with a presence–absence opposition. In the concept of the unconscious we find an alterity that is not 'a hidden, virtual, or potential self-presence' (Derrida 1982: 20). In his view the unconscious makes identity impossible.

Theorists specifically concerned with the subject formulate this in a rather different way. They emphasise the split between the unconscious and the conscious that comes about in the process of infantile repression. As has been pointed out by many commentators on Freud, this stands as a refutation of the idea of a unitary subject (see, for example, Mitchell and Rose 1982). If Freud's topographical accounts of the psyche encourage a conceptualisation of the unconscious and the conscious as separate entities, it might be better to focus on the conception of them as systems in a dynamic relation of tension, and bearing the traces of each other. Consciousness can be understood as the moment of the desire to know, the desire for identity and wholeness, and the unconscious as that which undoes identity. The crucial point is that the former is dependent on repressions, which are its very undoing. Consciousness necessarily bears traces of the unconscious, despite denials. And Freud's own work has been read in precisely these terms: his pronounced rationalist and scientistic views are contested by his account of the unconscious.

Given my interest in the connections between the body and the unconscious in meaning processes, something must be said about the difficult question of Freud's understanding of the relation between the psychic and the somatic. What constitutes the unconscious is ideational representatives of the instincts or drives; representatives which, in turn, have a determinative effect on aims and object choice. Freud also distinguishes between two aspects of the representative – the idea and the affect. He is insistent that some phenomena, such as dreams, are psychical rather than somatic (Freud 1973a [1916]: 129). For semioticians, Freud's theory of psychical mediations, meaning processes within the subject, and the reality of fantasy have been enormously important in refuting notions of unmediated experience (see, for example, Silverman 1983). However, the problem is, does Freud reinvent a mind-body distinction? (see Laplanche 1985: 48–65).

In the *Three Essays on the Theory of Sexuality* Freud (1977a [1905]: 82–3) defines the instinct (libido) as a 'psychical representative of an endosomatic, continuously flowing source of stimulation' and says that 'this concept' lies on the 'frontier between the mental and the physical'. If we take 'frontier' to refer to point of contact or interface, this certainly suggests that despite the conceptual distinction there is a complex interconnection between the psychic and the somatic. In fact all of Freud's work points to a conception of psychical energy is embodied. The effect (and affect) of unconscious processes, and Freud's constant concern with the experience or feeling of pleasure and unpleasure, the principles that move psychical processes, suggest such an understanding of psychical energy.

Now to the question of the narratives of the subject in Western culture, or more precisely, the narrative of Oedipus. Apart from brief references to the Greek legend, in, for example, the *Introductory Lectures* (Freud 1973a [1917]: 373–5), Freud does not give an explicit account of the Oedipus myth; the myth that he does give an account of is that of the primal feast, which is structurally similar to Oedipus. The latter came to inform all of his analyses, to such an extent that the common feminist claim is that he was implicated in resubmitting female patients to the law of the father. But feminists also take the view that Freud's work provides a particularly clear account of the nature of phallocratic or patriarchal culture: 'Freud is describing an actual state of affairs', he is not inventing female or male sexuality (Irigaray 1985a: 70).

Versions of the Oedipus myth can be found in texts, mainly written later in life, that Freud regarded as sociological. I want to address the question of the status of these texts and how they might be read in relation to his psychoanalytic texts proper. They include: *Group Psychology, Civilisation and its Discontents, Future of an Illusion, Moses and Monotheism, Totem and Taboo*, and the essays on war. Freud did not regard these as his important works, and possibly his own evaluation has led to their not being taken seriously by either cultural theorists or social scientists. Sociologists, and more commonly, anthropologists, do read them, but usually find them to be amateurish or to contain anthropological data that has been discredited, concluding that Freud is an analyst of individual psychic processes and not of culture or society. Cultural theorists and those working in the humanities note the outdated form of theorising in these texts, and that it sits oddly with the theory of meaning to be found in *The Interpretation of Dreams*, which Freud himself regarded as his most important work. Culler is an exception, and I want to pursue his view that the sociological texts should be read in relation to Freud's major works (Culler 1976: 74–6; see also Lacan 1977: 281; Gallop 1982: 23–8). If we do take them not at face value as scientific accounts of the development of society, but rather as versions of the myths of the culture, they then become extremely useful in throwing light on the connections between discourses that would fix the subject and the particular trajectories of individuals. A tension between these can be discerned in all of Freud's analyses.

In these explicitly sociological writings Freud uses a form of argument that looks like a search for origins, indeed he presents stories of origins rather like those of the contract political theorists of the seventeenth and eighteenth centuries. This mode of social theory does certainly stand at odds with Freud's modern form of analysis of psychic processes. But, as Culler has pointed out, to reject these texts on such grounds is to miss the point. In connection with *Totem and Taboo*, Culler says that it is crucial to remember that this was written after Freud's psychoanalytic interpretations, which are written back into the 'founding story'. Rather than being read as an explanation in the manner of a search for origins, *Totem and Taboo* should be read, in a certain respect, atemporally. For example, to substantiate claims about the social consequences of the ambivalent relation to the primal father, Freud (1985b [1913]: 223) cites the rituals of obsessional neurotics. In cases such as the rat man, Freud (1979 [1909]: 117) interpreted obsessional neurosis as symptomatic of ambivalence towards the father. Thus, he reads 'individuals' and culture symptomatically, in relation to and against each other, moving back and forth between them.

Culler's proposal for how we read these texts is perhaps a little defensive. We could think of the search for an original drama in terms of an originary drama in the now; such stories might be understood as generative 'models' which continually create the conditions of their own self-reproduction. Thus Freud's sociological writings can be understood as accounts of the myths of Western culture, and as themselves, mythic. What, then, do they tell us about the nature of contemporary culture, and indeed, the effects of psychoanalytic discourse? Here I am taking up Lévi-Strauss's understanding of myth: whether or not Freud presented the events of *Totem and Taboo* as 'real', or indeed believed them to be such, is besides the point; this story stands as a version of one of the most powerful myths of Western culture, one endlessly replayed on stage and screen and in art. Freud (1985b [1913]: 222) does in fact say that we do not have to believe that the event of killing and eating the father actually took place, the wishful fantasy is sufficient, and, we might add, is real. There is no doubt that the story of incorporating, being incorporated, and the primal killing of the father, is a constant psychic theme in our culture.[6] On the cultural significance of this myth there is agreement between Lévi-Strauss and Freud: the taboo on incest – father–son rivalry over the possession of women having led to the terrible event – marks the shift from nature to culture, the precondition of culture being exogamy. Not only is this the founding myth, but there is a universality to it. As Lévi-Strauss (1968: 218) said of Freud's version of the Oedipal myth (and *Totem and Taboo* can be read as yet another version of this), it is no more or less true than others, there is no original of which others are copies. It is always at work.

If we take stories of origins as mythic versions of Western culture, what do Freud's stories – that of the *resolution* of the Oedipus complex being the most significant – suggest about how he understood the culture, and about the ways in which he, himself, was subject to it? In Freud's accounts this is indeed a phallocratic and patriarchal culture, characterised by the law of the father, different paths of sexual development for boys and girls governed by the law of castration, a taboo on mother–son incest, and the exchange of women between men. Despite Freud's (1985a [1930]: 294–5) extremely critical comments, particularly on the damaging effects of the sexual repression demanded by civilisation, he nevertheless held with the importance of the resolution of the Oedipus complex. And, in this regard, as feminists have pointed out, his own analyses involved considerable repressions.

Yet feminists also regard Oedipus as the most powerful fiction of the subject, the normative story of Western culture, and they take Freud's account of how the subject is culturally inscribed in and through this story as a starting point in analyses of the sexed subject. This is a case in point of differences between Foucault and feminists, and specifically the different ways in which multiplicity is used. The feminist argument is that there is something totalising and singular about the phallocratic order, and indeed their use of this term presumes this. In this view, Foucault's conception of multiplicity evades the issue of the repression of multiplicity in the singular positioning of the subject. Feminists such as Irigaray claim that there is simultaneously a singularity to the order, and multiplicity: singularity requires a negation – and thus a repression – of multiplicity. If it is the case that Freud is implicated in the rewriting of this narrative, both in his writings and in his practice, his analyses – particularly the case studies – also stand as testimony to both the persistence of this narrative *and* its undoing. As Irigaray and Cixous have insisted, it is not a matter of proving Freud wrong, but rather of discerning within his analyses the ways in which Oedipus fails. This includes bringing to light the repressions in Freud's texts, that is, applying a Freudian analysis to Freud. Their argument is that in defining femininity in masculine terms, with reference to the masculine standard, Freud represses the specificity of female sexuality. Thus, in Irigaray's (1985a: 73) view, the feminine is the repressed which underpins culture, which leads her to propose that the feminine might *be* the unconscious.

Reading Freud through Lacan, feminists have been particularly concerned with the connections between meaning and language and the constitution of the sexed subject. The Oedipal story is read as a story of language and the subject. The law of castration has the effect of division and differentiation, it instigates the presence–absence principle of language, and marks the different relations to language of boys and girls. In short, the cultural or symbolic order is sexually differentiated and hierarchised: language works not just by differentiation, but by sexual differentiation (Mitchell and Rose 1982). The central issue here is the structure of binary opposition, and difference defined negatively in terms of sameness. The feminine is defined as lack, as not-man, as a means of maintaining the pretence of the presence of a masculine subject.[7] While psychoanalytic theory brings these operations of language to light, deconstructive feminists are concerned to find 'leverage points' for dismantling the structure of hierarchised opposition (Jacobus 1986: 20–1).

Freud's (1973b [1933]) essay on 'Femininity', the earlier papers on which it is based, and the case study of Dora (Freud 1977b [1903]), have produced a considerable body of feminist critical rereadings (including Irigaray, Jacobus, Kofman, Gallop, Spivak, Cixous). Rather than go over this ground, I will simply give some indication of the feminist questions asked of these texts, and the leverage points to be found in Freud. How might the masculine–feminine structure in Freud be deconstructed? For example, attempting to define femininity in terms of the Oedipus complex led Freud to argue that there was a good deal of difficulty in the acquisition of femininity, that it was rarely successfully achieved. We could say that his theory demonstrates a certain impossibility of femininity; or, as feminists have put it, that femininity is masquerade (Doane 1982). Does this then open up possibilities for bringing to light the pretence of masculinity; if the feminine is masquerade, what, by extension, are the implications for the masculine? As Jacobus (1986: 21) says, if femininity is masquerade because it is defined with reference to a male sign, might not that definition itself in turn be masquerade, 'imposture'? If the notion of masquerade suggests that there is, somewhere, an authentic, it perhaps needs to be stressed that this is regarded as a strategic move against any notion of presence.

The implication of Jacobus's comment is that Freud's theory is itself imposture. Does what he identifies as the difficulty in the development 'of a little girl into a normal woman' (Freud 1973b [1933]: 150) come of his own imposition of the Oedipus structure onto the development of girls, or is it that Freud recognised an inadequacy of Oedipus to the therapeutic task in the case of women? Freud (1973b: 163) finds that the castration complex moves girls into the Oedipus complex – the reverse of the situation for boys – and that there is nothing compelling girls to resolve this complex. Despite his attempts to define the feminine, Freud (1973b: 165) is forced to conclude that it is unstable.

The 'difficulty' is that Oedipus is a story about boys; the incest taboo is specific to mother–son relations; the castration complex does not impose itself as a law on girls in anything like the way it does on boys. As many feminists have pointed out, it cannot work as a threat for women as they have nothing to lose: their subjectivity is not constituted through fear of loss. Is there a sense, then, in which women are not subject to the law? To put this question is not to doubt its operation as law and the effects of hierarchised opposition, nor indeed women's complicity in the law of the father.[8] It is rather to ask whether this is a possible means of making trouble for that opposition. It works by a definition of the feminine in masculine terms, and yet even in these terms there is a difficulty in getting the feminine to stick. This

raises the question asked by Irigaray of the possibility of disruptive excess on
the side of the feminine. I will return to this issue, and to the question of how
feminist formulations bring the body and the unconscious together in their
understandings of what is disruptive to the cultural order and the unified
subject.

If the basis of culture is supposedly the mother–son taboo, there is also
something paradoxical in this. The threat of castration compels the boy to
give up the Oedipus complex, it is repressed, 'and in most cases entirely
destroyed' (Freud 1973b: 163). However, the boy, unlike the girl, is
supposedly not confronted with a problem of object choice, he retains his
initial one – his mother. What is repressed is also 'retained', what is taboo is
also the most socially sanctioned of relationships – that between mother and
son. With apparently no irony, Freud (1973b: 168) says: 'A mother is only
brought unlimited satisfaction by her relation to a son; this is altogether the
most perfect, the most free from ambivalence of all human relationships'.
What he does find ironical is that a man looking to a wife to satisfy his
Oedipal attachment finds that his son is getting what he wants: 'One gets an
impression that a man's love and a woman's are a phase apart psychologi-
cally' (Freud 1973b: 168). For all that the Oedipus narrative is meant to
produce a couple, man and woman, the couple fails, two halves do not make a
whole.

The bad timing that Freud, almost as an aside, makes reference to, makes a
correspondence between the terms masculine and feminine impossible
(Gallop 1982: 22–4). As Irigaray (1985a: 27) says: 'the Oedipal interdiction
seems to be a somewhat categorical and factitious law ... when it is
promulgated in a culture in which sexual relations are impracticable because
man's desire and woman's are strangers to each other'. They only meet
indirectly through the woman as mother, with the child, preferably boy, as
mediation. (A female child – imperfect mediation – is to become, in Irigaray's
view, archetypal mediation, but mediation that must be denied.) Maternity
fills the gap in a repressed female sexuality; and the man is identified with his
son (Irigaray 1985a: 27). But, Irigaray says, even if categorical, it nevertheless
provides the means for perpetuating the authority of the father. Thus, we
might say that the Oedipus narrative both does and does not work. This
fiction of the subject has certain effects – the perpetuation of the law of the
father, the positioning of woman as mother or object of exchange – but
written into the story is a failure. In this fiction of the subject we also find the
fictionality of the subject: the feminine is excluded; the masculine subject
cannot be made whole or complete, although the fantasy of this persists.

Freud's reference to 'the enigma of woman' in the essay on 'Femininity' has
been taken up in some readings as providing an opening for dismantling the
opposition between masculine and feminine. Freud (1973b: 165) says the
enigma 'may be derived from this expression of bisexuality in their lives', and
at the beginning of the essay he describes the task of psychoanalysis as one
that does not try to 'describe what a woman is' but rather inquires 'how she

comes into being, how a woman develops out of a child with a bisexual disposition' (Freud 1973b: 149). A crucial point here is that the original bisexuality is quite different from the later bisexuality, the shifts between masculinity and femininity after the Oedipus complex. This later bisexuality is defined with reference to the masculine, but what is 'originary' for women is a bisexuality that is also originary for men. This is a view that Freud (1977a [1905]) first elaborated in the *Three Essays on the Theory of Sexuality*, written before he took up the Oedipus complex. As a first step, then, in unsettling the structure of masculine–feminine some have suggested something like a reappropriation of a different origin – bisexual rather than masculine. Jacobus (1986: 20–1), following Heath (1982) and Kofman (1985), argues that positing bisexuality for women 'makes them not a derivative of men but rather a model for sexuality in general'. In this light the masculine as well as the feminine is masquerade. Freud's conception of bisexuality provides 'the beginning of an alternative representation, against the fixed sexual order' of man and woman. This is a point of leverage, but Freud also recuperates the order, 'neutralising' differences under identity, by defining bisexuality in masculine terms (Jacobus 1986: 21; see also Clément 1983: 83; Cixous 1986: 84–5). In Freud's account polymorphous perversity is a stage prior to sexual differentiation. Thus we might reformulate this bisexuality as a sexual indeterminacy, an originary indeterminacy even. Then the issue becomes one of different indeterminacies, in so far as they are differently embodied. And perhaps in this lies the possibility of moving beyond the fixings of masculine and feminine.

Lacan's rereading of Freud posits a direct connection between the castration complex and language. It is through the castration complex that the subject is inaugurated into the symbolic order; the phallus is the mark of separation and differentiation, that is, the principles by which language works. Lacan's concern is to show that there is no identity in language or the subject, and his work has contributed much to a project of bringing to light the pretence of the logos, and the ways in which this is based on a sexual differentiation in which woman is defined negatively in relation to man, as lack. Language operates through absences, making the presence of the subject an impossibility. The feminine is the absence in language. The issue for feminists has been how Lacan is implicated in the phallocentrism he describes. This turns crucially on the question of the phallus as transcendental signifier (Lacan 1982: 74–86; Gallop 1982: 36). If the pretence of the logos is phallic, for Lacan it is also the phallus as mark of differentiation which is instrumental in exposing this pretence. It is on this point that feminists such as Irigaray, Cixous, Gallop and Jacobus have argued that Lacan is phallocentric (disputed by Mitchell and Rose (1982)). The question is: Why the phallus, and why castration as the moment of splitting and differentiation?

As part of the general concern to interrogate the phallocentric basis of language and meaning, one strategy adopted by feminists has been to rewrite the story of separation, identifying instances other than those involving the phallus that might consist in separation and differentiation. While not disputing the cultural significance of the phallus, the concern here is again to identify repressions, and in refiguring differentiation in the account of language and the subject, to open up the possibility of alternative principles of meaning based on a different conception of differentiation. Thus, feminists have asked the rather obvious question: Might it not be the case that separation comes much earlier than the castration complex, for example, at birth or even in the womb? (See, for example, Jacobus 1976: 147; Benjamin 1986: 82). Freud (1977a [1905]: 98, 144–5) himself regarded the separation from the breast as a crucial informative experience of loss and absence (see also Laplanche 1985: 19–20). Why should this necessarily be read as simply prefiguring the castration complex as the decisive separation from the mother? Locating the basis of meaning and language in experiences such as these rather than the castration complex dislodges the phallus and makes the mother *and* child 'agents' of separation (Benjamin 1986: 82). It also has significant implications for principles of meaning. For example, it disrupts the privileging of sight. The castration complex turns on seeing, or seeing nothing (Freud 1973b: 158–9; 1977a [1925]: 336–7; Jacobus 1986: 113; Doane 1982: 79–80). The alternative points of separation involve senses of touch, sound, smell and taste (although in Freud's own accounts in the case studies it is possible to read these senses, particularly that of sound, as having a part in the castration complex). It could be said that it is in the very nature of a separation constituted through sight that a desire for identity is invoked; other senses imply different principles of relation between terms or elements, notably those of contiguity and metonymy.[9]

Lacan's famous essay on the fantasy of identity, 'The Mirror Stage', addresses the connection between sight and identity. This is a story (although Lacan would have given it the status of science) of the economy of the imaginary, the retroactive fantasy of an originary wholeness of the subject. The principle of meaning in the imaginary is that of resemblance, a coalescence of the signifier and the signified, a direct correspondence: 'That image is me'. It specifically refers to the 'ego of the infant constituted on the basis of the image of the counterpart', the specular ego (Laplanche and Pontalis 1973: 210). But, neither the imaginary nor the mirror stage should be read in a narrow developmental way.

The mirror stage is a story about the instability of the 'I'; the subject is neither the origins of the 'I' nor centred. The mirror 'reduplicates' the child's body; but, the assumed image of the body does not 'correspond' to the uncoordinated bits and pieces body of the child (Lacan 1977: 1–2). The 'inner' body is fragmented; the external is the 'total form of the body' (Lacan 1977: 2), fixed, in the image. *Identification* with the imago is thus constitutive of the fantasy of identity. Identification with the mirror image provides the fantasy of a coherent autonomous subject, but this subject is constituted in a split: the image splits the child – inner and outer. Furthermore, the subject forms an image of itself by identifying with an other's perception of it (which is an operation very like Foucault's understanding of self-surveillance). That is, the 'I' does not come from within the self, but is conceptualised when the subject is mirrored back to itself from the position of the other – from someone and somewhere else. Thus, Lacan (1977: 6) says, the moment of recognition of self is the moment of misrecognition (see also Gallop 1985: 82–90; Clément 1983: 84–96). We might reverse this: the moment of misrecognition is the moment of recognition. The mirror founds the fantasy of identity: the possibility of a correspondence between subject and object. But the very process of mirroring makes this a fantasy: there are not two but three terms involved; the image of self is dependent upon the (imagined) gaze of an other (see also Benveniste 1971: 220–2). The process of referral of the image through the mirror and the other shows that the subject does not stand alone.

In the introduction to this chapter I suggested that psychoanalytic theory had a methodological significance with respect to the particular. Freud's case studies are exemplary analyses of the particular. They are his stories of the particular histories of individuals; and, if he regarded Oedipus as universal, he nevertheless took the view that there was a particularity to every repetition of it. His entire analytic project is based on this assumption, and indeed, the development of psychoanalytic theory comes out of specific analyses. If Oedipus sometimes looks as if it functions as a 'model' in Freud's work, it should be remembered that he came to the significance of this myth through analyses, and, however much it informed further analyses, he had to be convinced that a specific instance was a repetition, maintaining an openness to the analysand.

Both Foucault and Freud took the individual as an object of analysis, although in very different ways. However, both their approaches run directly counter to any individualism. It is the recognition of the particularity of any object, be it an individual or anything else, that calls for analysis rather than 'theory'. A concern with the particular also has implications for how we think about change. If narratives such as Oedipus are imposed on or write the subject, they do not simply do so; in any particular combination of codes and elements there is the possibility of a rewriting. In Foucault's account, the subject is positioned in a complex, and possibly contradictory, network of discursive practices. In this specificity, or what he refers to as multiplicity, of positionings of the subject, lies the possibility of refusal. In Freud's account, civilisation demands the repression of wishful fantasies that are reactivated through chains of association. Any instance of this is particular; while there are rules of association, the possibilities of combinations are vast, and so too are the possibilities for disturbance.

I want to conclude this section by addressing these issues in relation to Freud's (1977b [1905]) case study, 'Dora'. This is probably the most widely read of the case studies, certainly by feminists (see, for example, ICA 1984; Bernheimer and Kahane 1985). It is a particularly striking case of the positioning of a woman in phallocentric culture: Dora is the object of exchange between men – her father, Herr K. and Freud – in what emerges from Freud's account as nothing short of a family nightmare. There is an impossibility here. What choice did Dora have in her objects and identifications? There were the men engaged in exchange relations, or women who were objects of exchange or 'mother', and defined as 'nothing'. Without a speaking position, Dora's body spoke in hysterical symptoms; which is why, together with her dismissal of Freud and denial that he was a love object for her, some feminists regard Dora as a case of refusal (Cixous 1986: 99, 147–55).

'Dora' is read as much as a story about Freud as one about Dora. One of the things that makes this case study particularly interesting is Freud's position both in the text and in the analysis, together with his account of the writing of the story. Feminists have drawn attention to Freud's oversights and repressions. In a sense the text invites this sort of reading: Freud actually refers to some of his oversights, clues are provided, and there are gaps in the text which open up the opportunity of asking Freudian questions of it. The most obvious example is the other text, the story told by the footnotes. It is here, below the line, that Freud (1975 [1905]: 152, 162) discusses at some length his belated discovery of Dora's homosexuality and attraction to Frau K. He accounts for this in terms of Dora's disappointment in father substitutes; a regressive masculinity complex is relayed through the Oedipus complex.

One of the questions feminists have asked in connection with this is: What of the possibility of woman's desire independent of the masculine, and how might the relation to the mother be figured differently? The 'mother' is noticeably absent in 'Dora', with, for example, the repetition of 'I get nothing from her'.[10] Then there is the afterthought about transference, which invites the question, not addressed by Freud, of his counter-transference onto Dora, and the possibility of his desire to take up a feminine position (Freud 1977b [1905]: 157–60). As a way of saying that he speaks directly, as a man of science, about the body and sexuality, Freud (1977 [1905]: 82) says '*J'appelle un chat un chat*'. His repressions are very clearly around female sexuality, and Dora was certainly an enigma to him. This points to the desire to write this story, to narrativise. Dora did not want Freud to find an end to her story; she walked out, dismissed him, putting *him* in the position of the governess, contrary to his view that she was 'governess' giving notice.

Why did Freud choose to write up a case that he admits to having failed at in some respects? Marcus (1985: 88) has argued that it is precisely Freud's therapeutic failure, and Dora's refusal, that provokes the desire to tell the story. This comes back to Weber's argument about the desire to totalise, to get a whole, complete picture; and the way in which Freud's work both demonstrates this desire, and the impossibility of its realisation. Freud wanted to make complete what he insisted was a fragment; the case study is titled 'Fragment of an Analysis'. This is rather disingenuous, given the description of his task as one of providing a coherent story. But, it does bring to light the conflict between fragmentation and the desire to make whole, to tell a coherent story of self. For Freud (1977b [1905]: 45–7) the problem with patients is that they tell incoherent stories; his role is to produce a complete story, 'intelligible, consistent, and unbroken'. At the end of successful analyses patients will accept this story as their own, symptoms will be converted into speech (Marcus 1985: 71–2). In short, they have to be able to speak the story. 'Dora' was not successful; Dora did not accept Freud's story. Perhaps this impelled Freud to make a coherent narrative, as a response to the fragments of his analysis. Dora eluded Freud: what is at stake is *his* self-coherence.

Marcus (1985: 64, 70) claims that Dora is comparable, in the complexity and non-linearity of the narrative structure, with the modernist novel, and with Borges. The text reflects on itself, it provides a story of the story. In a way it admits to being fiction, and yet claims to be real at the same time. In this regard it is a 'model' of cultural analysis: the fact–fiction opposition is broken with, and the position of the writer-researcher is not denied. As a consequence, the repressions in the text are relatively easy to discern. The reader is invited to ask: 'Where is Freud in this text?' He tells us that he is speaking 'frankly' about himself, questioning his role; thus we are invited to look for what is not spoken about frankly. Freud acknowledges the desire for completion, but writes in such a way as to open up further analyses. And indeed this text has had the effect of cultural production – rewritings of the story which would 'inscribe' femininity differently (for example, the film *Sigmund Freud's Dora: A Case of Mistaken Identity*, made by McCall, Pajaczkowska, Tyndall, Weinstock (1979), and Cixous' play *Portrait of Dora* (1979)). For feminists such as Cixous, Dora is particularly significant because the refusal, and what eludes Freud, is a bodily speaking of the unconscious. However Dora's hysteria is interpreted, as resistance or oppression or both, this case has been taken as something of a model for the idea of 'writing the body', a bodily inscription of difference that disrupts knowledge, based as it is on the repression of the feminine. The unconscious, embodied, escapes the order of discourse, including psychoanalytic discourse. Nevertheless, it is Freud's telling of this story that has opened up the possibility of such feminist formulations.

Bergson: the centred subject

In Chapter 5 I will be giving a detailed account of Bergson's theory of duration and methodology of multiplicity, which have important implications for how we think the subject. Here, I want to make reference to a section in *Matter and Memory* (Bergson 1950b) where he directly addresses the question of the centred subject, and effectively displaces the subject through a strategy of reversal. Where, for example, Lacan starts from the centred and proceeds to dismantle, Bergson's claim is that to take the centred as the starting point is mistaken. He does not dismiss the importance of the notion of the centred self, but he argues that it cannot be accounted for by taking self as the reference point. 'My belief in an external world does not come, cannot come, from the fact that I project outside myself sensations that are unextended: how could these sensations ever acquire extension, and whence should I get the notion of exteriority?' (Bergson 1950b: 43). In some respects this is similar to the Lacanian view that a notion of identity, our body as 'our representation' (Bergson 1950b: 43) is acquired relationally. But in Bergson's approach there is no originary wholeness of the imaginary. Despite the fact that the imaginary comes retrospectively via the symbolic, for Lacan it is the subject of the imaginary that is to be decentred.[11]

Bergson (1950b: 43) asks how is it that in the aggregate of body-images that comprise the material world we come to give our body a privileged position. It is not the external world that is problematic, but how we ever come to a notion of the self as the centre. Bergson (1950b: 43–4) says: 'If you start with my body, as is usually done, you will never make me understand how impressions received on the surface of my body . . . are able to become for me independent objects and form an external world'. This is to make a disarmingly simple point, but one that radically refutes a conception of the subject as source of meaning and action: how, if there is only the internal of the self to start with, could any sense of the external come about? In Bergson's account there is first of all an aggregate of images, and in this aggregate, centres of action. How my body comes to stand out as a centre through which actions are referred can only be understood if we start from the periphery and move to the centre, rather than the reverse. To start with the centre and move to the periphery presents insurmountable problems: the idea of an external world, constructed artificially, piece by piece, 'out of unextended sensations', though we can neither understand how they 'come to form an extended surface, nor how they are subsequently projected outside the body' (Bergson 1950b: 44).

> Why insist, in spite of appearances, that I should go from my conscious self to my body, then from my body to other bodies, whereas in fact I place myself at once in the material world in general, and then gradually cut out within it the centre of action which I shall come to call my body . . . ? (Bergson 1950b: 45).

This mistaken view of the self arises, he says, because extensity is taken as homogeneous empty space, that is, an external world without qualitative distinctions, which makes possible the notion of projecting the self and its qualities onto that world. On the contrary, what characterises the material world is qualitative difference in Bergson's view.

Through the education of the senses we acquire a notion of our body being acted upon and in turn acting. But this process of development of the senses takes place within a system of bodies acting: if there are so many possible kinds of action of my body in response to the body-images around it, the same must be so of the other bodies. Through the senses the body interprets actions of bodies such that it in turn can exercise actions on other bodies (Bergson 1950b: 46). Bergson does not privilege sight; he is concerned with the complexity of the senses and their relation to actions. Crucially, the data of our senses are 'the very qualities of things'. In claiming this, Bergson disrupts the notion of a qualitative distinction between the internal and the external, and a conception of knowledge as consisting in consciousness knowing the material world that is qualitatively different from itself. Our senses, characterised by qualitative difference, are *of* that material world.

Bergson, like Foucault, emphasises bodies acting in relation to each other: a materialist, relational and mobile conception of 'the subject'. In Foucault's understanding of the system of power there is always the possibility of change; Bergson's concept of qualitative difference makes a further contribution to an understanding of the potential for transformation, a process that is embodied.

Irigaray: commodities as mirror of self?

The idea that the self is constituted through a working on nature such that the products of one's labour will reflect self, that the self is externalised in objects which mirror the subject, runs through modern social theory from Hegel and Marx onwards. Taking up Hegel's conception of alienation, Marx argued that the specific form of these products under capitalism was the commodity. Feminists, sexualising Marx, have argued that woman is in the position of commodity; the subject of labour is masculine. What is to be highlighted here is the close connection between the commodity form and identity. Deconstruction, in part, consists in an undoing of the principles of meaning of the commodity – sameness, interchangeability – of which Marx so clearly provides an exposition in Chapter 1 of Volume 1 of *Das Capital*. Bringing to light the sexual underpinnings of commodification, showing how woman as commodity is mirror, is an important move in this project. I want to demonstrate how this contributes to an undoing of both the subject and the social with reference to Irigaray's reading of Marx.

Irigaray makes connections between the sexed subject and the economy through a rereading of Lévi-Strauss on the exchange of women together with Marx on commodities. In 'Women on the Market' her argument with respect to Lévi-Strauss is that the cultural order is homosexual, masked by a heterosexual economy of exchanges of women between men. She claims that all systems of production and exchange (of women, signs, commodities) in patriarchal societies are referred back to men, they are men's business, valorise men's desires (Irigaray 1985a: 171). What 'the anthropologist' calls the passage from nature to culture, is the institution of the 'reign of hom(m)o-sexuality' which is prohibited in practice, and 'played out through the bodies of women'. Heterosexuality is an alibi for the 'smooth workings of man's relations with himself, of relations among men' (Irigaray 1985a: 172). Women as reproductive use-value and exchange value (signs), 'underwrite the symbolic order as such' (Irigaray 1985a: 173).

The idea that women underwrite the social order, constitute an infrastructure, is a constant theme in Irigaray's essays (1985a: 30–3, 84–5). In 'The Power of Discourse' she claims that being external to the laws of exchange and yet included in them as commodities, women are in a position to elaborate a critique of political economy. This would involve an analysis of 'the impact of the economy of discourse on the analysis of the relations of production' (Irigaray 1985a: 85). 'Women on the Market', written three years later, could be seen as part of that project, asking of Marx, for example: What is the repressed of this discourse on the economy?

Irigaray rereads Marx's analysis of commodities in an attempt to show that it can be understood as an interpretation of the status of women in patriarchal societies. For commodity she substitutes woman. For commodities to be exchanged they must be treated abstractly, in a quantitative rather than qualitative way. An exchange relation requires that two commodities have a common property that is neither one nor the other; they must both be reducible to a third term. In Marx, the third term is abstract labour, labour in its quantitative aspect. What this quantitative aspect consists in, namely labour time, is highly significant for the discussion of time in Chapter 5: if labour is quantified, it is so through a quantification of time. Thus it could be said that the quantification of commodification requires a suppression of time.

Irigaray rewrites Marx on abstract labour: 'when women are exchanged, woman's body must be treated as an *abstraction*', and the third term in this case is the phallus. Specifically feminine qualities are irrelevant to these exchanges. Women's bodies are abstracted, and they are compared in terms of a common feature: as products of 'man's labour' (Irigaray 1985a: 175). Woman's exchange-value is a 'mimetic expression of masculine values' (Irigaray 1985a: 180). 'Man endows the commodities he produces with a narcissism that blurs the seriousness of utility, of use . . . commodities can have no relationships except from the perspective of speculating third parties' (Irigaray 1985: 177). In this symbolic order women's bodies mirror the desire for exchanges among men: the specific qualities of women's bodies have to be suppressed. In 'Commodities among Themselves' she says that 'women exist only as an occasion for mediation, transaction, transition, transference between man and his fellow man, indeed between man and himself' (Irigaray 1985a: 193). Homosexual relations, including the incestuous relation of father–son, are veiled by this mediation, indeed must be veiled if the value of the standard, the phallus, is to be maintained and not reduced to penis, 'means to pleasure'. It is interesting to note that in *Totem and Taboo* Freud (1985b [1913]: 205–6) claims that when the brothers instituted the law against incest, renouncing the 'women they desired and who had been their chief motive for despatching their father . . . they rescued the organisation which had made them strong – and which may have been based on homosexual feelings and acts'.

In 'Women on the Market' Irigaray presents an analysis of the different social positions of women in terms of their 'natural' value and 'social' value. As 'mother' woman is positioned within reproductive nature, excluded from exchange. The incest taboo operates with respect to mothers, their role is to maintain the social order which would be threatened by their circulation. The virgin is pure exchange value – the sign of relations between men, what is really at stake in social exchange. The prostitute is both use-value and exchange-value, or at least usage that is exchanged: the qualities of her body have value 'only because they have already been appropriated by a man', and because they serve as a locus of relations between men (Irigaray 1985a: 185–6).

In Marx, human society is characterised by the submission of nature to man's labour. In Lévi-Strauss, the passage from nature to culture is based on the exchange of women between groups of men. In these discourses of Western culture women's reproductive capacities lie on the side of nature; in the symbolic order women have value only in so far as their bodies are abstracted and reflect man's labour, man who is the subject of production and exchange relations. However, this process of abstraction means that man's relation to himself and other men is constituted through mediation, and it is woman who mediates.

In these essays on social and economic discourse Irigaray is bringing to light the mediations in economic relations, and specifically the mediations of the commodity (although clearly not herself speaking as a commodity). She makes this argument more generally about the logos and the operations of language: the self-presence of the masculine subject is dependent on mediations which must be hidden in order that the pretence of presence be maintained. The mirror, which allows the subject to reduplicate itself by itself, most often remains hidden (Irigaray 1985a: 75). Thus, woman functions as a negative mirror image: her specific qualities are repressed so that the subject can reflect itself; the feminine is defined through a negation.

The commodity as mirror has been a source of fascination for social theorists (see, for example, Baudrillard 1975). There are numerous reread-ings of Marx's account of the inverted mirror image of the commodity in 'The Fetishism of Commodities', frequently taken as a starting point in analyses of modern cultural forms. For Marx the commodity did not mirror the labour of the worker, given the double alienation of the ownership relation. In a sense, though, Marxism retains the fantasy of the imaginary: the possibility of a true mirroring relation between the subject and object of production, the object as an expression of self – a coalescence of the signifier and the signified. While Marx presents a critique of the quantification of the commodity form, feminists such as Irigaray take this a step further in pointing to the qualitative which is repressed, the specificity of femininity. In turn, this disrupts the fantasy of a true mirroring relation between man and the products of his labour, a mirroring of masculine qualities which requires a quantification or abstraction of the feminine.

Other theorists who have addressed the sexual dimension of commodities include Simmel, Benjamin, Eco (1977: 26), and Spivak (1988: 154–78). One of Benjamin's figures of modernity is the prostitute, which he produces by combining Marx's reference to the soul of the commodity with Baudelaire's 'prostitution of the soul'. If prostitution of the soul comes of the lure of commodities, the prostitute as sexual object is in a sense the archetype commodity (Benjamin 1973: 55–7; see also Buck-Morss 1986: 118–27). Simmel (1982 [1900]: 376–80) makes a similar connection between the commodity and prostitution. Prostitution is a relationship in which all 'individual differences are eliminated'. The 'economic counterpart of this kind of relationship is money'; money is a quantification and objectification which transcends qualitative differences, or in Simmel's (1982: 376–7) terms 'individual distinctions'. He speaks of this as an analogy: in money we can discern the essence of prostitution, and prostitution takes the form of money. Simmel's analysis of money as the paradigm of modernity – interchangeability, abstraction, quantification – is remarkably like Irigaray's account. What emerges from Simmel's essays in *Georg Simmel: On Women, Sexuality and Love* (Oakes 1984), is the idea that the basis of modern culture is a sexual differentiation. Objective culture is a product of men's activity: a projection and externalisation of their subjective into the objective world of commodities. This consists in a projection of self into an external understood as homogeneous, which, in turn, produces a detachment from self. Thus, in what is a strikingly Hegelian formulation, Simmel claims that mediation characterises a masculine way of being, while women live in immediacy (Oakes 1984: 24–5; Simmel 1984 [1923]: 103, 117–21). And closely connected with this is his claim that the feminine is a moment 'prior to the division into subject and object' (Simmel 1984: 132). The convergence with Irigaray will become clear when the question of mediation and immediacy – and that of subject–object – is addressed in the following chapter. This turns on the issue of the connection between the body and meaning processes.

In arguing that the *matter* of women's bodies underpins the social order, and that the specific qualities of these bodies must be repressed as a means of disguising this process, Irigaray makes a direct connection between the unconscious and the body as the site of potential disruption to the order. Qualitative difference presents a disturbance to the singularity and sameness of the social order and the self-presence of a masculine subject. In the following chapter her argument about the body 'inscribing' a different way of meaning, consisting in difference and multiplicity, will be addressed. What, we might ask, are the possibilities of the body? Of bodies?

One of the central assumptions in this discussion has been that 'the subject' is relational. The following chapter pursues this question through an investigation of the self–other relations of knowledge, that is, the structure of power and desire that is constitutive of meaning and knowledge processes.

4

POWER

The theme of this chapter is power and desire in knowledge. If knowledge consists in a mirroring relation, what is the structure of desire in such a relation, and how is this desire linked with power? Desire refers to inter-subjective relations between self and other which motivate knowledge processes; in a sense, knowledge and meaning *are* desire. Making connections between power and desire contributes to an understanding of the mechanisms of power-knowledge, the structure of power relations in knowledge, and what is involved in strategies that would deconstruct knowledge. If these can be understood as strategies of counter-power, to use a Foucaultian term, they are also constitutive of and constituted in a different structure of desire. While the structure of desire of representation is negative, that of transformation is positive: desire is basic to different ways of meaning, and the production of different subjects. Thinking of knowledge and meaning in terms of desire immediately draws attention to the subject of knowledge as a subject of desire, and indeed a bodily subject rather than one characterised by a speculative consciousness. The very process of countering knowledge-power consists in a transformation of the subject of desire.

The first part of this chapter addresses Hegel's account of power and desire in knowledge in the master–slave story. Contemporary French philosophy comes out of the Hegelian philosophical tradition, and it is this tradition which is the principal object of deconstruction. A theme which appears in the writings of French philosophers, including feminists, is the idea that the Hegelian scenario of power and desire in knowledge and structure of self–other relations prevails in Western culture, in philosophical practice, but also in practices of everyday life. Butler (1987: x) says, with reference to contemporary French philosophy: 'Hegel's subject of desire remains a compelling fiction even for those who claim to have definitively exposed his charades.'

The second part of this chapter considers critical rereadings of the Hegelian tradition (particularly those of Irigaray and Cixous), and feminist strategies of confronting the power of Hegelian discourse. Hegel is read not only for what he has to say about power, but also for the operations of power in his discourse. Hegel's story of mastery, the certainty of self-consciousness and the power relations that, in his view, are essential to this, is simultaneously a story of his philosophy. The critical target of French feminists is the desire for mastery in Hegelian philosophy. The Hegelian concept of mastery has the double sense of power ('lordship' in the English translation) and knowledge (to grasp). In proposing a different desire, or relation between self and other, feminists are also proposing different principles of meaning, forms of relations between elements. Relations between (and within) bodies, and the significance of different senses to such relations, are crucial to this way of meaning.

Hegel: power and desire

The key text for this discussion is 'The Truth of Self-certainty', particularly the section 'Lordship and Bondage', in *Phenomenology of Spirit* (Hegel 1977 [1807]); but first, some general remarks. As some Hegel scholars emphasise, he should be read as fiction, which, far from a devaluing of his philosophy as 'fiction', 'shows the essential role of fiction . . . in the quest for philosophical truth' (Butler 1987: 23). Among other things, this is to say that despite philosophy's claims about its status as knowledge, it is not and cannot be free of the tropes of fiction or literary texts. Hegel's fiction contributes, then, to a bringing to light of the operations of philosophical discourse. As a story there is also the possibility of a rewriting in the retelling, what in fact Hegel was doing in retelling philosophical stories. This relates to my general concern with the potential openness of storytelling over 'theory'. In recounting stories by, for example, Hegel and Freud, and the retelling of these by Lacan, Cixous and Irigaray, I want to emphasise that these are different stories of Western culture, that there is no *one* story, and certainly not one that is the true story. In a sense they are all true, and in reading them across and against each other we can discern a multiplicity of determinations and subject positionings.

Hegel's fiction of the subject of desire and knowledge tells us something about the fictional status of the subject. This fictionality is a consequence of the impossibility of unmediated self-knowledge; and, thus, an account of the search for such knowledge in the form of a story serves precisely to highlight the mediations of language in philosophy. The master–slave story is a narrative, with one event leading to another, curious twists, and contradictions to be resolved. The significance of the story, particularly the irony in it, will be missed if we do not follow specific turns of events. The full import can only be grasped through an imaginative – which does not preclude critical – engagement with it. And then it is a truly fantastic story; for the 'error', or more precisely the failure, is inscribed in the very structure of the story. It can be read as a story of ourselves, and as such is a compelling fiction. In summary it is this: the human subject or self-consciousness strives for identity of itself with itself, for a unified independence, and self-reflection or knowledge. *The Phenomenology of Spirit* is about the development of Spirit, or self-consciousness; the emergence from lower states of consciousness and immersion in the sensuous world to the truth of self-certainty: philosophy's reflection on itself. One of the most important assumptions in Hegel is that self-consciousness requires a relation to an other self-consciousness. We can only know ourselves through a relationship to an other that is the same, but different. Unlike the Cartesian approach to knowledge, there is no singular, originary, knowing 'I'; knowledge, for Hegel, is necessarily inter-subjective. Self-consciousness is always mediated; independence is dependent on a relation to an other. As Butler (1987: 7) says, this is the irony: self-consciousness 'knows itself only as a structure of mediation'.

This relation to an other points to the significance of desire in Hegel's account of knowledge. The process of knowledge is motivated by desire: what moves the show along is the relation of self to other, and the desire to be desired, the desire for recognition and a mirroring of the self by the other. In this sense knowledge *is* desire: 'self consciousness is *Desire* in general' (167).[1] Desire is rational in that it consists in the search for knowledge, but this is not a conception of rationality defined in terms of an end or goal in the way that purposive rationality is defined. The desire for knowledge is in a sense deceptive, and the quest for knowledge endless. Indeed, it could be said that there is no narrative closure in Hegel's story, even if the desire is for such a closure. The dialectic makes any resolution temporary.

The Hegelian idea of unity of opposites is crucial to an understanding of the nature of resolution. The unity of opposites is never a stabilised or static unity, but one that is in a constant process of dissolution, or resolution that is simultaneously dissolution, a splitting apart of the two sides of the opposition. Connected with this is the idea that in the unfolding of Spirit and movement to higher stages there is also a regressive movement: a resolution at a higher stage and a lapsing back to lower forms of consciousness. The stages in the unfolding of Spirit are not left behind; lower ones continue and coexist with higher ones. In Freudian terms – and one of my strategies will be to read Freud and Hegel together – we might say that the ever present possibility of regression contributes to the deceptive nature of desire for knowledge. This raises the important issue of temporal structure: although Hegel narrativises, much as Freud provides developmental accounts, it must be emphasised that all the moments or stages are simultaneously 'present'.

One of the implications of the idea of unity of opposites is that Hegel's understanding of the relation between mind and body is quite different from the mind–body dualism of the Cartesian model of knowledge. To conceive of knowledge in terms of desire rather than as a speculative, intellectual activity, implies a certain corporeality in knowledge processes. In Hegel, mind and body are not different kinds of stuff, qualitatively different in substance, but rather, different moments of the self: self-consciousness is the reflective version of the body. If this is a disembodied moment it must, none the less, be understood as one side of the split unity of mind and body which *is* consciousness.

The process of the coming together and splitting apart of the unity of opposites is the dialectic: the indefinite movement of moments of simultaneous negation and conservation. Above all else, the relation of consciousness to the other is a negative relation (36, 37). To grasp a unity requires a negation on the part of self-consciousness of what is other than itself: that is not me. But negation also implies dissolution. If the other is superseded it is no longer there as mirror to self. Thus the satisfaction of desire annuls the precondition of self-certainty. This is a negativity of which there is no final resolution. It is in the dialectic that the deconstructive moment in Hegel can be found: the dialectic of knowledge contributes to the undoing of that very knowledge.

In 'The Truth of Self-certainty' Hegel is giving an account of the emergence of self-consciousness out of less advanced stages of consciousness, a moment in the unfolding of Spirit from nature.[2] In the lower forms, such as sense-certainty and perception, consciousness is immersed in the sensuous, in what is other to it, and has no notion of itself. It might be noted that this is comparable to Freud's developmental account of the subject; the infant at the breast, for example, makes no differentiation between itself and the outside sensuous world. Such a distinction is brought about by the experience of loss. For Hegel, also, lack is constitutive of desire. What distinguishes *self*-consciousness is differentiation of self from otherness: 'self-consciousness is the reflection out of the being of the world of sense and perception, and is essentially the return from *otherness*' (167). And, with 'self-consciousness . . . we have . . . entered the native realm of truth' (167). The movement towards truth involves the double moments of negation and unification. First, the negation of otherness, 'the difference is *not*'; the 'sensuous world is preserved' for self-consciousness through negation – 'that is not me'. Otherness is superseded, incorporated into self. The second moment is 'the unity of self-consciousness with itself'. And this is the unity in difference: truth is this unity amid differences: 'difference which *in itself* is no difference' (167).

The basic Hegelian idea of unity of differences or the unity of 'what is distinguished' runs through the account of the emergence of self-consciousness. This unity splits into the antithesis of self-consciousness and life, which are two sides of the same coin. Self-consciousness is the unity of differences which is life, but life is 'this unity itself' (168). Thus with respect to life 'I' am one of those differences, a vanishing moment; but 'I' transcend these vanishing moments, self-consciousness is the unity of differences. These are two moments of 'I', self-consciousness, split as life and self-consciousness. The subject in Hegel is thus simultaneously a unity and split. Truth, or the attempted resolution of this contradiction, consists in a negation of differences in the unity: difference which is no difference.

Self-consciousness finds itself confronted with life: for certainty of self it must overcome this otherness (172). This is a negation: 'superseding this other that presents itself to self-consciousness as an independent life' (174). This is the satisfaction of Desire; but a satisfaction of desire is necessarily self-defeating. Without the other and desire there can be no self-consciousness: 'it is really because of that relation [the negative relation to the object] that it produces that object again, and the desire as well' (175). Thus self-consciousness realises that the essence of desire is something other than itself, and in order for the other to be there for desire it must 'effect the negation within itself', a self-negation (175). '*Self-consciousness achieves its satisfaction only in another self-consciousness*' (175). The negation of the sensuous world as other is not sufficient for truth, for that would involve an absolute negation of otherness; there would be no other to mirror self. Thus the object of self-consciousness must be independent in the negativity of itself, it must be a living self-consciousness (176). This is necessary for self-consciousness to mirror itself; it can only achieve self-reflection through the recognition that another independent self-consciousness is capable of offering. 'But the truth of this certainty is really a double reflection, the duplication of self-consciousness' (176). 'A self-consciousness exists for a self-consciousness' (177), and in this way the unity of itself in its otherness becomes explicit for it. Desire is the 'self-identical essence' (177).

From this duplication of two self-consciousnesses engaged in overcoming the sensuous world and self-negating, and the consequent mutual recognition, a struggle emerges. This is the master–slave, or lord–bondsman struggle. Hegel begins 'Independence and Dependence of Self-consciousness: Lordship and Bondage' with an account of duplication and recognition. There is a double movement of two self-consciousnesses, 'each sees the other do what it does', for each the action is directed against itself as well as against the other (183). And what this action is is supersession of otherness of itself and of the other independent being in order to become certain of itself (180). And in doing this it supersedes its own self, 'for this other is itself' (180). Hegel refers to this as an 'ambiguous supersession of its ambiguous otherness' which is also an 'ambiguous return to self' (181): ambiguous, because in overcoming its otherness it returns to self, is equal to itself, but simultaneously supersedes self. However, the other also gives it back again to itself in a self-negating process, and thus lets the other go free (181). Each confronts both itself and the other, and is dependent on the other for recognition of itself, but must also negate otherness in order to return to self. 'They recognise themselves as mutually recognising one another' (184). This involves both mediation and immediacy: each is for itself and the other an 'immediate being', but is so only through 'mediation' (184). This is, of course, the irony, that 'oneness' (185) is dependent on recognition, that independence involves dependency.

There is an inherent instability in this situation, where each needs from the other what the other needs, and the need is contradictory: negation of otherness and recognition from the other. This leads to struggle, and then a power relation: one recognised, the other recognising (185). How mutual recognition should necessarily produce this inequality is a major question in critiques of Hegel. But it is important to suspend these critical questions for the moment, to make sense of how this inequality relates to questions of mediation and dependence. The truth of self-certainty is dependent on a certainty of the other, and this is what produces a life and death struggle (186–7). It is important to note that what drives this inter-subjective relation is death, facing the fear of death. Each must simultaneously 'seek the death of the other' and stake its own life in order to transcend life (187). This is the only means of raising their 'certainty of being *for themselves* to truth': by showing that they are not attached to life (187). The life and death struggle is one of the dramatic moments in this story; what are the possible outcomes? In going through this struggle both consciousnesses face death, and thus learn from this experience that life is as essential as pure self-consciousness (189), the two sides of the split unity. In this regard both are independent, and in a potential position of attaining truth of self-certainty. However, the outcome of the struggle is unequal, unless it ends in death, a lifeless unity and a negation which supersedes without preserving. Both would be left free, but only as things, and no longer in a relationship (188). Death is the uninteresting outcome, the story would end there. Inequality arises at the point at which one consciousness, in the face of death, decides that life is more important. This consciousness is then attached to the life side of the split unity.

The unequal outcome is necessary to keep desire alive. The consciousness that gives in has been fearful, has faced the fear of death, 'its whole being has been seized with dread' (194). In this account it is possible to see something of the passion and corporeality of Hegel's understanding of the search for truth. And the close connection between death and desire. What emerges is two opposed shapes of consciousness – one independent, the other dependent. The former is 'lord', 'the other is bondsman' (189). In this relation of subjection we see how for Hegel desire for knowledge is inextricably tied up with power. Knowledge necessarily involves power as a consequence of the negative structure of desire. Knowledge consists in self-identity or sameness, which requires the negation of otherness, but an absolute negation of otherness produces a negation of self; a symmetrical relation of sameness also brings an end to desire and movement, and hence the search for knowledge. Thus inequality and power must be added to the system of relations between consciousnesses in order to maintain the movement of desire. In the logic of Hegel's story it would not be possible to retain knowledge, free of power. This brings to light the self–other relations involved in all knowledge processes, and the structure of power and desire in which these are inscribed. Although Foucault's insistence on the connection between power and knowledge has been influential in contemporary discussions of these issues, it is to Hegel that we owe the idea of desire as crucial to the motivation of knowledge, and as the link between power and knowledge, binding them together.

Back to the story. The crucial turning point has not yet come. Things are not settled by the life and death struggle, the power relation has to be played out. And there are paradoxes in this relation; knowledge is not a smooth process. These paradoxes turn primarily on mediation, and the relation between immediacy and mediation, which has important implications for conceptions of knowledge and meaning more generally. It should be noted that an attempted resolution of the immediate/mediated opposition runs through *The Phenomenology of Spirit*. For Hegel, Spirit is mediated. This is implicit in his view that states of consciousness that are lower than self-consciousness are not differentiated from the sensuous world. In contrast to this immediacy, knowledge is founded on mediation: 'Being is then absolutely mediated' (37).

Hegel begins with the master's side of the story, and presents the position of the slave from this perspective. The master's consciousness is mediated with itself through another consciousness, a consciousness that is bound up with the independence of things. 'Things' of the material world, nature, are the objects of desire. The master puts himself into a relation with both things and the other consciousness: he is the power over both, having won the struggle, and 'he holds the other in subjection' (190). But the relation is also one of dependency, for his relation to the thing is mediated by the slave. And, his relation to the slave is mediated by the thing. He is simultaneously mediation and immediacy, related immediately to each of these through mediation of the other (190). As his relation to the thing is mediated by the slave, his immediate relation becomes one of 'sheer negation of the thing'; in enjoyment of it he annihilates it (190). This is a negation without preservation, or, as Marxists would have it, unproductive consumption. It is a very different matter for the slave, and this, as we shall see, is the key to the paradox. Certainty of self requires recognition and a mirroring of self by the other. However, this recognition 'is one-sided and unequal' (191). What the master sees is not an independent consciousness but a dependent one that possesses his 'independence in thinghood' (190), and hence one that is incapable of giving him the recognition he desires. His mirror is a slave consciousness; in short, no mirror at all. He is therefore 'not certain of *being-for-self* as the truth of himself' (192). Thus an irony: the status of independent self-consciousness necessitates facing death, but what emerges from this is a relation of inequality, and hence the impossibility of mirroring, which is the very condition of certainty of self. The conditions of knowledge are contradictory. The master's victory is also his downfall.

Hegel then turns to the other side, the slave's perspective: 'we have now to consider what as such it is for and in itself' (194). Implicit in this consciousness, even if it is not yet aware of it, is 'pure-being-for-self'. He has 'trembled in every fibre of [his] being' (194) in the face of death; he has experienced the 'pure universal movement, the absolute melting away of everything stable' (194). Thus the slave is potentially an independent self-consciousness. Like the master he also relates to the thing negatively, taking away its independence, but not annihilating it. And in this regard the slave's relation to the thing is very different from that of the master's. Through his service the slave actually brings about dissolution, and thus rids himself of his 'attachment to natural existence in every single detail' (194). What he does is work on the thing, which simultaneously preserves it. Through his work, the slave becomes conscious of what he truly is, and moves out of immersion in life. If the victory of the master obviates his need to deal with things, it is the slave's work on things that leads to a reversal in the relationship. Mastery becomes servitude. To make matters worse for the master, he gets the rough end of the deal with respect to recognition. For when the slave looks to the master he sees an independent consciousness, the mirror works in this case: 'The *truth* of the independent consciousness is accordingly the servile consciousness of the bondsman' (193). The independence it sees is implicitly itself.

While the slave comes to know what he truly is, for the master there is only the fleeting satisfaction of desire in negating the object, but no permanence or objectivity. Through externalising self in the object, the slave achieves a permanency and objectivity. In fashioning and shaping the thing he overcomes its otherness – the thing is himself, externalised. And this externality is seen 'by him to be the truth' (196). The consciousness of the worker 'comes to see in the independent being [of the object] its *own* independence' (195). Here, then, is a mirroring relationship which supposedly works: an immediate relation of correspondence between the subject and object of knowledge. This would appear to be the satisfaction of the desire for self-presence.

What seems least believable in this story is the idea of stability through work. After the build-up to the reversal, the telling of the master's side and then the slave's, this comes as an anti-climax; moreover, it does not seem very Hegelian. Can we really accept the notion of a stabilisation, and through work? What comes of the relation to the other and desire, the very essence of the movement of Spirit? In the mirroring relation between subject and object this crucial third term, the other, seems curiously to have disappeared.

As in Foucault's account of power, it might be better to think of this as a moment of stability in an inherently unstable structure. Although Hegel tells the story in narrative form, one event following the other, it is not meant as a literal chronological sequence. And the quest for knowledge is an ongoing process. In his Hegelian formulation, Foucault makes this explicit: a power relationship is a constant struggle to the death between free, acting, or, in Hegel's terms, independent, subjects. When power is fixed and there is no longer the possibility of a reversal, it is not a power relationship but a relationship of violence (Foucault 1982: 220–4). It is reasonable to assume ongoing movement and instability, bearing in mind Hegel's assumption that any satisfaction of desire brings a stasis and lapsing back to lower forms of consciousness. A certain impossibility in the attainment of knowledge produces a movement, albeit one characterised by resolution and dissolution. The mediation of the self through a relation to an other is indispensable to knowledge and the truth of self-certainty. It is in this regard that Hegel's story of knowledge undoes itself: self-identity or presence is dependent on mediations, and thus impossible.

Hegel and Foucault bear comparison as they both make a direct connection between power and knowledge. For both, those exercising power are as trapped in it as those over whom it is exercised. And power works through bodies. This comes out in Hegel in 'the trembling body' of the slave, and, more ambiguously, in the working body: ambiguous, because through externalisation, the slave rids himself of attachment to bodily forms, and acquires knowledge. In the moment of subjection, however, he is in the sensuous world. Where there is a divergence between Hegel and Foucault is in the emotions that move the body. For Hegel, the negativity of terror and the emotion of fear are constitutive of knowledge processes; fear and desire are intimately connected. Foucault does not exclude terror as one of the modalities of power-knowledge, but he emphasises what is frequently overlooked: the connections between pleasure and power, and the positive forms of power. In Hegel, power *is* productive of the working subject, but this is essentially a negative form of power. However, there is something in Hegel's account which points to a problem in Foucault: the implications of reversal. It is quite clear in the master-slave story that a reversal does nothing by way of changing the structure of power relations. Foucault's general concern is to make trouble for the Hegelian Same–Other relation, but in refusing it he also underestimates the power of negation and the potential for a return to the Same in reversal.

Sartre and Lacan

Before turning to feminist questions asked of Hegel's master–slave story, I want to give some indication of the Hegelian influence on French philosophy, specifically through a brief account of the ways in which Sartre and Lacan rewrite the master–slave story. In 'The Look' in *Being and Nothingness*, Sartre (1969 [1943]) makes two modifications to Hegel's story that are important for an understanding of knowledge. First, he explicitly specularises the struggle: the eye becomes central in what, for him, is a struggle of competing looks. And second, there can be only one subject of the look; the other is object, in immanence. The power struggle between looks is a struggle for the position of the subject of the look. The focal point in Sartre's account of the master–slave struggle is the paradox that the self is both dependent on the gaze of the Other and yet this gaze is fundamentally threatening to self.

Sartre (1969: 256) speaks of the world as 'a kind of drain hole'. The subject is decentred by the appearance of the Other which has a drain-hole effect with respect to 'me': an absence or something that escapes. This wonderful metaphor brings to mind the psychoanalytic account of femininity: what threatens the centred masculine subject and must be displaced onto woman is lack or a hole. 'The Other is defined . . . by the absence of the world which I perceive, an absence discovered at the very heart of my perception of this world' (Sartre 1969: 256). At this point the Other is an object, part of that world, so he asks: To what can the 'original presence of the Other' be attributed? It is the possibility of my 'being seen by the Other'. 'It is in and through the revelation of my being-as-object for the Other that I must be able to apprehend the presence of his being-as-subject' (Sartre 1969: 256). Thus there is the permanent possibility of a substitution of a subject who sees me for the object seen by me. ' "Being-seen-by-the-Other" is the truth of "seeing-the-Other" ' (Sartre 1969: 257). The Other then is the one who on principle looks at me. I am dependent on the gaze, I am as I am seen: 'I have my foundation outside myself. I am for myself only as I am a pure reference to the Other' (Sartre 1969: 260). But this gaze objectifies me, fixes my possibilities, denies me freedom. Hence the struggle; the gaze must be resisted for transcendence, and can be, in so far as I am a free subject. This is a struggle that cannot be avoided (except through sleep, love or the mirror); there is no escape from the potential threat of the gaze. Thus selfhood is a constant struggle against the objectifying look of the Other. Although it is implicit in Hegel, Sartre draws attention to the structure of the self–other relation as a subject–object relation.

In Lacan, we find a similar conception of the self–other relation, but in his case it is explicitly sexualised: the Other, the lack, the place to which desire is addressed is the feminine; the subject is masculine. And one of Lacan's major contentions is that desire, by definition, can never be satisfied; truth and wholeness are impossible. Lacan's reworking of Freud is not only semiotic but also Hegelian. What he draws from Sartre is the significance of the gaze. In 'Of the Gaze' Lacan (1979: 84) emphasises that the gaze is not a seen gaze 'but a gaze imagined by me in the field of the Other', which also brings to mind Foucault's 'eyes that see without being seen' and forms of self-surveillance. For Lacan, Hegel's master–slave dialectic is the model of sociality: the entry of the subject into language or the symbolic order inaugurates the self–other relation. He places an emphasis on the mediation of knowledge through the desire of the other and language (Lacan 1977: 5).[3]

It is not surprising, then, to find that Lacan questions Hegel's account of stabilisation through work and the implication that a correspondence between the subject and object of knowledge is possible. Lacan alters the end of the story: stabilisation is itself illusory. And he claims that this 'development' is in keeping with Hegel. Lacan's contention is that the slave waits for the master's death; having given way in the face of death, knowing that he is mortal, he also knows that the master is mortal. Thus he accepts labouring and renunciation of pleasure in the meantime, holding out for the uncertain moment when the master will die (Lacan 1977: 99). His labour is doubly alienating (and in this regard Lacan is close to Marx): first, the product of his labour belongs to another (which Hegel seems to overlook); and second, the 'recognition of his own essence in his handiwork eludes him' (Lacan 1977: 100). Lacan claims that 'he himself "is not in it"', that is, the slave does not acquire self through externalisation of work. Lacan makes an argument similar to that about the fantasy of identity in 'The Mirror Stage': finding oneself mirrored in an object is illusory precisely because it involves a denial of the referrals through the mirror and the mediating relation with the other. It is a refusal to acknowledge that a mirror image is dependent on the gaze of an other, 'real' or imagined. Lacan claims that the slave is not 'in' the product of labour, but 'in' the anticipated moment of the master's death. After this moment he will live, but prior to this he identifies with the master and thus is himself already dead (Lacan 1977: 100). Lacan is pointing to the intersubjective relation that seems to disappear at the 'end' of Hegel's story, but he is also emphasising the workings of death in that relation. In Lacan's Hegelianism, negation becomes death.

The connection between death and desire emerges in Lacan's reading of Freud's *Fort! Da!* story together with Hegel's master–slave story, in an account of the subject's entry into language, the same moment at which desire is inaugurated and, indeed, the unconscious is founded. *Fort! Da!* is Freud's famous story about children's games of repetition that can be interpreted as an attempt to master absence and presence: *fort* = gone, *da* = there; disappearance and return. The child compensates for the loss of the object of libidinal attachment by miming – itself staging the disappearances and returns. By repeating the unpleasure the child 'masters' (Freud 1984 [1920]: 285) presences and absences. In a move from passive to active the gesture is defiant: 'I don't need you, I'm sending you away myself' (Freud 1984 [1920]: 285). The child will make the mother absent – negate her. In retelling this story Lacan emphasises that mastery is a mastery of absence through a negation. There is an interesting footnote in Freud (1984 [1920]: 284) that anticipates Lacan's version. In his observation of the game, Freud noted that using a mirror the child could make *himself* disappear, he could make his mirror image gone 'by crouching down' beneath the mirror. Via self-reflection the child puts himself in the place of the other-mother, in an attempt to master absence and make himself present to himself. In both Sartre and Lacan the mirror functions in much the same way, providing the illusion of self-sufficiency and escape from the gaze of the other.

Freud emphasises the repetition of the game of absence and presence. It could thus be said that repetition points to the failure of mastery. It is in 'Beyond the Pleasure Principle' that Freud (1984 [1920]: 308–9) introduced his theory of the death instinct: an 'urge to restore to an earlier stage of things', an 'inertia'. He claims that it was observing children's repetitive games that partly prompted these thoughts. The desire for origins is directly connected with the compulsion to repeat in Freud's discussion of the death instinct. The desire for a repetition of the same, and to hold still or fix an element (above all else one's mirror image), is integral to the desire for mastery, to know. In Freud this consists, in part, in a desire to know one's origins and to re-appropriate them. As we shall see this connection between origins, death and repetition of the same is extremely important to deconstructive and feminist concerns.

Lacan (1977: 103) claims that in the repetitive game in which the subject masters its 'dereliction' we might recognise 'that the moment in which desire becomes human is also that in which the child is born into language'.[4] There are two steps in the desire of this moment. The subject masters loss by 'assuming it', that is, putting himself in the place of the lost object. But in doing so he raises desire 'to a second power' for his action 'destroys the object' in 'the anticipated provocation of its absence and presence' (Lacan 1977: 103). By putting himself in the place of the object he negates it, 'negativizes the field of forces of desire', in order to become 'its own object to itself' (Lacan 1977: 103). The negation of the other is also the death of desire, and thus the other must be brought back to desire. Lacan (1977: 104) says that in addressing himself to a real or imaginary partner, the child will see the effect of the negativity 'of his discourse': 'since his appeal has the effect of making the partner disappear, he will seek in a banishing summons the provocation of the return that brings the partner back to his desire'. Starting with the negativity in Hegel's desire, Lacan (1977: 104) pushes this to the limit – 'the intermediary of death can be recognised in every relation in which man comes to the life of history'. In part this rests on his contention that symbolisation involves 'the murder of the thing' (implicitly in this text, the mother; elsewhere in Lacan, explicitly, the feminine) which is constitutive of the 'eternalization of his desire'. That is, language operates through absence, and a mastery of absence involves negation. Hegel's 'master–slave' and Freud's *Fort! Da!* are then, for Lacan, the stories of inter-subjectivity, desire and knowledge, in this culture, and in them is the figure of death:

> It is in effect as a desire for death that he affirms himself for others; if he identifies himself with the other, it is by fixing him solidly in the metamorphosis of his essential image, and no being is ever evoked by him except among the shadows of death (Lacan 1977: 105).[5]

The connection between death and the feminine in the Hegel–Lacan structure of desire is a major issue for feminists. In the *Phenomenology of Spirit* this connection is made explicitly in 'The True Spirit. The Ethical Order', where Hegel claims that the universality of pure being-for-self is death (452). However, this universality, as opposed to the particularity and immediacy of an individual's death, can only be ensured by the family, which in Hegel is 'the unconscious' (450) and the feminine (457). The nether world of the family, 'the blood relation', is the precondition of the universality of the realm of the community, self-consciousness (452). Death has a central role in connecting these two spheres. However, in this section Hegel also refers to a famous case of a blood relation that, in honouring the dead, committed a crime: that of Antigone (469–75).[6] Particularly as this brother–sister relation came of dangerous desires, we might read this as a return of the repressed. The 'community' is dependent on the 'family', but this nether world also disrupts the law. Does Hegel's reading of this story throw some light, then, on the idea that it is the fear of death and the feminine that constitutes desire, that founds the symbolic order?

Feminist questions

Deconstructive feminists make the claim that the power of philosophical discourse is dependent on the negation or repression of the feminine. Their deconstructive strategy consists in demonstrating how these repressions operate to effect the pretence to self-identity in knowledge. So, of Hegel's story of the pursuit of knowledge and self-identity, the question to be asked is: Where is the feminine in this text? Is the structure of desire masculine, and if the feminine is repressed how does this contribute to pretensions to truth and identity?

The most common feminist view is that the master–slave story can be seen as a 'model' of masculine–feminine relations. Even if there is no explicit reference to Hegel's master–slave, the structure of this power relation is frequently taken to be the structure of sexual relations. This relation is assumed in feminist politics based on one version of reversal or another. The liberal feminist version is to put women where men now are; the radical feminist one is to replace patriarchal power with the power of women. Structurally the same story. What we learn from Hegel is that reversal changes nothing of the structure.

A more subtle and complex argument can be found in Benjamin's (1984) reworking of Hegel's story. She does take master–slave to correspond to masculine–feminine, but is using Hegel as a suggestive starting point for an analysis of the fantasy of erotic domination in contemporary Western culture. Combining Hegel, de Beauvoir, Bataille and object relations psychoanalysis, she provides an account of a splitting of masculine and feminine, two poles in a unity; and the attempted resolution through relations of erotic domination. The 'ideal' for her would be the two sides of the split existing within each subject, in a relation of tension. This would constitute desire without inequality, and a resolution of the contradiction between independence and recognition. Although Benjamin's strategy is not one of simple reversal, her approach to oppositions is resolution of a split unity. In this regard the Hegelian structure is not disrupted, although inequality and subject–object are removed from it, and there is a notion of acceptance of the other. We are left with two subjects that combine characteristics of masculine and feminine; while the oppositional definition of these, autonomy versus nurturant and so on, remains.

De Beauvoir is the most important example of a reading of the master–slave relation as masculine–feminine. Addressing Sartre's version of the story, de Beauvoir argues that: man is in the position of master, the looker, in transcendence; woman is in the position of slave, the looked at, in immanence. In Sartre, there is a struggle for the position of subject; in de Beauvoir's view, there is no struggle between the sexes, women having given up the ideal of transcendence and being complicit in their objectification. The main critical point that has been made about *The Second Sex* (de Beauvoir 1972 [1949]) is that the opposition transcendence–immanence is taken as given (Lloyd 1983: 8–9; 1984: 96–102). De Beauvoir does not question transcendence as a human goal, and hence one that women should also strive for. She does not see the masculinity in Sartre's definition of transcendence – that it is defined in opposition to and as a negation of immanence, the feminine. By accepting a series of hierarchised dichotomies de Beauvoir takes as her reference point the masculine, transcendence. However, there are some interesting contradictions in her work that prefigure contemporary French feminism: although woman's body is to be transcended, she nevertheless speaks positively about woman's sexual pleasure, and claims that in this regard there will always be differences between men and women even with transcendence (de Beauvoir 1972: 740).

One way to approach the question of the sexual dimension of the master–slave story is to ask if there is anything explicit in Hegel that would suggest that this story is not sexually neutral. A simple feminist response to this is that women have not reached self-consciousness, and thus that the struggle is between men. But there are grounds on which a stronger argument can be made for the case of two male consciousnesses. Lloyd (1983: 3–5) has argued this with reference to sections in the *Phenomenology* where Hegel does discuss male–female relations (446–63). Hegel argues that as a consequence of women's location in the family and their taking as universal what for men is the particular, there is conflict between men and women: woman is 'the everlasting irony [in the life] of the community' (475). The sphere where men are located, the public, the state, is the proper sphere of sustained self-consciousness (Lloyd 1983: 5); woman remains immersed in life. Lloyd's argument is that this struggle and the master–slave struggle should be read as two versions of the story of the unfolding of Spirit, and, if read in conjunction with each other, it becomes clear that the master–slave struggle is not gender-neutral, but indeed about male consciousnesses. 'Women are outside the drama' as they are relegated to a sphere that is not associated with sustained self-consciousness (Lloyd 1983: 5).

However, this issue can be addressed by looking at the specific text – the master–slave story – itself, without reference to other sections of the *Phenomenology*. On the subject of desire and the structure of desire, what becomes explicit in Lacan is implicit in Hegel: the masculine characteristics of these. Desire is negative, structured around lack, and involves an overcoming of otherness. If desire is addressed to what is different, this is also a difference which is the same; desire is for a return to self, self-sameness. Difference is defined in an oppositional relation to the same: identity requires a negation of otherness and difference. The place of otherness thus looks like the feminine:

the place to which desire is addressed but which must be overcome for self-certainty. In the master–slave struggle both self-consciousnesses are independent, they have the attributes of a masculine subject. This, then, presupposes that there is a feminine against which the masculine is defined: a repressed term. Lloyd (1983: 9) makes this point more generally in relation to Hegel, Sartre and de Beauvoir: transcendence, or self-consciousness, 'is a transcendence of the feminine', immanence, immersion in life. The moment of truth in the story – the account of work on the object – is of particular significance. The object of desire, matter, nature, is worked on so as to mirror the subject. Here we find the illusion of the mirror: an immediate relation of correspondence between the subject and object of knowledge. What is repressed are the mediations of the subject by the mirror, the object – the feminine.

In Hegel's story there are both masculine and feminine moments in the slave. The master sees a dependent consciousness; although the slave is in some ways independent, it is also immersed in life, and in particular its independence is associated with the independence of the object. This could be understood as a feminine moment. Both self-consciousnesses must overcome otherness in self as much as external otherness; both master and slave are engaged in a negation of the feminine. In this regard the slave is in a masculine position. Furthermore, the slave position is an active one. What could be said about the effects of the reversal for the master is not that this leads to a feminine position, but rather that it is a story of the fantasy of masculinity – that a unified knowing subject is possible. On the question of the inequality in the master–slave struggle and the temptation to read this as sexual inequality: it is about sexual inequality in so far as the moments I have referred to are feminine. This is to say that a power struggle between men, in a mutually defining relation, is dependent on an asymmetrical power relation of masculine–feminine, the negation of difference, otherness. The common place of master–slave in our culture is a struggle between men, Hegel's story. Women are not in the position of subject. Thus, French feminists have suggested that there is something of the feminine that eludes, escapes.

It is clear that master–slave does not neatly map masculine–feminine in Hegel; there is a sexual ambiguity. There might, then, be something misplaced in a feminist project that would pin down the masculine and feminine in the story. Hegel's story does suggest that the desire for mastery is masculine, but it also points to a complexity in the sexualisation of power relations. And might we not take this as one of its strengths?

Cixous and Irigaray: an other desire

Turning now to French feminists, I will start with Cixous as she directly addresses the Hegel–Lacan structure of desire. At the most general level it is the negativity of this desire that she takes issue with, and regards as masculine. The desire for identity and self-sameness, structured around a lack, is the desire of a masculine subject; the otherness of the feminine is to be negated such that this subject can be a presence to itself. Cixous' strategy is one of a writing practice that inscribes a different desire and is based on different principles of meaning. She is not engaging in critique, then offering an alternative; rather, she is doing the alternative in the writing. In this respect it is difficult to talk about her ideas: her explicit concern with language and transformation serves to highlight the impossibility of translation, what exegesis aspires to.

With Cixous it is very tempting to simply quote her as the only way of 'representing' what she does with language. Furthermore *écriture féminine* is understood as writing the body, reinscribing the body, which brings to the forefront the effects, of reading Cixous, on the body. This is an account of a writing that I find very pleasurable.

The 'alternative' desire is one that accepts rather than negates otherness, both within the self and in the other; it goes out to the other rather than returns to self. The other is absolutely other, not a difference recuperated to the same. This desire is structured around 'more'; a desire that keeps on going without end or resolution. Thus *écriture féminine* is a writing practice that is concerned with the openness of texts, movement, and multiplicity, in contrast with texts of closure and singularity. Part of Cixous' strategy is to write 'half way between theory and fiction' (Cixous and Clément 1986: 136). She understands this as a means of breaking with the discourse of mastery, a pedagogic mode that is 'objective' (Cixous and Clément 1986: 136–7). Thus her writing contributes to a disruption of the opposition between theory and fiction; she does not regard stories of the culture as false, but rewrites them and writes other stories.

If Hegel's story is one about coming to consciousness, Cixous' story can be understood as one of the unconscious, written with the body. But, it is not a question of either/or: both stories are going on at once. It is possible to discern the workings of both negative and positive desire in knowledge and meaning processes.

The text I am looking at is 'Sorties: Out and Out: Attacks/Ways Out/Forays' which is the section written by Cixous in *The Newly Born Woman* (Cixous and Clément 1986 [1975]). Cixous reads and rewrites the myths of Western culture, and is probably best known to English-speaking feminists for her 'Laugh of the Medusa'. There is a section from that essay in 'Sorties' including the much quoted reference to writing the feminine: 'Let them tremble, those priests; we are going to show them our sexts!' (Cixous 1986: 69). Her response to desire structured around a fear of castration that associates femininity with death is: 'wouldn't the worst thing be . . . that, really, woman is not castrated . . . All you have to do to see the Medusa is look her in the face: and she isn't deadly. She is beautiful and she laughs' (Cixous 1986: 69). With reference to Freud's 'dark continent' (a metaphor that condenses femininity and the other of imperialism), she says that woman has been made 'to see (= not-see)' herself 'on the basis of what man wants to see of her, which is to say almost nothing' (Cixous 1986: 68). Characteristic of her reversal-displacement strategy, Cixous (1986: 68) proclaims 'the "Dark Continent" is neither dark nor unexplorable'. This statement is made in the context of a critique of a desire which 'is fragile and kept alive by lack' and 'threat'; and a concern to find a place for woman's desire and her body in which 'she has not been able to live' (Cixous 1986: 67–9).

It is via the commonplace 'gesture of History', the master–slave scenario, that Cixous makes connections between the negation of woman and other power relations. The same operations of power are at work in the inter-subjectivity of the 'personal', and in relations between 'races', classes. Of the irony of the master–slave dialectic, she says that 'the body of what is strange must not disappear, but its force must be conquered and returned to the master' (Cixous 1986: 70). Society reproduces the Hegelian system, the mechanism of the death struggle, and there is a 'dreadful simplicity' to this (Cixous 1986: 71). It is there in the exercise of all economic-political power: there are no masters without slaves: 'no "Frenchmen" without wogs, no Nazis without Jews' and so on. The other is defined by the 'same', by what rules; and is organised in a hierarchical relation to it. Cixous' formulation of the connections between different oppressions is quite different from that of Marxist feminists. The debate among the latter has always tended towards a reductionism: which came first or was determinative – class or gender. Cixous is not reducing all oppressions to sexual domination, but rather drawing out a structural homology: there is a repetition in the structure of power which has the form of masculine–feminine, subordination and negation of one term to privilege a dominant term. She *does* contend that relations of production, power and signification are intelligible as masculine–feminine; but in connecting the libidinal economy and the political economy she is refusing the 'false question of origins' (Cixous 1986: 81).

Cixous asks what is the 'Other' if it is truly other. This other cannot be defined, theorised; it 'doesn't settle down'; it is what escapes, it is elsewhere. As she puts it: 'There is nothing to say' (Cixous 1986: 71). This is a refusal of defining questions, and specifically the question: 'What is woman?' To pin 'woman' down as object is to constitute her as an other that is recuperated to the same. 'There is nothing to say' alludes to what cannot be put into representation, refuses the powers of discourse. And, to where this elsewhere is that escapes the repetition of the dialectic: for Cixous (1986: 72), it is in writing: 'where *it* writes itself, where *it* dreams, where *it* invents new worlds'.

Yet as she rereads the stories and myths of the culture she can find no woman to identify with, there is no place for her desire; and everywhere the battle for mastery rages between classes, and on an individual scale. But is this system 'flawless'? No, something escapes; her desire suggests that already 'it is letting something else through'. Cixous (1986: 78) expresses her desire thus: 'I want to become a woman I can love'. She looks for a different kind of desire, one that would take the risk of the other and difference, that would involve recognition of each other rather than 'feeling threatened by the existence of an otherness'. A desire that is not 'in collusion with death' but goes into the unknown (Cixous 1986: 78). The claim that it is possible to imagine an elsewhere is based on what escapes the order now, exceptions to the rule in ways of relating. Her primary example in 'Sorties' is bisexuality, not in the sense of a fantasy of unity, but beings who accept the other in themselves and the other, and a multiplication of the effects of desire (Cixous 1986: 84–85). One of her main examples here is Genet's writing (Cixous 1986: 84); and she refers to mythic figures whose sexual ambiguity allow her hers (Cixous 1986: 78). Cixous (1986: 122) cites Shakespeare, 'who was neither man nor woman but a thousand persons'; and she, Cixous, has lived all his characters. 'Sorties' concludes with a eulogy to Antony and Cleopatra as embodying a different desire: 'Still More – Encore – Never Enough' (Cixous 1986: 122–30). Theirs is a desire that transcends death: 'they live still' (Cixous 1986: 130). Over the top perhaps, but wonderful because it is a familiar story read differently.[7]

Cixous critically rereads Hegel and Freud together; implicitly this is a critique of Lacan's reading of Hegel and Freud. Neither Hegel nor Freud, she says, are making things up, unfortunately. We are still living under the 'Empire of the Selfsame' which is 'Man's law' (Cixous 1986: 78–9). The commonplace logic of desire, the subject 'going out into the other in order to come back to itself' is at work 'in our everyday banality' (Cixous 1986: 78). Sexualising Hegel via Freud, she questions the requirement of inequality for desire in Hegel, and the slippage from sexual *difference* to inequality. Her argument is that difference with an equality of force could produce desire without negativity: 'keeping the other alive and different' (Cixous 1986: 79). This relates to the argument above, that it is a consequence of Hegel's system of sameness that power and inequality must be introduced to produce the movement of desire. In Hegel and Freud difference is always opposition: identity–difference, a hierarchical valorisation of one of the terms in an economy of sameness. Desire is desire to reappropriate 'that which seems able to escape him' (Cixous 1986: 80). Her justification for making the connection between Hegel and Freud, sexualising Hegel's desire, is that the 'selfsame' is based on a fear of loss, expropriation, the need to reappropriate the not-mine; which Cixous (1986: 80) reads as the fear of castration, characteristic of masculine subjectivity but not feminine subjectivity. In this sexualisation of the master–slave relation, Cixous is implicitly taking the slave position as that of the moment of objectification, the constitution of the other in negativity – the feminine. This could be understood as a deconstructive version of de Beauvoir's sexualisation of Hegel–Sartre.

Cixous argues that there is something about the economy of female sexuality that inscribes a different desire. Insisting that there is no direct correspondence between men and women on the one hand, and masculine and feminine on the other, she claims that it is not impossible for men to come to desire differently (a desire of difference), although there is more at stake in accepting the other – the feminine – in themselves, given the constitution of

masculinity through fear of loss. On the other hand, femininity is not organised around fear of loss or of the other. While this receptivity is precisely what
leads to woman's dispossession, it also makes possible a relation to the other
that is not negative. This alternative desire is inscribed in and by *écriture féminine*. How does she speak of this desire? As a desire that keeps the other alive,
that goes out to the other, without returning to self; a desire without an end or
goal (Cixous 1986: 86–7). Furthermore, as a desire that does not privilege the
phallus, it also does not privilege the specular (Cixous 1986: 82). In a disruption of oppositions, Cixous (1986:89) says 'Woman (I) have no fear of elsewhere or of same or of other.' The crucial point is that desire structured
around openness to the other is the desire of an openness in writing.

In breaking with the phallic economy and the question 'What does woman
want?', Cixous (1986: 82) asks 'How do I pleasure?', and 'How does
feminine *jouissance write* itself?' It is not fear that is productive of this way of
meaning, but the pleasure of *jouissance*. The idea of writing the body is
central to this conception of writing: 'Write yourself: your body must make
itself heard. The huge resources of the unconscious will burst out' (Cixous
1986: 97). Cixous regards this as a disruption of the empire of the Selfsame:
there will be some 'elsewhere where the other will no longer be condemned to
death'; and a jamming of sociality – an inter-subjectivity defined in terms of
couples and oppositions (Cixous 1986: 96–7). Inscribing the body differently
prefigures the possibility of radical transformations of the libidinal economy.
'Let us imagine a transformation of each one's relationship to his or her body
(and to the other body)', and then, femininity and masculinity 'would inscribe
quite differently their effects of difference' (Cixous 1986: 83). That is,
feminine and masculine would not be as they are today, which is 'the same
thing'.

There is an exhilaration and passion in Cixous' writing. It is indeed
possible to get some tangible sense of what writing the body is about. You can
feel it, and Cixous' subjectivity. But she has no illusions about the difficult
process of transformation. For example, in the exchange with Clément she is
more insistent than Clément on the collusion of power and knowledge, and
the ways in which 'we' are caught up in mastery, particularly in teaching
practices (Cixous and Clément 1986: 144–5). Woman has always functioned
in man's discourse, and it can only be disrupted from 'within', but it is 'time to
displace this "within", explode it . . . ' (Cixous 1986: 95–6). Which is most
definitely not a matter of putting oneself in the position of mastery, for that
would be repetition rather than transformation. There is a tension in her
writing between the refusal of mastery and the acknowledgement of 'our'
implication in this desire. In terms of a methodology of multiplicity, about
which more will be said later, the important point is that both forms of desire
have an effectivity (and, possibly, an affectivity) simultaneously.

In Irigaray's writing a different economy of desire is also proposed in
connection with female sexuality and eroticism. As with Cixous, the body is
central to the question of different ways of meaning. Female sexuality, the

repressed of Western culture, presents a disturbance to the order of discourse. The essays to be considered here are: 'This Sex Which Is Not One' (1985a), 'And the One Doesn't Stir without the Other' (1981), and 'When Our Lips Speak Together' (1985a), the latter being a good example of a writing that disrupts the distinction between theory and fiction.

At this point something needs to be said about difference, which is crucial to an understanding of what Irigaray and Cixous are doing with meaning. The writing practice that they are concerned with is based on a conception of difference that is not defined in relation to the same: a radical difference of the absolutely other. This bears directly on Derrida's conception of *différance*. The *a* of *différance* refers to the process of deferral in system, the deferral and referral of elements in a chain: an element signifies 'only by referring to another past or future element in an economy of traces' (Derrida 1987: 29). It is this process that makes identity and sameness impossible. Elements in a relation of opposition, for example, are marked by the traces of each other, which, in turn, is the undoing of a negation that would effect identity. The structure and movement of *différance* is not 'conceivable on the basis of the opposition presence/absence' (Derrida 1987: 27). This can be taken not so much as a critique of structural linguistics as a bringing to light what is implicit in Saussure, namely the impossibility of holding oppositions apart from each other. *Langue* is marked by *parole*, synchrony by diachrony (see also Weber 1987: 9). However, this does place emphasis on the *practice* of meaning: structure is inseparable from the movement of *parole*, diachrony.

Thus Derrida (1987: 26–7) claims that *différance* is a new concept of writing that consists in a systematic play of differences, 'of the traces of differences'. A text is produced through an interweaving of traces of elements in a chain or system; it is 'produced only in the transformation of another text' (Derrida 1987: 26). French feminists sexualise *différance* in their claim that female sexuality points to a different structure of desire and signification. When Cixous talks about a desire that doesn't settle down she is emphasising deferral, difference that cannot be pinned down as it is constituted in and constitutive of a signification process in movement, without end. Her re*writing* of stories can be understood as the transformation that Derrida speaks of, but she emphasises that this is bodily, and a sexual transformation.

Difference in this sense is closely connected with the idea of multiplicity in French feminist writings. Difference and multiplicity are counterposed to sameness and singularity. 'This Sex Which Is Not One': this sex which has been defined in terms of the masculine, negatively in relation to the same and thus without specificity; this sex which is not singular, but multiple. There is a double moment to femininity; it means in two different ways. Here I want to focus on the 'positive' moment or way of meaning: multiplicity of desire and meaning. It is in this moment that Irigaray identifies something that escapes the dominant phallic economy. Female autoeroticism is of particular significance to a disruption of knowledge in this economy, characterised by the oppositions presence–absence, subject–object; identity; and privileging the specular. Irigaray's (1985a: 24) 'critique' turns on the issue of mediations.

> As for woman, she touches herself in and of herself without any need for mediation, and before there is any way to distinguish activity from passivity. Woman 'touches herself' all the time, and moreover no one can forbid her to do so, for her genitals are formed of two lips in continuous contact. Thus, within herself, she is already two – but not divisible into one(s) – that caress each other.

Irigaray is counterposing this way of meaning, lived in the body, to mediation in the phallic economy: mediations of woman and language. If we go back to Hegel for a moment it will be recalled that mediation is the basis of the irony: desire in knowledge is for immediacy, for the presence of the object of knowledge; but, as Hegel insists, immediacy is always mediated. More generally, knowledge both is dependent on mediations and requires a denial of this dependency.

It would be possible to read this quotation from Irigaray as a desire for immediacy and a denial of mediations, maybe even a desire for the presence of the feminine. But it is more fruitful to locate this in terms of a way of meaning based on different principles, which she is operationalising in some respects. A good deal of Irigaray's work is concerned with bringing mediations to light. This could be understood as the first move in deconstruction – that of reversal. In this passage from 'This Sex Which Is Not One' she makes a further move of displacing the opposition mediation–immediacy. The conception of meaning as meaning lived, in the body, breaks with the oppositions of the metaphysics of presence, such as subject–object. For example, in claiming that when woman touches herself there is no 'possibility of distinguishing what is touching from what is being touched', Irigaray (1985a: 26) is disrupting the subject–object distinction, and the mediations of this relation. If you like, mediation is immediate, or the immediacy of contiguity mediates in such a way that correspondence is impossible.

Thus, it is important to emphasise that in her critiques of mediation Irigaray is not arguing for immediacy – the other side of the opposition, and a desire for presence – but displacing the opposition itself. Her approach to meaning as embodied is reminiscent of Bergson's refusal to distinguish between the body as matter and as image. By explicitly addressing the question of the mediations of the body in immediacy, Irigaray's work throws light on the idea of writing the body which is Cixous' central concern. The body is both inscribed and inscribes. This conception of the connection between the body and meaning is to be radically distinguished from a notion of representing the body, which presumes the body as a presence. Furthermore, the idea that the body, or anything else, is mediated by meaning systems assumes that there is something prior to these to be mediated.

Crucial to Irigaray's argument is the question of how the body means if the sense of touch displaces that of sight. More precisely, it raises the question of what is the significance of the body 'meaning', for sight involves a distancing from the body, and even a repression of the body. Apart from the issue of there being 'nothing to see' (Irigaray 1985a: 26) of woman in a specular economy, sight consists in a fixing of the meaning of an 'object'. In Sartre's account the subject of the look fixes the object of the look; the structure of the look is the structure of desire. In Lacan, the illusion of identity arises with respect to the specular: the fixing, solidifying, of the image in 'the exteriority of the total form' (Irigaray 1985a: 116–17). Thus Irigaray counterposes the fluidity and movement of touch to the stasis and solidity involved in sight. In 'The Mechanics of Fluids', she argues that in an economy of solids there is a concern with the 'object', and with the question 'What does it mean?' (Irigaray 1985a: 115). Fluids elude 'Thou art that' (Irigaray 1985a: 117); and there is no possibility of identity (Irigaray 1985a: 109). It is only with a distinction between the subject and the object in a specular economy that a fantasy of identity is possible.

The touch of female autoeroticism relates directly to deferral. In this regard Irigaray (1985a: 110–11) always emphasises contiguity and metonymy (fluid) over metaphor (solid). In 'This Sex Which Is Not One' she puts it: 'What she says is never identical with anything, moreover; rather, it is contiguous. It touches (upon)' (Irigaray 1985a: 29). 'Nearness' makes identity impossible. 'She herself enters into a ceaseless exchange of herself with the other without any possibility of identifying either' (Irigaray 1985a: 31). Here, then, we have the process of referral and deferral of traces: no element is simply present, it cannot be identified. There are no distinct boundaries of self and between self and other. In this context Irigaray has an interesting critique of counting, which is directly related to her critique of economic calculation and quantification in Western culture (and has clear echoes of Bergson, which will be discussed in the following chapter). Woman is a mystery in a culture that counts everything: numbers, units, individualities. Counting is based on spatialisation and specularisation, and an assumption that each element is discrete, a unit that can be identified in and of itself. 'She is neither one nor two. Rigorously speaking, she cannot be identified either as one person, or as two. She resists all adequate definition' (Irigaray 1985a: 26). This argument about a multiplicity that has nothing to do with quantification is made with reference to female sexuality. Of woman's sex organs, Irigaray says she has at least two, but they are not 'identifiable as ones', she has sex organs everywhere, her sexuality and pleasure is plural, 'multiple in its differences' (Irigaray 1985a: 28). Multiplicity and diffuseness disrupt sameness, a sexual economy that focuses on one sexual organ; and 'upsets the linearity of a project, undermines the goal-object of a desire' (Irigaray 1985a: 30).

In 'And the One Doesn't Stir Without the Other' we again find the theme of solid versus flow in connection with the specular and mirroring. This essay is about a mirroring relation between mother and daughter in a phallocratic order.

> With your milk, Mother, I swallowed ice. And here I am now, my insides frozen . . . You flowed into me, and that hot liquid became poison, paralysing me. My blood no longer circulates to my feet or my hands, or as far as my head. It is immobilized, thickened by the cold. Obstructed by icy chunks which resist its flow. My blood coagulates, remains in and near my heart (Irigaray 1981: 60).

The flows of milk and blood are solidified, immobilised; hot becomes cold. This is the effect of the mirror: *la glace*: ice, mirror. 'Imprisoned by your desire for a reflection, I became a statue, an image of your mobility' (Irigaray 1981: 64). (The look of the Medusa? St Theresa?) Mirroring involves separation of self from an other, loss of self and the mirror reflection, 'two dead selves' (Irigaray 1981: 64). This is a critical rereading of Lacan's account of the mirror phase: the distinction between external and internal, and the 'death' that is a fixing of the image, immobilisation. The negativity also comes from a desire that would incorporate the other, negate the other through assimilation. 'We've again disappeared into this act of eating each other' (Irigaray 1981: 62). And (with echoes of Klein) a desire structured around lack produces 'a filling up of holes'; thus, not lack, but a surfeit, being stuffed full, and stuffed up: an 'immobilised body' (Irigaray 1981: 62). This consuming and being consumed is suffocation; 'I want out of this prison' (Irigaray 1981: 60).

Irigaray suggests an alternative to this production of woman's desire in phallic terms – lack, negation, immobility, death. For example, 'You/I exchanging selves endlessly and each staying herself. Living mirrors' (Irigaray 1981: 62). This is a desire with referral and movement, without negation, and without subject–object. She speaks of a game of exchanging images, without end, and says that 'we don't need an object to throw back and forth at each other for this game to take place' (Irigaray 1981: 62). This can be read as a critique of both the presence–absence opposition of *Fort! Da!*, and the mediation of self–other relations by an object in Hegel. The trap of the single function of mothering produces this choice: 'If I leave, you lose the reflection of life, of your life. And if I remain, am I not the guarantor of your death' (Irigaray 1981: 66). As opposed to a scenario of life of one requiring the death of the other, and thus death of both, she says: 'And what I wanted from you, Mother, was this: that in giving me life, you still remain alive' (Irigaray 1981: 67). What emerges from this piece is an ambivalence towards the mother: Irigaray does not simply positively revalue the mother or mother–daughter relations. But in this last statement there is also, perhaps, something of a desire for release from the death wish.

A key mechanism of the power of discourse is that of dichotomous oppositions; the structure of desire in the Hegelian tradition is oppositional.

The power of discourse is both dependent on and effective of the subordination of the feminine. 'When Our Lips Speak Together' (1985a) is
exemplary of a strategy of disruption of oppositions. Most significant is the
play with the I/you: the speaking position moves constantly, there is no fixing
of subject and object, nor any clear boundaries between subjects. 'You' is
both the other of autoeroticism and the other subject. In this sense an
inner–outer distinction constitutive of the specular 'I' is disrupted; there is
endless referral. 'I/you touch you/me, that's quite enough for us to feel alive',
and 'We – you/I – are neither open nor closed' (Irigaray 1985a: 209). 'Neither
one nor the other', and 'both simultaneously' are key devices employed in this
strategy. For example, with colours, and numbers: 'You are all red. And so
very white. Both at once . . . we give birth to all colours: pinks, browns,
blonds, greens, blues'; and 'Neither one nor two. . . And the strange way they
divide up their couples, with the other as the image of the one' (Irigaray
1985a: 207). The sea is a metaphor for the indeterminacy of internal–
external, and flow and movement. (In Cixous (1986: 90–1) the waves and
shore are repetition that is difference.) 'These movements cannot be described
as the passage from a beginning to an end. These rivers flow into no single,
definitive sea. These streams are without fixed banks, this body without fixed
boundaries' (Irigaray 1985a: 215).

    Mobility is strange to anyone claiming 'to stand on solid ground'. This
'essay' is about principles of meaning that are not based on a desire for an end,
a fixing; it also puts these principles into practice. Fluidity, touching of lips,
and so on, can be understood as metaphors for metonymy. Representation
consists of a desire for duplication and mirroring: a repetition that is the
same, an original and a copy; and self-objectification. On the other hand,
'between us, one is not the "real" and the other her imitation; one is not the
original and the other her copy' (Irigaray 1985a: 216). With reference to
touch rather than sight, she says that in our bodies we are already the same,
and doubled, two. This is not the immobilising repetition of representation,
but a repetition that is difference, constituted in the movement of deferral.

    Both Irigaray and Cixous are writing about and writing the principles of
meaning of transformation, and for both of them this way of meaning is
bodily. Cixous explicitly draws out the structure of desire in this form of
signification, but it is also implicit in Irigaray: a positive desire that would not
negate other in order to return self, and is kept alive through the process of
endless referral. Difference is qualitative, no repetition is the same. Irigaray's
work is important for the direct connections that are made between these
principles of meaning and the body. Whereas for Hegel knowledge requires
an emergence from and negation of the sensuous world, for Cixous and
Irigaray writing, which is to be distinguished from knowledge, is sensuous.

    'Jamming the theoretical machinery' and 'jamming sociality' can be
understood as strategies that counter the powers of phallocentric discourse.
(And, in the view of these feminists, Hegel is phallocentric, something that is
made explicit in Lacan's sexualisation of Hegel's structure of desire.) But, I

think we still need to ask the question: What are the assumptions about the nature of the counter-power of deconstructive strategies? These could not be understood as strategies of 'being rid' of or done with power. It would be reasonable to assume that the conception of power in deconstruction theory is not incompatible with Foucault's positive conception of power. And this can be further specified with respect to the body. For Foucault, power works positively through the body and is productive of counter-powers of the body. For Irigaray and Cixous, the counter-power of women's bodies is directly connected with phallocentrism in that it is the repressed of this order. The power of discourse is productive of counter-power. Unlike Foucault, the feminists do take the view that power works negatively: precisely what they are concerned to counter. But what they have in common with him is a conception of pleasure as counter-power (Irigaray 1985a: 32–3). After all, it is woman's pleasure on which the issue of counter-strategies turns for Cixous and Irigaray. And it is the specificity of this pleasure that makes the strategy not a simple one of reversal of masculine power and desire.

The concern with the disruptive body of pleasure is not peculiar to feminists. For example, Barthes (1986: 43) is making much the same point when he speaks of 'subjectivity' making 'structure hysterical': a bodily disruption to the order; the 'energy' of 'infinite Displacement'. Both Barthes and the feminists understand *jouissance* as just this. However, this raises the critical question: Why specifically female *jouissance*? In positing this as the counter to a singular order is there a danger (one that Irigaray and Cixous constantly warn of) of reinventing precisely what multiplicity refuses?

If, via Bergson and Foucault, we think of power in terms of actions of bodies on bodies, it could be asked: What makes the body act in a disruptive way? Foucault's conception of the body as a site of forces and the psychoanalytic conception of drives, and hystericisation, are not reducible, but do both make a connection between power and energy in the body. However, the energy of the unconscious would seem to come closer (than Foucault's account) to specifying what disrupts the *structure* of power. When Cixous speaks of the resources of the unconscious bursting out in a writing of the body, is this not a counter-power and a power of qualitative difference? Implicit in the 'unleashing' of a positive desire there is also a positive conception of power. This pleasure-power counters the negative structure of power and desire, and desire moved by fear (Cixous 1986: 97).

A positive desire destabilises the double of a mirroring relation, makes impossible a correspondence or representation: the self–other relation is constituted in movement. In this chapter it has been argued that this movement is bodily; the following chapter addresses the time of transformation, and the ways in which time presents a disturbance to the order of discourse and the double of the mirror.

5

TIME

Time is the substance I am made of . . .

(Borges 1970: 269)

'Writing the body' is a central concern in contemporary cultural theory. Following Barthes (1977: 179–89), my contention is that this involves a materialist conception of meaning. If the body is one of the components of a materialist semiotics, another one, I wish to suggest, is time. This chapter investigates the ways in which embodied meaning is temporal; it treats the connections between time and memory and the body, and the implications for conceptions of meaning processes.

The body is very much on the agenda in contemporary cultural theory, but time has received rather less attention. Nevertheless, the idea of transformation is a temporal conception of signification. In his reformulation of Saussurian semiotics, Derrida (1987: 26–9) emphasises movement in structure: deferral refers to temporal relations between elements. Approaches to knowledge and meaning can be distinguished from each other according to their temporal assumptions: whereas representation would hold elements and system still, a conception of writing as transformation acknowledges the time of meaning.

Transformation and writing the body are based on a positive desire that consists in a metonymic movement towards the other. This should be distinguished from Lacan's understanding of desire as metonymic, and indeed the movement of desire in Hegel. In the case of negative desire this principle of meaning operates only in so far as desire cannot be satisfied, but the desire is for identity and an end. The metonymy of a positive desire involves the displacement of various oppositions in the Hegel–Lacan structure of desire: immediacy–mediation, subject–object, internal–external. It is important to note that each of these oppositions is based on spatialisation, a distance between subject and object, and specularisation. But what happens to meaning and the subject when we turn to the other axis, that of time–touch, what Irigaray understands as metonymy as distinct from metaphor. (Metaphor, in this understanding of the term, consists in substitutions of the same, likenesses. The principle of association in metonymy is not sameness. The argument is that time and touch make an identity or sameness between discrete elements impossible.) The strategy of displacement of oppositions is itself a temporalisation. With reversal the structure stands still if on its head; with displacement (Krupnick 1987: 1–17) there is a movement of elements in relation to each other that involves 'permeation' or 'contamination'. One of my concerns is to demonstrate the temporality in this movement of permeation which is displacement, and the connection between a positive desire and time.

My project has been informed by the concerns of the French feminists. Reading Bergson has thrown light on some of the central ideas in their writings, in particular the significance of the body and time to different conceptions of meaning and knowledge. Bergson's philosophy is particularly important for the way it brings together questions of time and the body, and, in this regard, I will argue, makes a significant contribution to cultural theory. Furthermore, his temporal 'methodology of multiplicity' opens up considerable possibilities for cultural analysis. Although he applies multiplicity in a debate with philosophy this can be extended to cultural processes and texts more generally. In some ways I have found Bergson more suggestive than Irigaray or Cixous for developing an interdisciplinary approach to cultural analysis. For in his account of multiplicity I can get a sense of how this idea, much in vogue in feminist writings, might be applied in analyses of a diversity of texts.[1]

In some important respects Bergson's philosophy prefigures the contemporary ideas of transformation and writing the body. It can, for example, be read as a critique of a philosophy of identity and presence. His conception of duration as consisting of a movement and permeation of elements makes the presence of any single element impossible. And memory plays a significant part in this: 'Perception is never a mere contact of the mind with the object present; it is impregnated with memory-images' (Bergson 1950b [1986]: 170). As for Derrida (1982: 12), the movement in relations between elements undermines notions of causality, totality, and an end. For example, Bergson is critical of the idea that 'the present contains nothing more than the past, and what is found in the effect was already in the cause' (Bergson 1913 [1907]: 15). He can be located in the tradition of thought concerned with infinity, the unforeseeable, or in terms of contemporary theory, the 'play of the signifier', with no end point of meaning. Of finality he says: 'life transcends finality, if we understand by finality the realisation of an idea conceived or conceivable in advance' (Bergson 1913: 236). This relates to his conception of life as a process of qualitative differentiation. The temporality in this concept of difference has obvious parallels with Derrida's *différance*, with similar implications for system.

Bergson's conception of qualitative difference is related to a critique of notions of negation and difference defined negatively in relation to sameness. Negation, he claims, comes of the idea that what I see before me is something more than I want to see; hence the notion of 'disorder' (Bergson 1913: 233). This is remarkably like the feminist claim that negation is a repression of difference – specifically, in their view, of sexual difference. Bergson also distinguishes between singularity and multiplicity, arguing for the latter. While he does not deny the existence of singularity and negation, his critical concern is with a philosophical privileging of negativity. Rather than the negative of 'disorder', he argues that there is more than one order, a multiplicity of orders. Although his philosophy represents a critique of the Hegelian tradition, Bergson does not have a concept of desire. None the less, his conceptions of positive differentiation, the infinite and the unforseeable, are compatible with a positive desire.

Having already introduced Bergson's approach to the body, I will move on to his methodology of multiplicity, his theory of time and duration, and the connection he makes between duration and memory. I will then give an account of Freud's conceptions of memory trace and the temporality of the unconscious, and draw out connections with Bergson's ideas. While Bergson has a theory of time and the body, what Freud 'adds' to this is his understanding of memory trace as specific to the unconscious: relations between memory traces are governed by the principles of meaning of the unconscious. In this context reference will be made to Benjamin's discussion of Bergson, Freud and Proust on memory, and his use of the Proustian distinction between voluntary and involuntary memory in cultural analysis. I want to propose that one way of thinking cultural processes in multiplicity is to take up this distinction between voluntary and involuntary memory.

Bergson: multiplicity and duration

This discussion will make reference to the following Bergson texts: *Time and Free Will* (1950a [1889]), *Matter and Memory* (1950b [1896]), and *Creative Evolution* (1913 [1907]).

Bergson's methodology of multiplicity consists in dissociation, in taking any 'object' and dissociating its different moments, or, as we might say, its different ways of meaning. For Bergson it is not a question of either/or: we can discern different processes simultaneously at work. To give the most pertinent example, that of multiplicity itself: there is a multiplicity which is quantitative, the one and the many, and there is qualitative multiplicity (Bergson 1950a: 75–80). Thus, Bergson makes a qualitative distinction between two types of multiplicity: he applies multiplicity to multiplicity. To think in multiplicity involves making a distinction between, on the one hand, the singular, homogeneous and quantitative, and, on the other, the multiple, heterogeneous and qualitative. We could, for example, think of the subject in these terms: the subject as simultaneously singular and multiple. This is very close to the way Irigaray conceptualises the feminine, as both positioned by singular discourses in which the feminine is defined negatively in relation to the masculine, and as the repressed difference, or multiplicity, which 'exceeds' these discourses – the 'something more' in Bergson's terms. The singular and the multiple mean in relation to each other. For example, for both Bergson and Irigaray, the notion of multiplicity comes of a critical response to the oneness privileged in philosophical discourse, and in this sense, is dependent on that notion. The general critical point is that the singular suppresses the multiple, it denies dependency through a negation.

For Bergson, the quantitative implies a negation; it consists in starting from a general order, the same, rather than a 'difference in kind between two orders' (Deleuze 1988 [1966]: 46). Contrary to the sameness assumed in a negative philosophy, Bergson (1913: 248) argues for a distinction between kinds of order that are not reducible to one another. These orders are respectively the singular, quantitative, and the multiple, qualitative. They also correspond to a space–time divergence. In general, the dissociations that he makes are along these divergent lines of space and time. Multiplicity is temporal.

In the Introduction to *Matter and Memory* Bergson acknowledges that this approach is dualistic; but he contests dualistic approaches that negate one term in order to privilege the other. The very basis of such a dualism is called into question with the idea of multiplicity. He does, however, regard one side of the singular–multiple dualism as the 'good side'. Needless to say, this is the multiple, the principle on which dissociation works. Where a negative philosophy, based on binary oppositions, would have an end, the process of dissociation and reassociation is endless. The movement of this process is thus to be distinguished from the stop–start of the dialectic.

What, then, is the connection between multiplicity and time? The dissociation that Bergson makes here is time–space. Time is thought either spatially or temporally, and his argument is that the problems faced by philosophy stem, to a large extent, from thinking time spatially. The common conception of time is that it is abstract, linear, and homogeneous – homogeneous empty time (Bergson 1950a: 95; see also Benjamin 1969: 263). Each moment in this time is understood as a discrete element or presence, and it is presumed that it can be represented as such. Only if we spatialise time can we come to such a view; we should instead think time temporally, which means putting ourselves in time rather than standing outside: indeed, we need to live time rather than think it. This relates to Bergson's (1950b: 171) concern to develop a philosophy that is 'in life', the 'living reality' or 'becoming'. He counterposes this to philosophy understood as a matter of the intellect. Thus in his philosophy time and the body are inextricably linked: 'where anything lives, time is being inscribed' (Bergson 1913: 17).

In *Time and Free Will*, Bergson (1950a: 122) challenges 'the deeply ingrained habit of setting out time in space', and argues for a concept of duration that is not related to number or space, but is characterised by a qualitative multiplicity. Number is a collection of units which must be identical with each other, individual differences being dis*counted*; counting consists in placing these units in a succession in space, on a line. Number also implies a 'visual image in space' (Bergson 1950a: 76–9). The unity of the whole is comprised of a series of identical, discrete units (Bergson 1950a: 80–2). However, when affective psychic states are considered, it is clear that a distinction needs to be made between a multiplicity of number, and a multiplicity of states of consciousness. When we listen to the sounds of a bell we do not count them but gather a qualitative impression of 'the whole series', we are 'confronted by a confused multiplicity of sensations and feelings' (Bergson 1950a: 86–7). (We may of course count them, but this confirms Bergson's general point.) With this multiplicity there is a permeation of states that cannot be identified as discrete units. But mistakenly, when we think of time, we tend to range our states of consciousness alongside each other 'as in space', 'in a homogeneous medium' (Bergson 1950a: 90). Thus, affective psychic states are treated as a discrete series like number, which is to reduce the qualitative to quantity. There are, then, two kinds of reality, 'the one heterogeneous, that of sensible qualities, the other homogeneous, namely space' (Bergson 1950a: 97). As soon as we make time a homogeneous medium we abstract it from duration.

States of consciousness are not discrete, and 'even when successive, permeate one another' (Bergson 1950a: 98). Bergson makes this point in connection with the experience of listening to music. We perceive notes in one another, there is a 'mutual penetration', an interconnection of elements that cannot be distinguished, the notes of a tune melt into one another. (While this rather underestimates the complexity of the operations of listening to music, his principal concern is not with music.) This is the experience of duration, an experience of a being 'who was ever the same and ever changing' (Bergson 1950a: 101). Here, we find a conception of difference in repetition. The subject is the 'same' in so far as states of consciousness 'continuously' permeate each other; but it is also permeation that produces difference, much like the trace in Freud and Derrida. Each 'new' state of consciousness, in penetrating others, changes the whole. Thus in the movement which is duration there is qualitative difference. Pure duration is lived, as opposed to a separation of states as points on a line, or presences; in duration, past and present melt into each other without distinction (Bergson 1950a: 100). As soon as we fix on a moment, abstract it, it no longer endures; it is solidified, spatialised and impenetrable.

There are obvious echoes of this in Irigaray's distinction between solids and fluids. Irigaray frequently refers to fluids, and Bergson to melting. He speaks of 'the melting of states of consciousness into one another' and of duration as qualitative changes 'which melt into and permeate one another' (Bergson 1950a: 104). Even in the surface contact of solids there is no true interruption. Bergson says that affectivity, 'affection', is that part of the internal of our body that we 'mix with the image of external bodies' (Bergson 1950b: 60). Again there are continuities with Irigaray's emphasis on touch and contiguity as a means of disrupting the boundaries of identity.

For Bergson (1950b: 260), there is a permanent moving continuity, in which 'everything changes and yet remains'. And each duration beats to its own rhythm (Bergson 1950b: 272). Duration, then, is a qualitative multiplicity. In *Creative Evolution*, he presents a critique of mechanistic forms of thought which see only similarity or repetition:

> Thus, concentrated on that which repeats, solely preoccupied in welding the same to the same, intellect turns away from the vision of time. It dislikes what is fluid, and solidifies everything it touches. We do not *think* real time. But we *live* it (Bergson 1913: 48–9).

Bergson conceptualises relations between moments in time, relations between psychic states and relations between bodies in the same way – he moves back and forth between these in developing his argument. If the idea of body-images in motion is a basic premise, what is the connection between this and the time–space dissociation? A moving body occupies successive positions in space, but the process by which it moves from one position to another is one of duration which eludes space (Bergson 1950a: 111). Motion itself, the act, is not divisible, only an object is; space which is motionless can be measured, but the motion of bodies cannot. Movements cannot occupy space, they are duration. The flow on of the interval cannot be calculated. Mathematics cannot express a body in motion, only positions in space, which is to express 'something already done'. Concerned only with a static moment, the mathematician deals with a world that 'dies at every instant' (Bergson 1913: 23). Duration, on the other hand, 'is unceasingly being done' (Bergson 1950a: 119). Even if moving bodies occupy points on a line, one after the other, duration and motion have nothing to do with the line (Bergson 1950a: 120). Linear thinking consists in putting oneself, as an observer, outside duration (Bergson 1913: 327). To think of a body occupying points in space is to do so from a perspective outside the body, not from the perspective of the moving body. To be *in* the body is to be in time.

Some further connections with Irigaray can be drawn out here:

> Keep on going, without getting out of breath. Your body is not the same today as yesterday. Your body remembers. There's no need for *you* to remember. No need to hold fast to yesterday, to store it up as capital in your head. Your memory? Your body expresses yesterday in what it wants today. If you think: yesterday I was, tomorrow I shall be, you have died a little. Be what you are becoming, without clinging to what you might have been, what you might yet be. Never settle (Irigaray 1985a: 215).

In this passage from 'When Our Lips Speak Together' there is something of an injunction; to write 'Be what you are becoming' would seem to contradict precisely this form of becoming. Nevertheless, the implicit argument about time is worth considering. 'Keep on going . . .' is a movement, duration, unceasingly being done. 'Be what you are becoming': duration is a becoming; if you fix on a moment of the past, 'something already done' (Bergson), you are thinking: 'I have died a little'. Irigaray frequently makes critical references to counting, one after the other, and divisibility, and to this she counterposes a qualitative multiplicity that is not divisible. She speaks of being 'Always in motion: openness is never spent nor sated' (Irigaray 1985a: 210). Throughout 'When Our Lips Speak Together' there are references to moving bodies, and bodies without limits, borders. 'Moving bodies' is a refusal of the power of 'truth' which operates through a distancing from the body, and immobilisation. Movements cannot be 'described as a passage from a beginning to an end' (Irigaray 1985a: 214–15); they disrupt the teleology of linearity (Irigaray 1985a: 68). With reference to the embodiment of feminine texts Cixous (1981: 54) says: 'So the movement, the movement of the text, doesn't trace a straight line'. Duration, or time proper, is a property of the body in motion: a heterogeneous and qualitative multiplicity. The writing, textual practice, that French feminists advocate could thus be said to be in duration.

Memory

Bergson's analysis of memory in *Matter and Memory* is particularly complex as he proceeds from the dissociation of one composite to another in an attempt to identify the various elements of memory. His most important distinction is between memory images and the memory of duration: on the one hand, attempts to represent the past, have the past as a presence; and, on the other, memory that is lived bodily and in the movement of time. One form of memory represents the past, the other acts it (Bergson 1950b: 93).

To clarify the connection that Bergson makes between memory and duration, something needs to be said about his distinctions between the past and the present, and between memory and perception. A common and mistaken distinction is made between strong states, perceptions of the present, and weak states, representations of the past. This is to assume that they are qualitatively the same, and to proceed from the present. It was pointed out earlier (in Chapter 3) that he reverses the usual point of departure, by starting not with 'our body' but with the material world of bodies, and asking how from this we get to our body. He adopts a similar procedure with respect to the past and the present:

the truth is that we shall never reach the past unless we frankly place ourselves within it. Essentially virtual, it cannot be known as something past unless we follow and adopt the movement by which it expands into a present image, thus emerging from obscurity into the light of day (Bergson 1950b: 173).

This is an example of his method of intuition – placing oneself in the movement of life. We cannot get pastness out of the present by putting together likenesses from a present image. Memory and perception are qualitatively different (Bergson 1950b: 174–5). The present is sensori-motor, the materiality of existence, and is unique for each moment of duration. As memory materialises in the body, in movement, it ceases to be pure memory; it is lived in the present (Bergson 1950b: 178–9). It has moved from virtual, in the depths of the past, to actual, capable of provoking movements.

In connection with memory an obvious question to ask is whether Bergson has a 'concept' of the unconscious. Pure memory is preserved in a latent state, and here he uses the term 'unconscious' to describe that psychical state. Pure memory is virtual, which is actualised in the movement of becoming. In a sense this is the crux of the matter: the movement of life, a becoming which is duration is the process of actualisation of memory. However, the movement from virtual to actual is a process of differentiation, and thus pure memory could not be understood as a presence in 'the actual', or indeed in 'the virtual', despite his use of the term 'latent'. For the latent never arrives. There is no repetition of the same. In this regard Bergson's concept of the unconscious, although not nearly as sophisticated as Freud's, functions in a similar way to the unconscious in Freud. As Derrida (1982: 21) has said in connection with Freud: 'the alterity of the "unconscious" makes us concerned not with horizons of modified – past or future – presents, but with a "past" that has never been present, and which never will be'. What I think Bergson's account of memory has to offer is the emphasis on memory as bodily movement: 'hysteria' is *the* form of memory. Or, as Irigaray puts it, 'your body remembers' (Irigaray 1985b: 214).

Bergson frequently makes the claim that the present is the lived reality. But the present is not understood as a presence either. In fact he says 'nothing *is* less than the present, if you understand by that the indivisible limit which divides the past from the future' (Bergson 1950b: 193). He speaks of duration as the continuous progress of the past gnawing into the future. The pure present is 'invisible' (Bergson 1950b: 194). And here memory is directly connected with duration: memory is the prolongation of the past into the present, the very basis of becoming. This is duration, 'acting and irreversible' (Bergson 1913: 17). Notice that duration is invisible: what cannot be counted cannot be seen either. Duration is not 'one instant replacing another', but a prolongation of the past, a movement of the virtual into the actual. Otherwise there would be nothing but the present, a repetition of the same (Bergson 1913: 4–5, 48).

The memory of duration is not the memory of images: any representation consists in a spatialisation, a cutting out, an immobilisation. Representation of past, present or future is a denial of time. To think about the future consists of 'projecting into the future what has been perceived in the past' (Bergson 1913: 6–7). Contrary to this mode of thinking, in duration, each moment in its unfolding is indivisible, irreducible, and in a sense 'original' (Bergson 1913: 7, 326). In what could be read as a critique of the 'original and the copy' of representation, Bergson (1950b: 173) speaks of 'vain attempts to discover in a realized and present state the mark of its past origin'. This bears comparison with Derrida's (1982: 13) account of the present as an ' "originary" and irreducibly non simple . . . synthesis of marks, or traces'. Derrida acknowledges the importance of Freud's conceptions of trace and deferral; but it is also the case that Bergson's duration is comparable with temporal assumptions in 'the trace'. Bergson is critical of notions of causality; for example, the idea that a moment immediately before could be the cause of the present one. There is in fact no instant immediately before another one: the 'instant "immediately before" is, in reality, that which is connected with the present instant by the interval' (Bergson 1913: 23; see also 1913: 324–5).

For Derrida, every so-called present element is related to something other than itself, it keeps the mark of the past element, and is already 'vitiated' by the mark of a future element. But the interval must separate the present element from what it is not. The interval is spacing, 'the becoming-space of time or the becoming-time of space' (Derrida 1982: 13). Despite Derrida's different conception of the relation between time and space, what he and Bergson have in common is the idea that present elements are marked by the trace, and the significance of the interval to the relation between elements. The interval points to time and movement, and the impossibility of the presence of an element. Hence signification is understood as transformation rather than representation.[2]

What is the status of 'preservation' of the past in Bergson's understanding of memory? He claims that there is no limit to the preservation of the past: memory, or the 'piling up of the past upon the past', occurs at every moment, it is the essence of duration (Bergson 1913: 5–6). The issue here is whether preservation implies that the past is retained as a presence. In what sense, then, is the past preserved? For Freud, of course, the past is preserved; but, importantly, as memory traces, that is, in the system of the unconscious (Freud 1976 [1900]: 734). Bergson (1913: 5) argues that memory 'is not a faculty of putting away recollections in a drawer, or of inscribing them in a register. There is no register, no drawer'. He argues that notions of a container and the storing of memories come from thinking of memory in spatial rather than temporal terms (Bergson 1950b: 191–3). Thus, the psyche or unconscious is not a thing, and does not 'retain'. It could be said that Bergson refers to preservation in connection with duration precisely to counter any idea of discrete moments, past or present, as presences. In Bergson's theory of memory and duration the past lives, not in the sense of either a going back to a past moment, or a representation of it, but in the permeation of moments that moves us forward.

Duration and philosophy

Some brief comments should be made about Bergson's notion of philosophical intuition, a philosophy that is in duration, in the movement of life. He claims that his method of dissociation proceeds as life does. *Creative Evolution* is devoted to developing a philosophy of intuition, a method that is nearer to experience, the starting point of which is the recognition that a theory of life and a theory of knowledge are inseparable (Bergson 1913: xiii). He counterposes intuition to the intellect, which cannot think evolution in the sense of continuity, but represents becoming as a series of states. 'It does not admit the unforeseeable', but seeks and finds only causality and finality (Bergson 1913: 172–3). As evidence that the kind of effort involved in intuition is not impossible he cites the aesthetic faculty. Benjamin (1973: 111) claims that it was a 'poet' – Proust – who put Bergson's theory of experience to the test.

Precisely what Bergson understands by evolution, and indeed *creative* evolution, is obviously crucial for grasping the philosophical method he proposes. Basically, evolution is a process of positive and qualitative differentiation. Duration embodies a process of actualisation of the virtual, and it is difference that characterises this process. The very movement is one of differentiation: there is a difference between the virtual we start with and the actual at which we 'arrive' (Deleuze 1988: 96–7). Bergson (1913: 320) says, rather quaintly perhaps, 'Becoming is infinitely varied', that which 'goes from yellow to green is not like that which goes from green to blue: they are different qualitative movements'. Movements from flower to fruit, larva to nymph, and nymph to perfect insect are 'different evolutionary movements'. But, the crucial point is that, in his view, evolution is differentiation. Not only is a particular body characterised by differentiation, but there are qualitative differences between bodies. He cites what he says is a deceptively simple example of duration: sugar melting in water. 'I must wait until the sugar melts.' There is my duration, and that of the sugar melting; and a *waiting* (Bergson 1913: 10). Duration is a waiting, a deferral, and a mixing of systems, for which we could read intertextuality.

The idea of actualisation is radically different from the possible, counterposed as it is to the real. The virtual is, for Bergson, real. Creative evolution is a process without end, it is infinite. That the virtual is real is part of this conception of a process without end. And this relates directly to his view that philosophy should be intuitive rather than contemplative. If philosophy were to follow life, creative evolution, it would do without any notion of finality, or differentiation as negation, or cause and effect (Bergson 1913: 187). Once differentiation is understood as the movement of virtual to actual it is no longer negative, it is creative and positive (Deleuze 1988: 103). In 'vital activity' we see 'a reality which is making itself in a reality which is unmaking itself' (Bergson 1913: 261): actions that are making themselves in an unmaking. What could be a better description of deconstruction, and transformation?

With his conception of differentiation, Bergson disputes any idea of a whole as given. The illusion of a whole comes from a spatialisation of time in which 'things appear as ready made forms' (Deleuze 1988: 104). Duration is a movement of actualisation along divergent lines that do not form a whole; creation is a process of differentiation without goals. There are no ready-made lines as these are created in the action. As Bergson (1913: 17) says: there are no universal laws, there are only 'directions'. We might ask if this idea is commensurate with Freud or not. While Freud does have a conception of laws, they are not causally determinative, although neither is it a matter of 'anything goes'. Given the principles of operation of the psyche, there is a specific range of possible 'outcomes', but these cannot be predicted or read off cultural laws. Perhaps, then, Freud's 'laws', or principles, might be understood as 'directions'. For example, it could be said that the pleasure principle and the reality principle have no end; they are directions.

I have suggested that Bergson's theory of time is compatible with a positive desire, that is, a desire that accepts the difference of otherness rather than one that would negate the other. If this is so, it is important to distinguish the temporal assumptions in a positive and negative desire, respectively. What, then, can be said about time in Hegel? There is a passage, in the section of *The Phenomenology* discussed in Chapter 4 above, where Hegel explicitly makes a time–space distinction, not unlike that made by Bergson. But there is a crucial difference in their valuations of time and space and the respective assumptions about knowledge. In the split unity of life and self-conscious-ness, life is in the flux of time (Hegel 1977: para. 169). In so far as 'I' am a vanishing moment, I am also in this temporal flux. Life is the 'restless' movement of infinity, the 'fluid' of 'pure movement', which is 'Time'. But in-dependent self-consciousness, in its 'equality with itself', 'has the stable shape of Space' (Hegel 1977: para. 169). As a unity of differences, self-conscious-ness exists beyond the vanishing moments; it is outside time.

This account of the difference between space and time is remarkably like Bergson's, and Bergson may well be writing in response to precisely this formulation. For Hegel, in ceasing to be immersed in life, one develops temporal consciousness. Bergson argues for a philosophy that is in time, in the flux of life. These different views about the nature of philosophy are encapsulated in Hegel's lyrical account of the turning point of self-conscious-ness, 'where it leaves behind it the colourful show of the sensuous here-and-now and the nightlike void of the supersensible beyond, and steps out into the spiritual daylight of the present' (Hegel 1977: para. 177). The connection between a desire for presence, self-identity, and the *present* is quite explicit here: what deconstructive philosophers and Bergson claim to be the atemporality of knowledge. Bergson and Irigaray argue for a philosophy that is in 'the colourful show of the sensuous here-and-now'. Irigaray frequently makes references to the here-and-now which is to be distinguished from the present: it is the movement of time of the here-and-now that makes the present impossible.[3]

'I' as unity of differences is clearly a totalising moment in Hegel: the spatial axis of self would know the whole. But this is a split unity, and there is also a temporal moment of self. Taken together, these two moments are indicative of time in Hegel more generally. One of the reasons why Hegel is so important to contemporary philosophy is that he explicitly addresses the question of time and philosophy. The debate over whether there is temporality in Hegel's philosophy turns on the question of totality: Is his system closed, is it finite, with an end? In the progress of Spirit there is obviously movement, and even if the desire is for an end, there is something in the nature of the dialectic that makes this impossible – it goes on. This movement is one of negation and supersession; and to return to the example above, if vanishing moments are superseded, they do not disappear, they are not a succession but rather are incorporated, in the movement towards knowledge. This conception of the 'presence' of past moments is commensurate with both Bergson's and Freud's understandings of the temporality of psychic processes.

While it is acknowledged by philosophers in the tradition of positive desire that there is a temporality in this, what they take issue with is the Hegelian notion of the progressive constitution of truth (Levinas 1987: 127). Levinas's argument, much like Bergson's, is for a conception of the 'progress' of truth not external to time, but of the very essence of time (the actualisation of the virtual). There is no final point at which truth comes to a halt outside time. The philosophical dispute is whether this is the case with Hegel or not.

Butler takes a different view from that of Levinas. Basing her claims on the paradox in Hegel, namely the openness of an apparently all-inclusive system, she says: 'To be able to think Hegel's absolute, the infinite and the systematic at once, is to think beyond spatial categories, to think the essence of time as Becoming' (Butler 1987: 14). On this reading there is no finality, and she cites Kojève and Hyppolite who argue for this view: there is an indefinite movement of time, negativity is not resolved, there is an openness in the movement of Spirit. The question about this is, as she says, the issue of negativity and the satisfaction of desire in death. Positive readings of Hegel downplay these. Without attempting to 'resolve' this, it could be said that, in so far as there is negation and a desire for the solid and stable in Hegel, there is stasis, atemporality. But, negation is also what keeps the dialectic going. Thus the paradoxical in Hegel is also evident in the temporality of his philosophy. The dialectic is temporal even if it is marked by moments of stasis. However, it is in the very nature of desire that such moments fail to effect resolution.

Directly concerned to counter Hegel, Levinas proposes a positive structure of desire in connection with a theory of time. Without giving a detailed account of Levinas, I want to address the question of whether his theory of desire and the other makes an advance on Bergson's theory of time. Derrida (1978: 93), for example, in support of Levinas' theory of time, claims that Bergson overlooked the necessity of the other for time. For Levinas there is no time without the other, because to be without it is to be locked in self-identity, without movement. While it is the case that Bergson does not refer to the other, it is reasonable to assume that his conceptions of multiplicity and infinity, together with his concern with the movement of bodies in relation to each other, imply a concept of otherness. For Bergson, there is no unitary, singular self. And, he emphasises motion and flow explicitly in opposition to identity and sameness.

Levinas's opposition to Hegel is apparent in the title of his book, *Totality and Infinity* (1979 [1961]); Hegel represents the former, and his own philosophy the latter. Levinas is concerned with a relation to the other that defies any attempt at totalisation, a relation with the absolutely other that overflows thought, that is a surplus beyond totality (Levinas 1979: 22–5). This beyond totality is expressed in the concept of infinity, which is a transcendence. For him, consciousness is moved by infinity, and this is activity, or life. Thus he opposes the usual distinction between theory and activity, and hence the idea of representation: consciousness is not a matter of correspondence with the object. The relation to the other is not a question of knowledge of the other, or reduction of the other to the same; this other is not an object, and cannot be totalised (Levinas 1979: 27–8, 35, 49). The other is alterity, absolutely other, without limit.[4] The movement of transcendence, desire, is radically distinguished from negativity; infinity is not reducible to negation (Levinas 1979: 40–1). On the absolutely other as Other, he says:

> He and I do not form a number. The collectivity in which I say 'you' or 'we' is not a plural of the 'I'. I, you – these are not individuals of a common concept. Neither possession nor the unity of number nor the unity of concepts link me to the Stranger [*l'Étranger*], the Stranger who disturbs the being at home with oneself [*le chez soi*]. But Stranger also means free one. Over him I have no *power* (Levinas 1979: 39).

The parallels with Irigaray and Cixous are striking here: a constant movement in a relation to the other, a going out to the other, an other that cannot be reduced, that is beyond numbers. Furthermore, this is not a relation of power, at least not in a negative sense. The idea of the stranger disturbing a 'being at home' might be read as a metaphor of the disturbance by the unconscious to the homely of representation, a repetition of the same: Freud's 'uncanny', the un*heimlich* in a return to origins.

Levinas's conceptions of infinity, and infinity as activity, are close to Bergson's philosophy. But Levinas does depart from Bergson in his conception of time as the relation to the other. It is for this reason that he rejects Bergson's conception of duration as continuous: the alterity of the others' time is disruptive to my time. In his 1979 Preface to *Time and the Other*, Levinas (1987: 30) says that time is a relationship to the other which is 'a mode of the *beyond being*'. It is a relationship to the other that inscribes the impossibility of adequation and coincidence – a relationship with the 'In-visible' (Levinas 1987: 32). It might be recalled here that, in Bergson's view, duration is invisible. Levinas (1987: 32) says: 'Time signifies this *always* of non-coincidence, but also the *always* of the *relationship*, an aspiration and an awaiting'. For Bergson time is a waiting, and if he speaks of time as continuous, it is a heterogeneous continuity. The point of the melting sugar story is precisely the non-coincidence of durations. In Levinas (1987: 33) time is a movement, a transcendence, toward the infinity of the wholly other, which is not a linear temporalisation in any way. Thus the relation to the absolutely other provides a movement that Bergson's theory does not altogether account for, except with reference to the process of evolution. The important point here is that alterity temporalises, and undoes identity. Although Levinas makes this explicit, Bergson's theory of time, which Levinas substantially draws on, implies a positive desire. It is above all else time, constitutive of the positive relation to the other, that makes identity impossible.

Clearly in this approach to time and the other there is no death in the senses of an end to knowledge, representation, or a negation of the other. For Levinas and Bergson, time goes beyond death, the particularity of 'my death' (Levinas 1987: 114–16). Bergson (1913: 286) claims that creative evolution overcomes the 'most formidable obstacles, perhaps even death'. A philosophy based on creative evolution 'gives us more power to act and to live' (Bergson 1913: 285). Thus, meaning and knowledge processes in time are constituted in a positive structure of power and desire: in life rather than death. If there is a life–death dualism here, this needs to be understood in the context of multiplicity. An argument for 'life' is a refusal of negation, and thus an acceptance of both life and death. Negativity, on the other hand, consists in both a fear of death and desire for death.

Freud: memory and time

Freud and Bergson were contemporaries and made brief references to each other: Freud in *Jokes and their Relation to the Unconscious* [1905]; Bergson in *Matter and Memory*, which was published four years before Freud's major work on memory, *The Interpretation of Dreams* [1900]. For this discussion of time and memory the most relevant Freudian texts are *The Interpretation of Dreams*, 'Beyond the Pleasure Principle' [1920], and 'A Note upon the "Mystic Writing Pad" ' [1925a]. I shall focus on 'Beyond the Pleasure Principle', in which there is an abbreviated version of the theory of memory to be found in Chapter 7 of *The Interpretation of Dreams*, and which also anticipates important formulations about memory and time in the 'Mystic Writing Pad'. 'Beyond the Pleasure Principle' is of particular interest, not only because it is relevant to concerns about temporality and memory in contemporary theory, but also because of the speculations on the death instinct. A double reading is possible which corresponds to the different structures of desire: the death instinct as a desire for repetition of the same and a return to origins; and Freud's account of psychical processes which point to the impossibility of such a repetition.

Temporal assumptions that inform all of Freud's writings undo a repetition of the same. Overall these are of more significance than the brief explicit references to time. Taken together, memory and time are basic to
Freud's theories of psychic processes, and it is this aspect of Freud that has
been taken up by deconstructive theorists (see Derrida 1978: 196–231). The
Freudian concepts that have been most relevant to deconstruction are: the
distortion of dream-work; deferred action and memory traces; and overdetermination. Related to the principles of meaning of the unconscious, all
of these imply an understanding of meaning as transformation rather than
representation.

The effect of condensation and displacement – the distortion, or what deconstructive theorists refer to as displacement, of dream-work – is overdetermination: any manifest element has multiple determinations (Freud
1976 [1900]: 416–18). Overdetermination is temporal in that there is no
cause–effect relation between elements; there is no linearity of determination in this notion. No element is simply present, it is always overdeter-
mined; a manifest element does not represent a latent element, and a latent
element does not cause a manifest one. In manifest or present elements, in
dreams, in somatic symptoms, or whatever, there are traces of past elements
which have undergone a process of transformation through condensation
and or displacement. The work of interpretation consists in working backwards, applying these principles. Freud (1973a [1916]: 204) refers to this as
an 'undoing' of dream-work.

In the concept of deferred action temporal assumptions are quite explicit:
a previous experience takes on a new or revised meaning in the light of later
experiences. But, to put it in these terms is misleading in so far as it implies a
meaning, for example of a 'past', that takes on a new meaning, in a present.
In his reading of Freud, Derrida's emphasis on the delay and detour of
deferral, and the past that never was, avoids this problem. For example, he
says that 'the difference between the pleasure principle and the reality principle is only *différance* as detour', and that in Freud 'the movement of the
trace is described as an effort to protect itself by *deferring* the dangerous
investment' (Derrida 1982: 18). Most importantly, the psychic economy is
characterised by the detour that has no end.

This relates to the previous discussion about Derrida's (1982: 21) claim
that the concept of trace is incompatible with a notion of retention, implying, as it does, a present that becomes past. Freud, like Bergson, took the
view that the 'past' was preserved, but as with Bergson this should not be
read as the past as presence. Freud (1976: 734) is quite explicit that it is the
unconscious and memory traces that cannot be destroyed: 'it is a prominent
feature of unconscious processes that they are indestructible. In the unconscious nothing can be brought to an end, nothing is past or forgotten.' And

we have been inclined to take the opposite view that in mental life
nothing which has once been formed can perish – that everything is

somehow preserved and that in suitable circumstances . . . it can once
more be brought to light (Freud 1985a [1930]: 256).

The crucial point here is that that which cannot be destroyed is what is
unconscious, precisely what is negated in a desire for presence. Furthermore,
what cannot be destroyed is the process of deferral, the 'without end'.
   In the context of this quotation from *Civilisation and its Discontents* Freud
(1985a: 259) makes some interesting observations on problems of representing the mind, namely, that it is impossible to represent in pictorial terms the
preservation 'of all the earlier stages alongside of the final form'. The problem
is that we tend to represent historical sequence in spatial terms, and the same
space cannot have two different contents. In mental life there is a juxtapo-
sition of elements that cannot be grasped in spatial terms (Freud 1985a: 258;
see also Bergson 1950b: 193). Even in setting out his topography of the
psychical systems in Chapter 7 of *Dreams*, Freud (1976: 685) claimed there
was no justification for thinking that these systems were arranged in a spatial
order. His conception of relations between psychic elements seems comparable, then, to Bergson's conception of a permeation of psychic states that is
temporal rather than spatial. For Freud there is a psychic temporalisation that
is not spatial; and relations between psychic elements are marked by the
temporality of memory traces.
   What precisely does Freud understand by memory trace? In his schema of
the psychical apparatus there is a sensory end which receives stimuli, internal
and external, and a motor end of innervations or energy discharge. Psychical
processes advance from the former, from perceptions, to the latter (Freud
1976: 686). When he comes to the question of what happens to perceptions a
differentiation between systems is introduced: perceptions leave traces in the
psychical apparatus which are recorded in systems (mnemic systems) as
memory traces. There they stand in relation to other traces in the system, and
a new trace will produce modifications of elements (Freud 1976: 687). If
everything is preserved, it is also, we could say, forever changing. Traces are
organised in systems according to different forms of association, one of
which, it should be noted, is contiguity in time (Freud 1976: 688). The basis
of association, and the facilitating paths are located in these systems and not
in the Pcpt. system (perception). This concurs with Bergson's distinction
between memory and perception. Traces of a particular perception will be
laid down in different systems according to associations, and may be
reactivated in one associative context, while not in another. Laplanche and
Pontalis (1973) emphasise that in this conception of traces standing in
relation to each other within systems, memory trace is 'distinct from the
empiricist notion of . . . a resemblance to the corresponding reality'. A
memory trace is simply an arrangement of facilitations; there is no appeal to a
correspondence between a trace and an object (Laplanche and Pontalis 1973:
247–8).
   Memories are not only unconscious, but can produce all their effects while

in an 'unconscious condition'. Freud (1976: 689) claims that memory and consciousness are qualitatively different and mutually exclusive. Once a memory has become conscious it is no longer, strictly speaking, a memory. He developed this important argument in 'A Note upon the "Mystic Writing Pad"' and in 'Beyond the Pleasure Principle'. The perceptual system cannot retain traces as this would limit its capacity for fresh excitations; receptive capacity and 'retention' are mutually exclusive properties (Freud 1984 [1920]: 296; 1984 [1925a]: 430; 1976: 687). The crucial point is that becoming conscious and leaving behind a memory trace are 'incompatible within one and the same system' (Freud 1984 [1920]: 296); and further, that 'consciousness arises in the perceptual system instead of per-manent traces' (Freud 1984 [1925a]: 430; 1984 [1920]: 296–7).

It is 'Beyond the Pleasure Principle' that Benjamin compares with Bergson and Proust, drawing particular attention to Freud's claim that memory traces 'have nothing to do with the fact of becoming conscious; indeed they are often most powerful and most enduring when the process which left them behind was one which never entered consciousness' (Freud 1984 [1920]: 296; Benjamin 1973: 114). Benjamin claims that this corresponds to involuntary memory; and that Freud's distinction between remembering and memory is analogous to the distinction between voluntary and involuntary memory: 'only what has not been experienced explicitly and consciously, what has not happened to the subject as an experience, can become a component of the *mémoire involontaire*' (Benjamin 1973: 114).

The task of psychoanalysis is remembrance, which is in fact a form of forgetting. On this question, in *Dreams*, Freud (1976: 734) says that psychotherapy intervenes to make it possible for unconscious processes 'to be dealt with finally and be forgotten'. For example, in the case of hysteria, an association brings a memory to life in a motor discharge. It is only through the work of the pre-conscious, close to consciousness, that this memory can be brought to light and hence forgotten. Freud's account of the 'effect' of memory traces runs counter to the common view that memories fade with time, and on this point there is agreement with Bergson's refutation of the idea that memories are simply weak states of perception. In 'Beyond the Pleasure Principle' Freud (1984 [1920]: 288) refers to the repetition of repressed material as opposed to 'what the physician would prefer to see, *remembering* it as something belonging to the past'. Remembering is a characteristic of consciousness. Memory is unconscious.

Thus, as Benjamin suggests, Freud's distinction between consciousness and memory does seem comparable to the distinction between voluntary and involuntary memory. It is also comparable to Bergson's distinction between the memory of representation and the embodied memory of duration. Benjamin's (1973: 111–12) claim that Freud is more comparable than Bergson to Proust, is based on a comparison with Bergson's 'pure memory'. The memory of duration, the actualisation of pure memory, would seem to be more appropriate for a comparison with involuntary memory. However, in both virtual and actual forms, memory is implicitly unconscious.[5]

In 'Beyond the Pleasure Principle' Freud says that the function of consciousness is to provide a shield against external stimuli. There is no such protective mechanism against internal excitations, and one way that these are dealt with is by treating them as if they came from the outside (Freud 1984 [1920]: 300–1). It could be said that to remember, or to bring to consciousness, is a form of externalisation; once a memory is in the system of consciousness the protective shield can come into operation. As Freud (1976: 689) says, if memories become conscious they lose their sensory quality; the role of psychotherapy is to rid unconscious memories of certain affects by bringing them to consciousness. This is close to Bergson's view that representations of the past are without affectivity. Bergson (1950b: 132) distinguishes between affective states and their representation: 'A violent love or a deep melancholy takes possession of our soul'. These feelings *live* by virtue of the duration of permeation. But as soon as we attempt to isolate these feelings from one another, setting out time in space, they become lifeless and colourless: 'We are now standing before our own shadow' (Bergson 1950a: 133). Involuntary memory, or memory proper, is affective. In Proust and Bergson this memory is clearly temporal. For Freud, consciousness and the unconscious are characterised by different temporalities, and there is evidence to suggest that his conception of the time of the unconscious is comparable to Bergson's duration.

In 'Beyond the Pleasure Principle', with reference to his paper 'The Unconscious' (Freud 1984 [1915]: 191), Freud (1984 [1920]: 299–300) says:

> We have learnt that unconscious mental processes are in themselves 'timeless'. This means in the first place that they are not ordered temporally, that time does not change them in any way and that the idea of time cannot be applied to them. These are negative characteristics which can only be clearly understood if a comparison is made with *conscious* mental processes. On the other hand, our abstract idea of time seems to be wholly derived from the method of working of the system *Pcpt.-Cs.* and to correspond to a perception on its own part of that method of working. This mode of functioning may perhaps constitute another way of providing a shield against stimuli.

Freud says this is only a hint. But clearly it is a very suggestive passage. He is claiming that the unconscious is timeless in the sense of *abstract time*. And here a comparison with Bergson can be made, despite the fact that what Bergson regards as 'good', Freud, with his belief in science, values negatively. Abstract time is time externalised, spatialised. We have seen that Freud does not think that the psychic apparatus can be thought in spatial terms, particularly with respect to memory traces. What is interesting is the connection between abstract time and consciousness: for Bergson representation is a cutting out in space, it has nothing to do with time in the sense of duration. When Freud says to remember, to bring to consciousness, is to put something in the past, this could be read as a spatialisation: a putting on a line which is abstract or homogeneous time. His claim that abstract time is related to the way the operations of consciousness are perceived is also comparable to Bergson's account of theories of knowledge. And the suggestion that this abstract idea of time is a protective mechanism could be put in Bergsonian terms as a quantification instead of the qualitative, the affective.

Benjamin (1973: 117) also claims that the shock defence assigns to an incident 'a precise point in time'. Freud (1984 [1925a]: 434) says that the protective shield operates by interruptions, it breaks innervation and excitation. This is very like Bergson's idea of the sensori-motor circuit being broken by perception and representation. Freud refers to this as discontinuity, much as Bergson regards the cut out of representation as a discontinuity: 'I further had a suspicion that this discontinuous method of functioning of the system *Pcpt.-Cs.* lies at the bottom of the origin of the concept of time' (Freud 1984 [1925a]: 434). Freud is speaking of abstract time, and this seems remarkably close to Bergson's view that homogeneous empty time is characterised by the discontinuity of discrete identities. Perhaps then, when Freud says that time cannot change unconscious processes, that they are timeless, we could take this to imply continuity in the Bergsonian sense: the continuous permeation of heterogeneous psychic states. This is certainly how memory traces operate. When Freud speaks of the unconscious as timeless it is in contrast to a conception of time in which discrete moments or elements can be identified. The process of deferral of traces is 'timeless' in that there is no arrival at a presence in the present. For Derrida and Bergson this timelessness *is* time.

Multiplicity: voluntary and involuntary memory

Reading Freud with Bergson suggests that a distinction might be made between the voluntary memory of representation, atemporal and characterised by the operations of consciousness; and the involuntary memory of transformation, characterised by the operations of the unconscious. The former relates principally to the sense of sight and a distancing from the body, while the latter is affective, relating to senses of touch, taste and smell. In turn, this distinction also corresponds to the distinction between negative desire and positive desire. The argument that a positive desire is related to the principles of meaning of the unconscious is confirmed by Freud's (1984 [1915]: 190) claim that one of the defining features of the unconscious is that it knows 'no negation ... no degrees of certainty'. In the essays 'The Unconscious' [1915] and 'Negation' [1925] he claims that negation is a substitute at a higher level, for repression. Something can enter consciousness on the condition that it is negated, which is a means of refusing, while taking cognizance of, what is repressed (Freud 1984 [1925b]). This is the main point made by deconstructive feminists: that a repression becomes a negation. Or to put this the other way round, a negation provides a clue to a repression; it is the principal mechanism in the maintenance of a pretence to self-identity. In a binary structure, one term is defined negatively in relation to the dominant term: a negative mirror effects sameness. What is repressed is qualitative difference. A positive desire is understood as a disruptive return of the repressed or an otherness that cannot be contained or negated. In other words, an involuntary memory.

The temporality of meaning disrupts binary oppositions. This is one of the central points that Derrida makes about transformation: any element is marked by the trace of the oppositional element. The specific opposition that I want to draw attention to here is that between immediacy and mediation, the opposition that is the basis of the paradox of knowledge and self-certainty in Hegel. Time, lived in the body, displaces this opposition: the temporal body mediates in an immediacy. And memory traces are crucial to this; they mediate the subject in an immediacy that can in no sense be understood as an unmediated presence: the subject can never know the truth of self. It is only an opposition between mediation and immediacy that allows for this fantasy.

In Irigaray's strategy of displacing this opposition the feminine is crucial: the feminine is mediation (the negative mirror, the absence that founds language), but the specificity of female sexuality, repressed qualitative difference, points to an altogether different way of meaning which is not founded on this opposition.

As I have drawn parallels between Irigaray and Bergson, the question of the sexual assumptions in Bergson must be raised. Bergson's philosophy is not explicitly sexual, but I want to suggest that it is not sexually neutral in the sense of being implicitly masculine; rather it is sexually indeterminate. His argument for multiplicity, his refusal of negation, and his theory of duration obviate against a feminist deconstructive project: there is no negation of one term in order that the (masculine) subject might return to self. In Irigaray's terms, Bergson's philosophy could be understood as a writing of the repressed of female sexuality. But, in an important sense, to claim that Bergson's philosophy has the characteristic of the specificity of female sexuality is beside the point. French feminists identify this repression as a means of pointing to different ways of meaning, which have implications for different inscriptions of the subject. Just as Freud's notion of an originary bisexuality can be read as an originary sexual indeterminacy, the sexual indeterminacy in Bergson is perhaps a move beyond the discursive fixings of masculine and feminine. The positive force or bodily energy of *élan vital* might even be compared with *jouissance* – central to both Cixous' and Barthes' understandings of writing the body. And Bergson's conception of duration involves a refusal to predict the future in much the same way as French feminists refuse the question of the future of masculine and feminine.

In Part 3 I will be taking up a method of multiplicity in analyses of various social texts: identifying different ways of meaning or different moments in specific 'objects'. Following Bergson and the French feminists, the lines of dissociation will include: the singular and the multiple; quantitative and qualitative; negative and positive desire; voluntary and involuntary memory. These distinctions are characterised by different temporal assumptions. The crucial methodological point is that it is possible to discern the operations of different ways of meaning simultaneously: this is to think in multiplicity.

Benjamin is a 'social theorist' who in some respects provides a model for such an analysis with his interest in the ambiguity or double moments in the experience of modernity, and, specifically, the commodity form. I want to take up Benjamin's question: Within modernity and the experience of the commodity, is there a critical or disruptive moment, or, in his terms, a moment of redemption? Irigaray poses a similar question with respect to the quantification and abstraction of the commodity form (and it is possible to read Bergson's critique of quantification as a critique of modernity understood in these terms): What is the repressed qualitative on which the quantitative is dependent? For Benjamin, techniques of mechanical reproduction, based on the temporality of a repetition of the same, encourage voluntary memory. In so far as they reduce scope for imagination and involuntary memory, Benjamin (1973: 146–8) expresses a certain ambivalence towards them, as he does with all experiences of modernity. None the less, in these forms there is the possibility of something else. This something else is involuntary memory.[6]

Formulating this issue in terms of a disruptive moment involves something of a departure from Bergson that is necessitated if Freud's conception of the unconscious is taken into account. This bears on the major critical question that is asked of Bergson by those who are in general sympathy with his theory of time: the question of continuity and discontinuity in time (Levinas, Deleuze, Merleau-Ponty, Horkheimer, Benjamin). Bergson's view that time is continuous sits oddly with the notion that it is heterogeneous and multiple. Levinas, for example, agrees with Bergson's critique of mathematical time, where one moment succeeds another – what Bergson defines as discontinuity. But this, Levinas (1979: 283) argues, does not make time continuous. For him, multiplicity is a discontinuity: there are ruptures, recommencements, breaks. This is implicit in a multiplicity of acts, and the ever recommencing relation with alterity. The indefiniteness of this relation, together with the interval, makes time discontinuous: 'one instant does not come out of another without interruption' (Levinas 1979: 284). Bergson gives the interval as evidence of continuity in the sense that one element cannot be identified as discrete unto itself. For other theorists, such as Derrida, the interval also points to a break and a spacing. Merleau-Ponty claims that Bergson was wrong in explaining a unity of time in terms of continuity, since this amounts to denying time altogether. Continuity is a phenomenon of time, moments run into each other, but they are not indistinguishable; if they were, there would be no time (Merleau-Ponty 1962: 420).

In Bergson's account any break is in the order of the quantitative; in Freud, the unconscious produces ruptures, that is, they are in the order of the qualitative. Something of the double moment of rupture can be discerned in the ambiguity of 'shock' in Benjamin's writings. Developing Freud's account of the protective shield against external stimuli, Benjamin takes the shock, the failure of this mechanism, as characteristic of the experience of modernity. 'Shock' refers not only to the experience of modernity (and collapse of tradition) – the crowd, the machine, techniques of mechanical reproduction – but also to the creative process, which he associates with the unconscious and involuntary memory (Benjamin 1973: 117). Taking this a step further, it could be said that the shock, in breaking through the protective mechanism of the conscious, is a temporal disruption: the time of the unconscious, or duration, breaks the abstract time of consciousness. Freud's concept of the unconscious and the return of the repressed makes a contribution that is not there in Bergson's account of time or the unconscious.

In psychoanalytic theory, the break or rupture is produced, not by representation as it is for Bergson (and in an ambiguous way for Benjamin), but by the unconscious – what is not in discourse. Thus time might be understood as a *discontinuous* continuity. What I am proposing, then, is an approach to cultural analysis that draws on Bergson's multiplicity and duration, together with Freud's concept of the unconscious.

PART 3

WRITING THE SOCIAL

6

MEDIATION AND
IMMEDIACY

The cultural analyses in this chapter aim at developing an approach to meaning that moves beyond the opposition between immediacy and mediation. The trajectory of the chapter follows that of a deconstructive strategy: the first analysis brings to light the mediations of woman in man's relations with himself; the second is concerned with the potentially disruptive effects of mediations on the double of a mirroring relation; and in the third analysis the possibility of displacing this opposition is addressed. This turns on an understanding of signification processes in terms of the body in duration.

The master–slave dialectic: boss–secretary relations

the dialectic . . . is in fact, what is commonly at work in our everyday banality (Cixous 1986: 78).

Hegel's master–slave dialectic is a process at work in knowledge and in everyday relations of sociality. If Hegel's story is in a sense a 'true' story, it is, nevertheless, not the only story. There is no single story of the culture or social life, but rather a multiplicity of stories which are not reducible to one another. In this analysis, a social text (a transcript of an interview with a boss) is read with and against several stories or accounts of social life: those of Hegel, Freud and Irigaray. None of these texts functions as a theoretical model to be tested against the empirical. Rather, this form of analysis is understood as textual dialogue. For example, the story of boss–secretary relations is read, in part, as a version of Hegel's story, but this is not a one-way reading. Hegel's story is also reread against the boss–secretary story.

This is an analysis of a transcript of an interview with a boss, an analysis of his discursive production of independence of self-consciousness and the mediations on which this is dependent. Comparisons are made with his secretary's discourse: Do they tell the same story? And if not, what does this suggest about multiplicity? In all of this I am very well aware of the mediations of the interview itself, of the complexity of positionings in the interview relations, and that it was to me that they were speaking.

The transcript is of an interview with a 38-year-old, highly ambitious finance executive in a large company. This person is particularly single-minded, epitomising the 'rational, purposive worker'. In fact, it is his clear distinction between the public and the private that invites a deconstruction of his discourse. More commonly, there is a marked slippage between public and private in bosses' discourses, for example, in their descriptions of work in personal or sexual terms. Interviews with bosses were frequently conducted in armchairs with tea and coffee. But in this case he sat behind his desk. Indeed there was none of the usual lounge room furniture in this office. It contained nothing 'personal', and apart from company decorations on the wall, it was empty. The desk was likewise empty: it did not have a paper or file on it – ordered, no clutter, no distractions.

Here then, are his descriptions of his secretary's activities and qualities.[1]

```
[    take                shorthand
     answer              the phone
     shield      me      from junk mail
     managing            me
     managing            other people
     organisation of     my day
     organisation of     papers
     organisation of     work and the other side of that is
     management          skills of people
     handling            people
     being able to put people off without offending them
     and also
     keep me under control if I get side-tracked          ]
```

```
[    I have an enormous filing system
     which M controls
     and if I want a certain file . . .
     then I rely on her to find it for me
     I say remember that memo. . .
     Then she has to retrieve it for me
     I can't retrieve it
     I try not to keep any files                           ]
```

```
[    managerial work which is
     controlling my diary and
     controlling my mail and
     controlling appointments                             ]
```

Q can you give me some details on how that works? . . .

she sorts out what I have to see
she reads it all
and if she thinks it's *important* and she knows it's *important*
because mostly people would only send me *important* stuff
so *she will bring* that in straightaway . . .
she *has a bring-up* system which is very effective
say if I do some work then *I say bring that* memo *up*
and so *she has got* a system *out there* somehow . . .
she keeps a diary *out there*
and I keep a diary *in here*
and she tries to make them stay the same
I write in that the managing director says how about lunch . . .
similarly people trying to see me she puts in and *she knows* who I
    want to see and who I don't want to see . . .
she *reminds me* the day before a meeting if I have got a meeting
    coming up
she *reminds me* about lunches in advance
so that each day I know what is happening
or if I have to travel around the country seeing and interviewing
    people
she will tell me that next week you are going away don't forget
so *she organises* that
and *she organises* the airplane tickets and hotel accommodation
    and all that sort of stuff
. . .

she is getting tougher now and I am getting busier
and she is getting more discriminating with the sort of people
that *she allows* to get into *my* diary

What does he say his secretary does? What is most striking is the repetition of manage, organise, control. These look like boss-type activities, being attributed to a secretary. I will suggest that this apparent inversion has an important function in how he positions himself, and how he positions her in relation to him.

What are the objects of the managing, controlling, organising activities? The phone, junk mail, accommodation, airplane tickets, 'and all that sort of stuff': all things that he regards as a 'waste of time' – which is precisely how he describes making a phone call later on in the interview. Elsewhere he refers to files as 'junk'. The filing system example is a particularly clear case of what this is about. 'I have an enormous filing system' – it is his possession, 'which M controls'. As an extension of himself, she controls it. She knows what he wants and how to get it: 'She has a system *out there*'. 'Out there' is repeated, and set in opposition to 'in here'. He thus constructs a spatial separation between himself and her: he is inside, she is outside. He does not know, or want to know, how the system works. He literally does not want to touch files: 'I try not to keep any files'. He does not want to touch the materiality of his work: mess, clutter. So, what is going on with the inversion is a displacement of his disorder onto the place of the feminine: it is the disorder of *his* work that she puts into order (the system), rationalises. His room and desk are empty ('in here'), files are 'out there', with his secretary. He is pure abstraction, or as he says elsewhere, 'with no day-to-day cares of the world', 'removed from reality', 'thinking about business', 'being creative', 'whereas as a secretary you have to do the housekeeping first, keeping everything going'.

Here is a nice statement of woman as infrastructure, underpinning the system, keeping everything going. 'Housekeeping' as purposive activity is defined as such with respect to clearing away day-to-day mess, as opposed to, and as the precondition of, an 'empty desk'. He *thinks*, she *does*. The status of his 'thinking', abstract rationality, is raised by the inflation of her activities as 'organising', 'controlling'. At the end of the interview he told me a story about an executive who lost power in a takeover. As an indication of loss of power 'he had to pick up a phone book for the first time'. His own projection?

Running through this is a notion of contamination, the fear of contamination by his own mess; her organising is a matter of clearing away his mess – 'shit work'. Is he perhaps, then, in the position of child, and she in the position of mother, her organising activities being toilet training? (She is 53 and has been in the company longer than he has.) To pursue a Freudian account, his sitting behind the desk, being creative, could be understood as a fantasy of pregnancy, as male envy of women's reproductive capacities. This brings to mind Freud's case study of 'Little Hans', in terms of both the association between shit and babies, and Little Hans's fantasies of giving birth (Freud 1977b [1909]: 234–5, 245–7). The boss's repetition of 'bring up' makes an association between mess and childbirth. It suggests that he is in danger of throwing up, and that she is his imaginary controller. He must separate himself from disorder, his disorder, by displacing it on to woman. And yet, if men are to give birth, the puzzle is how? By shitting *or* vomiting?[2] In the light of this connection between shit work and the creative work of giving birth, it would seem that both order and disorder are mediated by the secretary; there is a double moment to this, just as there is an ambivalence about giving birth.

In Hegel's master–slave story the slave works on things, the inanimate world, for the master: the master's relation with things is mediated by the slave. In this boss–secretary story the secretary works on things, things that the boss will not touch. She is positioned by him as a consciousness without independence, positioned with the 'thing'. For the boss, to have a direct relation with things would be a mark of loss of power and independence: a consciousness that is defined in association with objects is a slave consciousness. When he speaks of the failure of other bosses it is clear that this is something that provokes fear in him, the fear of a reversal.

In attributing boss-type characteristics to his secretary, this man is defining her as an extension of himself; she is, in some respects, defined as an extension of his body. In his discourse she has no autonomy or specificity. 'Man endows the commodities he produces with a narcissism that blurs the seriousness of utility, of use' (Irigaray 1985a: 177). The dependence of his rationality on her emerges in these passages, but there is also a sense of the tenuous basis of this rationality.

The trivial objects which he will not touch have a further significance: they represent his links with others. The diary, mail, phone, files mediate his relations with her, *and* with other men in the company and the outside world. His relations with others are relayed through her, her 'control' of the diaries, appointments and so on. It is *his* diary, *his* filing system, *his* mail. But she 'controls' them, is an extension of them, is attached to them. All his possessions? She 'knows' him, must know him, which mail is important, whom he wants to see; she must be discriminating about who gets into his diary. Note the repetition of 'important'. He is saying quite directly: 'I am important'. Her task is to try to make the diaries stay the *same*, that is, to understand, know him exactly. She mediates all his relations. Thus his autonomy, separateness, abstracted rationality, is maintained: 'I can't just pick up the phone . . . I have to have somebody in between, and that person is a screen'. There is an interesting ambiguity about 'screen' here. It can be read as mirror of masculine desire: the screen reflects projection. But the 'in between' also implies a 'screening', that is, something is let through, penetrates, and something else does not. Among other things this gives a certain autonomy to the screen: in this regard the secretary is possibly not simply an extension of his body.

By positioning his secretary with things, as one of his possessions, this boss denies that his independence depends on her mediations. She is a negative mirror, simultaneously given boss characteristics and denied any autonomy. She mediates not only his relations with other men but also, and most importantly, his relation with himself. In his initial list of her activities, managing *him* comes before managing *other people*. She mediates his relation to *himself*: 'organisation of my day', 'organisation of [my] work'. He ends with 'and keep me under control if I get side-tracked'. He is in danger of getting side-tracked from his singular path. Management of him is about the maintenance of his body boundaries; for example, the lack of office furniture focuses on his body and his desk. He gives birth, via this desk (table), to idea after idea, deal after deal: producing the mediations which are finance capital. He makes money.

[I like M to *understand* exactly what *I am trying to do*
   so she *understands* fully what *I am trying to do* . . .
   what we are trying to do is make more money
   simple to explain
   and the techniques involved are often quite complex

but she can see what *I am trying to do*
and I have absolutely *no secrets from her* whatsoever
she knows that I would like to reduce this office from 100 to 10
    people . . . so I have *no secrets from her*
similarly I have my own private ambitions . . .
and she fully *understands* that too
and she is *my ally in achieving* my advancement inside the
    company
and she is *my ally in achieving* my objectives for the company   ]

[if she was *disloyal* I would definitely get rid of her
I have to have her total *loyalty* and discretion and
often *I bounce ideas off her* to see what she thinks
so I would tell her what I am going to do just to gauge her reaction
  . . .
so *I can ask* M about some of the things that *I am trying to do*
I get very involved in the technicalities and
sometimes I don't see the wood for the trees
and *she helps me* to try and explain complicated
things to somebody who wouldn't understand complicated things
so *I just ask her* what do you think a or b   ]

What his goals, purposive activities, are about is explicit here – 'simple', 'we are trying to make money'. The 'we' implies that he and his secretary are a unit, a body – boss and secretary. She is his ally: the voluntaristic kinship (alliance) of marriage. Note that 'what I am trying to do' is repeated, and that 'she understands'. That she understands him is completely unproblematic for him; he speaks for her without any recognition of her as an autonomous person. She keeps him to his goals (identified with those of the company), keeps him on his singular path if he gets 'side-tracked' or can't 'see the wood for the trees'. The basis of his autonomy is a dependence on her which cannot be acknowledged. It is denied through a negation of her. Autonomy, singularity, is with respect to other senior executives and 'the outside world', and her mediations ensure this. All her purposive activities ('keeping things working') are purposive with respect to him, his goals, ambitions; his purposive activities are so with respect to himself, and the company. (But to complicate this picture we might take into account his 'productions', as son, for her, as mother). Thus, the inversion of her controlling and his 'dependence' functions to maintain his autonomy, or at least the *pretence* of it. The rather more significant sense of dependence is veiled by the inversion, namely the dependence of dominance of one term on the subordination of the other. In terms of the *Fort! Da!* story, the child's dependence on the mother must be mastered, which requires a negation.

[Q would M ever give you information that she thinks might be
    useful in terms of making decisions?

yes one of the important attributes she must have
in her interpersonal relationships
is her *ability to get on with* the other secretaries
of other senior company officials
and if *she didn't get on with* them all
I would have a major problem
because the secretaries are important
the managing director's secretary for example *controls* his diary
and if *I wanted to* see him and *I offended* her
I would find it difficult
and *I would have to break through* that
which would be an unpleasant experience
I would have to go to the managing director
and say *I can't get to* see you
because your secretary doesn't like me
and then it would show
that I *was unable to handle* such a trivial relationship   ]

'Commodities can have no relationships except from the perspective of speculating third parties' (Irigaray 1985a: 177). And this is how this boss sees it: the relationships of secretaries with each other are instrumental to relations between men: 'and if *she* didn't get on with them all *I* would have a major problem'. This is a particularly striking example of mediation: his relations with other men in the company are mediated by secretaries. As Irigaray (1985a: 193) says, 'women exist as mediation ... transference between man and man, man and himself'.

However, some cracks in this can be discerned, even in his account. For, in speaking about 'her ability to get on with the other secretaries' is he not assigning her an autonomous sphere of action? Do commodities speak as commodities when they are in relations with each other? It might be the case that secretaries relate to each other via the mediation of their bosses (babies). (I am suggesting that the secretary is positioned as both mother and commodity.) His account of the consequences of failure of the mediation of secretaries supports Irigaray's argument about mediation maintaining the masculine standard, the phallus. The tenuous nature of this is suggested by it being a matter of 'liking'. He would have to 'break through' (forced penetration), go to the managing director and say 'I can't get to see you'. He would have to face him directly, and consequently would be diminished. It would show that he had failed at something 'trivial' – 'such a trivial relationship'. His boss's secretary had screened him out. In such a case the screen is not a mirror of masculine desire: it refuses projection. The desire directed towards the boss must be relayed through a screen which is feminine: seduction is required to get through to recognition by the master. But if this screen is the condition of man's relation with himself, does it not also have some autonomy?

What does his secretary say about her position as secretary? (Note the use of a different transcription technique. A new line comes after a pause.)

[Q   And would you like to describe your work?

well there is nothing very specialised in it
I don't think
I just do as I am asked to do

there is lots of little
other little tasks
that I sort of take over looking after
various records and things like that
that I am sort of responsible for
but apart from that
it is mainly secretarial

Q   and what do you understand by secretarial?

do as you are told (laughs)
whatever you are asked to do

Q   and what sort of things are you asked to do?

it is mostly typing
keeping his diary
that is sometimes tedious and frustrating

I sort of fit him in with other people
with other parts of the organisation
with the meetings and that sort of thing

I just sort of fit him in with it
it is not too difficult
but a little bit frustrating sometimes

we keep two diaries
I have got one
he's got a little pocket diary
and one of the tasks is keeping the two of them

there is a fair amount of typing
there is letters
well not letters
but memos
notes
filing
a certain amount of filing
just whatever else he asks me
what he dreams up for me to do   ]

The content looks the same as his description, but the form, the way in which her work is described, is remarkably different. She repeats 'little', everything about this is diminutive – 'little tasks'. If his account of her work functioned to inflate his position, her description, apparently about the smallness of secretarial work, simultaneously deflates his position. The diaries: he constructed the separation – 'out there', 'in here'; she refers to his diary as 'a little pocket diary', ('we, the motherly mistresses of their little pocket signifier' (Cixous 1986: 89)). She types memos, notes, not letters, something less than letters; it is not *his* records, files, just records, files. His description of her managerial skills is reduced to 'I sort of fit him in' which is 'tedious and frustrating'. She says explicitly what he implies: 'I don't think, I just do', but adds, and repeats, 'as I am asked to do'. In fact she 'is *told* to do'; she recognises what is going on. She is a part of his body, or is body to his mind: one *tells* the body what to do. He cannot work without her, she is his nervous system.

Many of the tasks she is asked to do she regards as 'beneath [her]'. The material position of her powerlessness is acknowledged, but his authority is not legitimated by her: asking demeaning tasks of her lowers him in her estimation. She never speaks of understanding him (there is a sense of not understanding, finding irrational), she simply obeys him. This is a very different perception of the relation. She gives an account, for example, of the 'slight effort' she puts into getting a lunch together for him. This would not show 'on the surface', but business lunches are no big deal to her. Business lunches, along with tea and coffee, are some of the tasks she regards as beneath her, but she speaks of them as being quite central to *his* work, thus by implication questioning the value he places on his work. In fact, she says that what is most important is 'keeping him happy', which hardly conforms to the notion of the abstract rationality of the purposive worker. It was she who raised 'tea and coffee', in answer to a question about tasks that she'd prefer not to do: 'I realise that it is a very essential form; part of being a secretary is to be able to cope with things like that'. She provides a detailed description of the routine of tea and coffee, highly rationalised in fact. This is part of his entertaining or business relations ritual, the domestic sphere in the public: a ritual that mediates between the public and the domestic.

He 'dreams up' tasks for her: the fantasy of self-importance, irrationality. She does not engage in any mystique about the importance of his job (it is men who sit around drinking cups of tea, after all). The masquerade of masculinity is primarily for the gaze of other men, certainly not this secretary.

[Q   what makes a good secretary?

being able to cope with your frustrations
and annoyances

your willingness to do whatever you are asked to do
because sometimes you get some strange tasks

your organising ability

you have to be able to organise your boss
get on well with other people in the firm
outside the firm
being able to present yourself well to visitors
and make them feel comfortable and at home
it's a bit like housekeeping really   ]

Again, there is a similarity in what they both say: organising the boss,
mediating his relations. But she likens this to housekeeping, involving
relations of support characteristic of the domestic sphere – making people
feel at home. When he refers to secretarial work as housework it is in
opposition to his 'creative work'. Nowhere does she describe his work in
these terms. Her reference to housework consists in a reversal, associating
him with the domestic, as opposed to the rational sphere of work.

At a later point in the interview I asked: 'In what way is it like
housekeeping?'

[well
running the
looking after somebody
I sometimes think
and I hope you don't
play this over to J
but I sometimes think that I leave the office
and I go home to my son
and he starts on about something
and I think which is worse
the office or the home

all I am doing is running around after somebody else
and that is basically what a secretary does
you do that at home   ]

She does not want him to hear this. Previously she has said of secretaries, 'You
must appear calm, cool, and collected on the surface', not show annoyances.
Now some of the calm has gone: she is not being secretary. 'Secretary' is
performance: 'presenting yourself well', 'making visitors feel at home'. It is
also like home to her; it means 'running around after somebody else'. Her boss
is positioned with her son, which could be understood as a refusal of his
authority. It is an inversion of his positioning of her, as mother, as part of
himself. She diminishes him, speaks of him as irrational, reduces 'work' to
'home'. Her only free time is on the train, where she reads, between the office
and home: she lives in the moment of separation. (From his account of travel to
work (see below), it is clear that the boss, on the other hand, would have the gap
closed between his two 'homes'.) She *is* support of the boss's position, performs
secretary; but, on the other hand, she does not accede to his definition of her or
himself. This secretary's discourse does not correspond to that of her boss.

Now to the issues of recognition and the struggle between self-consciousnesses. This is a rather more complex story than that of Hegel. The boss desires recognition from his secretary, but this cannot be the recognition of another independent self-consciousness for he has positioned her negatively in relation to himself, without independence. As Irigaray (1985a: 85) says, 'the "feminine" is never to be identified except by and for the masculine, the reciprocal proposition not being "true" '. He does not recognise her, and she only grudgingly recognises him. The struggle between self-consciousness is in fact to be found in relations between bosses. This boss defines himself in relation to, and desires recognition from, other bosses in the company, and 'the outside world'. He desires recognition from his boss above all else.

[Q just briefly what your current job entails

really assistant to the managing director primarily
responsible for accounting and finance and management control
involves me travelling around with him. . .   ]

He also refers to 'the service' that he gives 'his boss'. For the moment he is in the position of slave to his boss: he works for him. Bosses are to be serviced, but this does not imply that he regards his service as comparable to his secretary's service to himself. There is a crucial difference: he works in anticipation of taking his master's place.

[Q do you want to give some idea of where your future lies?

yes I would like to be managing director of the company one day

Q how long will that take?

I mean there are a few other guys with the same opinion . . .
there are other people of similar ages to myself
– the new guard
that are aspiring to be managing director . . .
I think that it is generally accepted that I think
that I will get there . . .
there is no way that people are trying to do each other in the eye
we are all working towards making the company a better
     company
and if I don't get the job then I don't get the job   ]

His relation to the managing director can be seen as a classic case of primary identification with the father: an ambivalent relation of identification and desire to take his place. He demands recognition from him, the form of recognition a father gives a son: 'You could be me'. He wants to appropriate his boss's status and name and that of the company. His ambition is always spoken of in conjunction with his objectives for the company. But, it would seem that he has some competition for the father's place. This is analogous to Freud's story in *Totem and Taboo*: the rivalry between the brothers for the father's place. Their individual goals are controlled by the company goals for which they are all working, the Law. This man has already identified with the place of the father (albeit the father who he knows will be killed off), and, as he puts it when the tape has finished: it's all or nothing, power or 'loss of power', and 'feeling a lesser man'.

In Lacan's Hegelian perspective, the boss as slave awaits the 'death' of the managing director. All his work now is in anticipation of this end. There is simultaneously a 'life and death struggle' going on between bosses of the same age: 'all or nothing'. When he says 'there is no way we would do each other in the eye', this should be read as Freud would, taking a negative as an affirmative. This is a struggle for the position of subject of the look and the word. He regards himself as the legitimate heir. But, of course, there is no end; 'heir' would only be a momentary resolution; positions cannot be stabilised.

Where, then, is the feminine in this struggle between (masculine) self-consciousnesses? Something of this is hinted at in his account of the implications of loss of power: loss of wife, 'wives are prepared to accept them as long as they are successful'; and loss of secretary, 'someone to do the photocopying'. (Note that it is 'them' and 'they'.) Masculine independence presupposes a negative definition of the feminine. The master–slave relation of boss–boss is not structurally homologous with the boss–secretary relation, but it is dependent on the negation of the feminine.

This bears on Irigaray's analysis of the social positioning of women: 'secretary' means in relation to wife, mother, virgin, prostitute.

> [I look towards M
>   as being an assistant
>   I wouldn't look towards her
>   as necessarily contributing ideas
>
>   I consider that she should organise me
>   so that I don't
>   and in fact my wife is complaining
>   about my increasing distance from reality
>   in the day-to-day cares
>   I don't have any
>   I get out of my car in the company garage
>   walk into my office
>   and everything is organised for me   ]

The mention of his wife comes midstream in an account of his secretary organising him – there has been no discussion of her, or his personal life before this point. It is apparently out of the blue that he makes the association of wife and secretary. This is of interest in this transcript because this man makes a very clear differentiation between work and the personal; many other bosses I interviewed did not, openly comparing wives and secretaries and/or speaking about secretaries in sexual terms. Despite his concern to speak an impersonal language of work, this boss expressed a preference for older women as secretaries because 'young girls' tend to want to go out at night, and away for weekends. The implication is that older women do not run around with other men, prostitute themselves. He prefers use-value to the risks of exchange-value. This is an important issue for his secretary. She is concerned about her age, aware of how important this is to the value of secretary. She was nervous before his arrival because he is so much younger than she is: 'Well somebody my age is going to think that anyway with a younger man coming in because a lot of them do like young attractive girls to work for them whether they have got the capabilities or not'. His wife, it should be noted, is as well qualified as he is, being employed in the same field in another company; they met through 'work'. (This comes out of 'routine information questions' at the beginning of the interview.) This paradox highlights the argument: men define other men in terms of occupation, but women in the semantic field – wife, mother, prostitute, ally and so on. The effect of this is to disguise men's affective relations with each other. Men are apparently autonomous, individuated with respect to each other, their identifications and rivalries are spoken of in terms of success at work, a language of rationality (which excludes, for example, gossip and sexuality). Masculine autonomy, rationality, presupposes a dependence on women, wives, secretaries, who are positioned as being without autonomy or occupation.

Some brief remarks should be made about positions in the interviews. Rather disconcertingly, I found the interview with the boss pleasurable, and even identified with him in some respects. There is evidence that recognition from academics is important to him. However, if I did represent 'the outside world' of the university, it would have been at the expense of my autonomy. My specificity as a sociologist and feminist would have had to be discounted for him to maintain a narcissistic relation to the university. Both the topic of the interview, 'secretaries', and the interviewer mediated his relation with himself. The speaking position was not the powerless one of the analytic relation. In the interview with the secretary I felt discomfort which was symptomatic of a general unease about the power relations of research and the constitution of the other to the subject of research.

I want to conclude this discussion with her view of women bosses:

[you have to get along a lot better with a woman
    I think
    that you are working with
    than with a man
    you could just wipe him off as being a man
    and they are all alike
    that sort of thing
    but a woman I think
    probably even though you are a woman as well
    you probably expect far too much of her   ]

Does the boss–secretary relationship only work if the positions are taken up by men and women respectively? Is the performance of secretary less tolerable if it is for a woman? 'You would expect more of her' – not to dream up silly tasks, to be more rational. Note the inversion here, of his discourse: it is all men who are alike, without specificity or qualitative distinction. In a similar way, she positioned her boss with her son, reversing the masculine positioning of secretary as wife, mother, prostitute. Being a woman, she implies, is to see qualitative distinctions among women. She is suggesting that she would expect a woman boss to not position her as secretary: 'You have to get along a lot better with a woman'. This is difficult if a woman takes up a masculine position. I wonder, then, if this says something about the interview: am I, as researcher, in a masculine position with respect to her; and did she expect more of me? In fact she spoke quite openly about the problems of working with men and the demands her son puts on her, which might suggest that she was inviting me, as another women, to be complicit. There is, then, a multiplicity of subject positions in the interview.

What conclusions might be drawn from this analysis in terms of multiplicity? To put this another way, if this secretary is defined negatively by the singular discourse of the boss, is there also anything of an elsewhere? She is off-centre to the desire for recognition, and the struggle between self-consciousnesses. This is reserved for men, or, more precisely, masculine positions. If she is outside the struggle by virtue of a negative positioning, she is simultaneously in it through exclusion. But, in some important respects, her discourse is elsewhere. If it does not amount to disruption in the sense that Irigaray speaks of, it nevertheless does not conform to his discourse. Even in her inversions something of the smooth functioning of his discourse is perhaps disrupted; and she does not simply take up his positioning of her. She performs her tasks to keep the job, but not as he imagines her doing so. In this interview there is little evidence of her offering him recognition or of her desiring recognition from him. In her discourse he was positioned as 'little', and with her son; his 'goals' were spoken of as trivial things. She asked me to be complicit in her desire to show up his pretensions and silliness. Irigaray's conclusion about women as mediation is that the possibility of withdrawal from this position makes it potentially subversive. What, she says, if the goods left the market, or got together? Clearly, this secretary is in no position to do this (even if she 'got together' with me for a moment, regulated by the rules of research). But just how important the smooth functioning of mediations is, comes out when the boss says: 'If she were disloyal I would definitely get rid of her'. For him, of course, there is an endless chain of substitutions as mediation. Unless, that is, he loses in the bigger struggle.

This analysis points to the instability in the quest for self-certainty, the tenuous nature of the position of master. But it also suggests a more complex set of relations than Hegel's binary master–slave structure; this relation is not a relationship in itself, but rather functions in a wider context of relations. Once the position of the feminine, on which this structure is dependent, is brought to light there is a displacement. The paradox of knowledge in Hegel produces an endless series of reversals. The repressed feminine is potentially disruptive to this structure: an elsewhere that refuses the position of mirror is 'outside' binary opposition.

Doubles and death: *Dead Ringers*

Duplication and death emerged as central aspects of desire in the Hegel–Lacan tradition. I want to pursue further the connections between identity, mirroring and the death drive through an analysis of Cronenberg's film, *Dead Ringers*. The title itself makes the connection. The questions to be addressed are: Can the film be read as the trajectory of masculine desire, and/or is this desire undone? Is there anything that escapes or exceeds it? Is a positive structure of desire prefigured in this film? Or in terms of multiplicity: Is there a 'double' moment of desire?

Before turning to the film I will briefly reiterate the main points in a feminist analysis of doubles and death. The central argument here is that the death instinct is at work in the mirror phase. Freud (1984 [1920]: 308) claims that the death instinct is 'an urge to restore to an earlier state of things', a return to inertia, stasis, quiescence, completion. In Lacan's mirror phase the phantasy of identity is effected through an identification with an image which is fixed. The total form of the body as exteriority involves a solidification and standing still of the body as object. Thus, Irigaray (1985a: 115–17) argues, the death instinct – characterised by the principle of constancy and homeostasis – is discernible in the constitution of identity via duplication. As a disruption of identity and the internal–external distinction on which it is based, she is concerned with flow, fluidity, and the indeterminacy of internal–external. The movement in this is a movement forward, as opposed to the movement of return that is the death instinct, looking for ends in origins. The mirror phase is itself based on such a desire for origins: the original and the copy, the irony being that the original is only discernible in the copy, and then it is in fact a misrecognition. In his critique of identity, Bergson also emphasises fluidity and flow in a disruption of the internal–external opposition: this is the multiple order of life rather than death which is associated with the static, singular order.

Feminists have argued that a desire for return to origins is masculine nostalgia. The key reference for this is Freud's (1985c [1919]: 368) famous passage in 'The "Uncanny"':

This *unheimlich* place, however, is the entrance to the former *Heim* [home] of all human beings, to the place where each of us lived once upon a time and in the beginning. There is a joking saying that 'Love is a home-sickness'; and whenever a man dreams of a place or a country and says to himself, while he is still dreaming: 'this place is familiar to me, I've been here before', we may interpret the place as being his mother's genitals or her body. In this case too, then, the *unheimlich* is what was once *heimisch*, familiar; the prefix *'un'* ['un-'] is the token of repression.

Freud is referring to the uncanny of the female genitals, and is making a direct connection between a return to origins (the death instinct) and the mother. In his account of the death instinct in 'Beyond the Pleasure Principle' this drive is not explicitly associated with the mother, although it is indirectly if we read his major example – *Fort! Da!* – together with the death instinct. In Lacan's Hegelian reading of *Fort! Da!*, the desire to master the absence of the mother entails her death, negation. In 'The "Uncanny"', a page before the quotation above, Freud (1985c: 367) cites the example of being buried alive, the terrifying fantasy that originally had nothing terrifying about it – intra-uterine existence. Freud rarely makes reference to this experience (see Freud 1973a [1916]: 117, 465–6; 1977b [1909]: 230–7; 285); and it is presumably a token of his own repression – the return of – that he does so in the context of the uncanny, associated as it is with death.

The feminist argument about this is that it is an appropriation of otherness to return to self: 'I will know my origins'. In reference to man's relation to his mother and its re-enactment, Irigaray (1985a: 25) speaks of a desire 'to appropriate for himself the mystery of this womb where he has been conceived, the secret of his begetting, of his "origin"'. (Why this is a specifically masculine desire is a question that might well be asked here. What, for example, of the double originary, the father as well as the mother? To formulate this somewhat differently, it could be said that there is a difference between masculine and feminine forms of resolution.) Cixous and Irigaray claim that there is a direct relation between the fear of death and the fear of the feminine – the two things which are unrepresentable – in a masculine desire for recuperation of loss.

In rereading Freud it could be said, then, that the terrifying of the intra-uterine is otherness, the otherness of the woman's body, which signifies origins and death. Where death comes into the picture is precisely with respect to the desire to know: to know the other is to negate it, but in negating the other the self is negated. One's own death is implicated in a desire for origins. This constitutes the uncanny: the connection between mastery, the death instinct and the maternal body. In an argument about the masculinity of this, Cixous (1986: 93) says:

> Not the origin: she doesn't go back there. A boy's journey is the return to the native land, the *Heimweh* Freud speaks of, the nostalgia that makes a man a being who tends to come back to the point of departure to appropriate it for himself and to die there. A girl's journey is farther – to the unknown, to invent.

In 'The "Uncanny"' Freud also talks about the double. Citing the work of Rank, he claims that the double 'was originally an insurance against the destruction of the ego, an "energetic denial of the power of death"' (Freud 1985c: 356). However, when the stage of primary narcissism has been surmounted the double takes on an uncanny reversal of aspect: 'from having been an assurance of immortality, it becomes the uncanny harbinger of death' (Freud 1985c: 357). Despite the different definitions of primary narcissism to be found in Freud, if we take the above to be a reference to a move from omnipotence to a stage of mirroring identification with an other, this could be glossed: I will live on in the other who is myself, but what if the other should die?

Dead Ringers is 'about' death in the double which could be read as masculine nostalgia for origins. But I will argue that this reading is too simple: there is something disturbing to this desire in the film. It is perhaps curious that it has not been a box office success, given the popularity of Cronenberg's *The Fly*. Might this be related to the fact that the monstrous in *Dead Ringers* is human, and indeed masculine? There is no projection of the monstrous onto the non-human or the feminine (see Creed 1990). And the horror works, in large measure, because there is an invitation to identify sympathetically with the double, the Jeremy Irons character(s).

Beverly and Elliot are identical twins, each other's mirror image: 'the subject identifies himself with someone else, so that he is in doubt which his self is ... there is a doubling, dividing and interchanging of self' (Freud 1985c: 356). There is a doubling in their names: throughout the film they are called, and particularly refer to each other as, 'Bev' and 'Elly'. They are one, two halves that make a whole, a split unity. They are also split from the mother, and the doubling of their names might be read as mastery of this loss: Evil and Belly. It is externally, in the exteriority of the mirror image, that Bev and Elly are identical; they are also differentiated and split. At the outset the mirroring runs smooth. For example, while still students of medicine, Elliot collects the prize for their invention of a gynaecological instrument; Beverly sits at his desk. On his return Elliot says 'You should have been there'; Beverly's response is 'But I was there'. However, this mutual mirroring is mediated, in particular, by women – patients and lovers. Clare, the patient who becomes lover, is in the position of the third term in the mirror phase: she grants the mirror image, it is referred through her. In a sense the spectator is also in this position, and, like Clare, we have some trouble telling them apart. The brothers exchange and share everything; through exchanges they share each other. But it is the mediations, on which the mirroring is dependent, that proves to be its downfall. The mediations of women that Irigaray claims must remain hidden for the mirror to work, become not only apparent but disruptive. Furthermore, the body is crucial to this. Where Lacan's focus is on the image, Bergson makes no distinction between image and body. Body-images do not allow for the fantasy of identity in the way that the image does, and the body is the site of disruption in this film.

There is a complex web of mediations, for mediation is also, necessarily, constitutive of the twins' relationship with each other. In this respect it has echoes of Hegel's master–slave story. And the stabilisation of this relation is temporary: what ensues is reversals, the failure of mastery, the death of one necessitating the death of the other. In the stabilised moment of the double, Elly is in the position of master and Bev is in the position of slave. It might not be too far-fetched to suggest that the reversal is inscribed in the naming: the privileging of Beverly in Bev and Elly. Prior to any reversal the master–slave scenario works like this: Elliot does the public performances, Beverly does the work for these; Elliot seduces women, Beverly fucks them. Well, in the process of seduction Elliot fucks women, but he is too clever for that and hands them over to Beverly, thus denying him any autonomy. Beverly works for Elliot, he mediates the world of things, objects. And what he works on is woman's body: matter to be transformed, to mirror man as the product of his labour. Beverly's labour is on the labour of women; the twin doctors work on women's wombs, they make infertile women fertile. They are the source, agents of birth (as in a sense all men are), appropriating the mystery of the womb, origins. Beverly says to a patient: 'We only work on wives, not husbands; you have to keep things simple, don't you agree? We just make women fertile.' So they are in the business of creating life – as a hedge against the death instinct implicit in appropriation of the womb? and the double? The double works, the master–slave relation is stabilised, as long as the mediations by women's bodies work. But the body, and women's bodies, cannot be fixed, objectified, made to 'stand still'.

> For a while, the double can freeze the instability of the same, give it temporary identity, but eventually it explores the abyss of the same, probing those unsuspected and unplumbable depths. The double is the unconscious depth of the same, that which threatens it, can engulf it. (Kristeva 1987: 147).

Oh yes, the abyss of the same. Once the double of Bev and Elly can no longer freeze them in an identity it does indeed explore the abyss; the return of the repressed sameness engulfs them. The doubling falls apart, reduplication of the mirror fails. The 'agent' of this process is Clare, a patient and an object of sexual exchange. (Note the alphabetical sequence of their names: B–C–(D)–E, with death in their midst.) Rather than mediating, Clare disrupts identity and sameness; she is the mark of separation. In this regard she can perhaps be read as phallic woman – she does not bleed, cannot have babies, and has three cervices. But even so, Clare is definitely not represented as monster or evil other who is to blame for disaster. All talk of women as monstrous, for example, as 'mutants', is very clearly the doctors' projections. The trouble with the double is the pretence of identity.

When Beverly expresses doubts about their sharing Clare without her knowing, Elliot's response is: 'She's an actress, a flake, you can't tell who she is'. As it is their masquerade which is at issue this sounds like projection. On Elliot's instructions Beverly goes off to fuck Clare; and when he returns from a very funny bondage scenario in which Clare is tied to the bed with surgical instruments, Elliot says 'Tell all'. Beverly refuses, he wants to keep it (her) to himself. Elliot presses him: 'But you haven't experienced anything until I have experienced it' – the first moment of separation, and an attempt, on Elliot's part, to hold on to identity. Already there are hints of the reversal to come, Elliot's tenuous grip on the position of master, and his dependence on Beverly; and the faltering of Beverly's mediation, his work, runs parallel to the faltering of the mediations by women.

When Beverly turns up drunk at Elliot's speech, this is the first real indication that the master–slave relation is destabilised. Just as Elliot is saying what a pity it is that his brother cannot be there because he works so hard, Beverly staggers to the platform saying 'Not so, not so' and takes the microphone: 'It's all a fraud – he's Beverly and I'm Elliot. He makes the speeches; I slave over the snatches.' An interchanging that is fraudulent? A suggestion that he will not go on working for Elliot? In fact, as the separation gets worse he loses his capacity to work.

Clare separates them. When she discovers the double dealing she calls a halt to their game of exchange; from having been object she now becomes subject of division and differentiation. After she has resumed a sexual relationship with Beverly, Elliot asks her to have one with him also, as otherwise she will disrupt the brothers' scene. When she refuses, he looks in the mirror, from the position of her gaze, and asks: 'Are we really that different?' Clare responds: 'Yes you really are'. Despite the externality of the mirror image, she differentiates. In bed with Clare, Beverly has a dream: Elliot is watching them fuck, Beverly says 'I don't want him watching', Clare says 'I'll separate you'. The brothers are connected by an umbilical cord. Clare bites through the cord and separates them. Beverly wakes terrified: in fear of separation? This dream has a reversal. When Clare confronts them together in a restaurant she says to Elliot: 'You can't get it up unless baby brother is watching'. After the dream Beverly moves out of the apartment he and Elliot share, and in with Clare. He is by now hooked on the drugs that Clare got him into, and being alone is intolerable. He does not want Clare to leave the apartment, and by the time she goes away to work on a film he is falling apart. Meanwhile Elliot deals with separation by getting twin call-girls up to his hotel room while he is at a conference. One of them is to call him Bev and the other Elly – 'so I can tell you apart'. Here is the mirror of a double: he will be double in himself.

Doubling fails to stabilise identity; it has been disrupted by a woman, and now women's bodies begin to elude them. This is particularly so for Bev, as it is he who works on them, and he has left Elly. He has declined into a junkie state. While Clare is still away he goes back to Elly: 'I've been hiding from you. I've been hiding from the wrong person'. Elliot tries to save him, get him off the drugs – an effort which will fail. Beverly's work on women's bodies gets more and more bizarre. Corresponding to the failure of identity there is a failure to appropriate otherness, which leads to more violent penetration, misuse of instruments, and eventually the use of very sinister instruments. For example, Bev inserts into a woman an instrument that is meant for external use – the instrument they first designed as students and for which they won the prize. At medical school they had been told that it might work on cadavers but it would be no good for live women. To know woman is to negate? This instrument is significant in another respect: the play with the internal–external distinction that runs through this film. Their identity is constituted in externality, but as this fails the boundaries between external and internal become distinctly blurred. It is this disruption to the internal–external scenario that makes the film disturbing. In the scene just mentioned, the woman cries out in pain; Bev tells her that she feels no pain, she agrees, and he suggests that she might have been having sex with dogs. As explanation to Elliot for the use of this instrument, Beverly says: 'It's not the instrument that's the problem, it's the body, her insides were all wrong.' The internal of woman's body is not mediating the externality of the mirror image.

Beverly commissions an artist to make some very whacky instruments. In the attempted use of these he falls on top of the patient, needing a hit; the woman nearly dies, blood flows, and the medical board bans the brothers from clinical practice. Irigaray (1985a: 25): 'Desire/need also to make blood flow again in order to revive a very old relationship – intra-uterine, to be sure, but also prehistoric – to the maternal.' Beverly's slavery has failed with separation; now he has been removed from the raw material of women's bodies. This failure of mirroring is projected onto women: looking out through venetian blinds (which reproduce the external–internal split on another dimension), Bev, almost climbing through them, says to Elly: 'There's something strange happening out there, they look alright on the outside but their insides are deformed; they're mutants.' (At a later point, when Bev is off to see Clare for the last time, he sees the instruments in the window of the art gallery. The title of the work is 'Instruments for operating on mutant women'.) It is not the brothers' sameness that is the problem; the uterus is at fault.

If their identity is constituted in externality there has always been a question of the internal of the body, and an intra-uterine dimension to their relationship. As children, when they discover that fish have sex without touching they ask a girl to have sex with them in the bath. She says: 'Fuck off, you don't even know what it is'. And the brothers: 'They're so different; it's because we don't live under water.' Already woman is other, and problematic as mediation. In one of Elly's rescue attempts he dances with Bev, holding him, with a woman between them. It does not work, Bev collapses. When Elly first examines Clare he says that there ought to be beauty contests for the insides of bodies: the internal of the body that escapes specularisation? The intra-uterine relation involves touch and sound but not sight (women's genitals and also loss of sight are given as examples of the uncanny by Freud). Once women's bodies are removed from them how is the intra-uterine fantasy to be dealt with? And their identity? Only their bodies remain. Men's distance from their bodies is effected through mediations (Irigaray 1985a: 24): without mediations, the immediacy of the body. In *Dead Ringers*, as in most of Cronenberg's films, things get disgusting around the body. It starts in an innocuous way when early in the film they eat takeaway pizza and drink out of elegant wine glasses, but food becomes mess that spills everywhere, breaking boundaries of the body and the public–private distinction. Bev shoots up in the clinic surrounded by packets of chips, half-eaten junk food and the like (and the receptionist resigns at this point). Things flow, in and out of the body, spilling, and the body flowing: the internal–external distinction becomes blurred. Bev's body is not the total orthopaedic body of the mirror phase, but the bits-and-pieces body. When Clare rings him on her return he is lying on the floor; his body is not the standing, erect body. He tries to shave in the mirror before seeing her, but somehow the mirror does not work: Elliot's image reversed, for by now Elliot is going through exactly the same process. The uncanny of the double.

The transformation of Bev's body is mirrored by the transformation of Elly's. This begins at the moment he attempts to rescue Bev, or, more precisely, their ill-fated identity: 'We just have to get synchronised again' – an identity in time, abstract time. Thus Elly gets into drugs, beginning with, as Bev puts it, 'You have to take uppers so I won't take downers'. And they synchronise through regression. The moment of horror is the realisation of the inevitable outcome. Elly says: 'What happens to you, happens to me.' He gets Bev to recite the story of the Siamese twins, or at least they both tell bits of the story. They know it. Joined at the chest, when one died the other died: the uncanny turn of the double, the harbinger of death. At this point fear becomes pity, sorrow: 'poor Elly', 'poor Bev'. Elly is no longer in position of master; he wears dark glasses so as not to be seen, the look is fearful, not the look of recognition. He awaits synchronisation, in what is to be a death of the master and the slave. In Hegel the death of one is implicitly the death of the other; in Lacan's twist on this, the slave anticipates the death of the master, and in this is himself certain to die. But the death in *Dead Ringers* pushes Hegel, and Lacan, to the edge.

Beverly goes back to Clare's, stealing his instruments from the gallery on the way. He waits expectantly for Elliot to ring, and when he does not, leaves to find him. As Beverly is leaving, Clare asks what the instruments are for, holding one up to her face, dividing it, and his reply is: 'Separating Siamese twins'. She says: 'You won't come back, he won't let you.' Separate–together is thus prefigured.

Bev finds Elly in the clinic, where the whole process of decline has taken place, and he finds him as himself, Bev. They have synchronised. If this is a sameness, it is not the identity of the mirror phase. Rather, it is the outcome of the failure of the mirror: the externality of the double has not guaranteed self-certainty, mediations have been disrupted and disruptive. In Hegelian terms the state of the brothers would be described as a lower stage of consciousness, immersion in life. And in many respects their trajectory looks like one of regression, and a return to the point of departure in order to appropriate it and to die there. But, I think, not simply so. Appropriation of the otherness of woman's body has failed: it is their bodies that remain, in relation to each other. And this is a relation between bodies that displaces the oppositions internal–external, mediation–immediacy. In so far as there is an immediacy of the body the 'lower stage of consciousness' is correct – if we accept, that is, the Hegelian framework. Another way to read 'immersion in life' would be in Bergsonian terms as bodies acting on bodies, the matter of bodies. In Bergson's philosophy these oppositions do not apply as he argues against the notion that consciousness and matter and the internal and external are qualitatively different: the world is comprised of body-images acting on, transforming each other, in motion. And if we adopt Bergson's methodology of multiplicity it could be said of *Dead Ringers* that what goes on is simultaneously regressive (stasis) and a transformative excess, something more. The corporeality, and movement, that has little to do with consciousness, is striking in this film.

In the clinic they are baby boys again, following each other, wandering about in their underwear, bodies that can barely walk or talk. They have a party, stuffing their faces with cake: 'Mother didn't get us any ice-cream'. Bev: 'Happy birthday'; Elly: 'it's not our birthday'; Bev: 'yes it is'. In a sense it is their birthday as it is to be their deathday: in death a return to origins. *But* this is effected through their bodies, rather than bodies of women, which have escaped, eluded them.

In the final scene Elly is on the examining table. Bev, who always did the operations, will now operate on his former master. Elly says 'Don't forget the good bit', the drugs. Before the first cut, Bev says: 'We're about to separate Siamese twins'; Elly: 'Why're you crying?'; Bev: 'Separation can be a terrifying thing'; Elly: 'We'll always be together'. Bev makes a cut in Elly's chest where the Siamese twins were joined, with the instrument that nearly killed the woman, and that Clare held up to her face. In the place where women's bodies were worked on, and with instruments for mediating women's bodies, they now operate on their own body. Blood flows, the body has been penetrated. When Bev wakes from a bad dream he finds Elly's body opened, the internal specularised, as in an opening image in the film of a pregnant woman's body opened, exposed. This can, of course, be read as a feminisation of the body, as indeed the process of transformation of their bodies can be read in these terms. So, again, the feminine as the place of monstrous other? The final scenes can also be read as a spectacular resolution of the Hegelian separation–unity opposition – simultaneously both, in death. Now they are the agents of separation and possibly birth. This is reminiscent of the way Bataille (1986: 21–5) pushes Hegel's death in desire to the limit: in death there is unity and continuity, a resolution to the fear of separation – except that in *Dead Ringers* there is both unity and separation.

Having attempted to leave and ring Clare, Bev returns to the clinic, takes an overdose and lies across Elly, where he cut him, in a foetal position, as in the images of twins in the womb at the beginning and end of the film. A split unity in death. But I think there is an ambiguity about whether this is an end in the origin. Their desire does not seem nostalgic, there is no fear of death; and, it is not the maternal body which is uncanny, as it is for Freud. There is something about the film that is scandalous to Freud: the disruption of the internal–external distinction that characterises the development of the ego, a distinction which Lacan held with even if he gave it an ironic twist. To Bergson's conception of permeation, however, this film is not scandalous. What is uncanny is the return of the repressed of sameness, the madness that comes of duplication. To know themselves as one has led to a transformation of the body, a breaking of the internal–external boundary, a violent cutting of the body, and a madness of truth in death. A journey that starts with the desire for identity, but ends in a death that goes well beyond the death implicit in the mirror phase. If the death instinct is at work in duplication (a desire for fixing an identity), the death in *Dead Ringers* points to the instability of duplication, the failure of the double to ensure identity. This is a death in duration.

In this analysis of *Dead Ringers* the question of cinematic mediation has not been addressed. Although beyond the scope of this project, the movement of film obviously invites questions about duration. However, the following analysis does address the issues of mediation and time in a specific signifying system – that of photography.

Duration and photography

'the Photograph – my Photograph – is without culture' (Barthes 1984: 90)

This analysis of photography focuses on Barthes' approach to meaning with particular reference to *Camera Lucida*. I will also draw out connections between Barthes' concerns with and approach to photography and those of Benjamin. My argument is that photography can be thought of in terms of multiplicity, or as meaning in two different ways: on the one hand, as the fixing of the past as memory in an image, which is associated with the specular and might be understood as a voluntary memory; and, on the other hand, as having little to do with the specular, invoking involuntary memory which is not representable – 'without culture'. In this way of meaning, photography produces a movement, a textual transformation, which is in duration.

It might seem strange to consider photography as an example of duration in light of the discussion about the atemporality of the specular, and the commonplace that, of all media, photography invites notions of representation, particularly representations of the past. If representation or the notion of representation is the supposed attraction of photography, it also provokes a desire to show that there is something else going on. This, I believe, in different ways, was the fascination that photography held out to both Benjamin and Barthes. Photography is a good case for applying Bergson's method of multiplicity: it invites questions of qualitatively different ways of seeing. If there is a desire for the fixing of an image, is there also a duration in photography – or, at least the possibility of duration?

Following the method of multiplicity, the question to be asked is: What kinds of desire are involved where photography is concerned? To be consistent with what has been argued it could be assumed that moments of both negative and affirmative desire will coexist. Addressing Barthes' response to photography, it will be argued that if his desire can be read as nostalgic in some respects, it is the affirmative that predominates. Thus, I am as much interested in desire, and time and the body – the affect – in Barthes' text as in what his argument suggests about time and photography. In *Camera Lucida* Barthes does identify different ways of meaning: the fixing of the photographic image which is a death, and a movement in photography which is associated with a different response to death, an overcoming of death. The approach to meaning in *Camera Lucida* is one compatible with a positive desire. 'Meaning' is located in affectivity, in the body. And the disturbing moment of photography is in the register of time. As with Bergson, time and the body are inextricably linked. Barthes' account of the specificity of photographic mediation, and his notion of the punctum as time gets at something of the possibility of duration in photography.

> The Winter Garden Photograph was my Ariadne, not because it would help discover a secret thing, but because it would tell me what constituted that thread which drew me toward Photography. I had understood that henceforth I must interrogate the evidence of Photography, not from the viewpoint of pleasure, but in relation to what we romantically call love and death (Barthes 1984: 73).

The Winter Garden Photograph is a photograph of Barthes' mother as a child. Looking through photographs of her after her death, he found the truth of her in this image. For once, photography had given him 'a sentiment as certain as remembrance', the experience of an involuntary memory (Barthes 1984: 70). Barthes feels grief and pain over his mother's death; he also attempts a resolution of his own death. He claims that this book is about mourning and desire (Barthes 1984: 27), as well as love and death. But, what kind of desire is involved in his mourning? *Camera Lucida* can be read as nostalgic, and the desire in the text as a desire for certainty in the face of death. But I think this reading is too simple; in so far as there is any desire for certainty, it is not the certainty of representation. The movement of the text itself undoes such a desire. His concern with involuntary memory indicates this: it is something about the disturbing of the unconscious that draws him to photography. But I am also suggesting that the temporality of the text contributes to an undoing.

Barthes is always 'present' in his texts – never more so than in this one. Perhaps this can be attributed to the fear, but not necessarily the denial, of death of the author; not the author as institution, but as writing subject. In *The Pleasure of the Text* Barthes (1975: 48–9) rewrote Bataille's 'I write not to go mad' as 'I write not to be afraid'. In *Camera Lucida* there is an ambivalence about writing, and a movement towards the affect of photography – love, grief. He says there will be no transcendence in his death: his particularity could only be universalised by writing (Barthes 1984: 72). But writing, always fiction, cannot authenticate itself, cannot give the certainty of 'that-has-been' of photography (Barthes 1984: 85). On the face of it this looks like the certainty of an unmediated presence; but, I will argue, Barthes' semiotics is more complex than this. First, there is nothing reassuring about 'that-has-been' (but something exciting and sad); it is not an effect of the protective operations of consciousness; and second, in Barthes' writing, authenticity and immediacy move beyond the mediation–immediacy opposition, with an emphasis on the corporeality of meaning. At the end of *Camera Lucida* he opts for the madness of the truth of photography, that is, for what escapes representation and language. This is comparable to Bergson's conception of duration.

The madness of photography has been repressed. With echoes of Benjamin's account of commodification, Barthes (1984: 13) says that photography has become a matter of ownership and property, and that it objectifies. In the fixing of an image there is death. Of himself in front of the photographer, Barthes claims that as an object already he does not struggle, unlike the photographer who struggles to prevent the photograph becoming death. There are intimations of his own death running through this book; after Barthes' death Calvino (1987: 300–1) was particularly struck by this passage and the account of the experience of being photographed. Calvino (1987: 305) cannot separate his reading of the book and the death of the author. Perhaps rather than fear, then, there is a resignation; but *Camera Lucida* cannot be reduced to Barthes' concern about his own death. In this same section, on being photographed, he says that what he likes is the sound of the camera, the abrupt click. He hears the living sound of wood that the first cameras, clocks for seeing, were made of. The photographer's organ is not his eye, which terrifies Barthes, but his finger (Barthes 1984: 15). The reference to the click is reminiscent of Benjamin's account of the shock which is the click of the camera – shock in the sense of the experience of modernity. But there is ambiguity in Benjamin's 'shock'; he also uses the term to refer to an involuntary memory. In some ways the double sense of shock is implicit in Barthes' account of the different ways that photographs mean; he, like Benjamin, is interested in what will disrupt the culturally given. Even as he is talking about objectification he hints at something else: sound rather than the eye, and the involuntary memory of hearing. In madness there is a refusal of the death of objectification, of the fearful gaze that turns a subject into an object.

In *The Pleasure of the Text* Barthes (1975: 57) argued for the *jouissance* of reading/writing over 'Desire and Death'. Now even pleasure in that sense is not enough, it will not give him the 'noeme' – the essence – of photography. To find the universal of photography and what distinguishes the photograph from other images, he must 'descend deeper' into himself (Barthes 1984: 60). This deeper is desire, associated with death, triggered by the image of his mother as child. From this photograph Barthes (1984: 73) decides to 'derive' all Photography. There is something extraordinarily disarming about his methodological claims: he will start with photographs that he loves, that exist for him, indeed a photograph that only exists for him, and proceed to the universal, the 'essence' of photography. But in making this claim Barthes brings to light what is implicit, if denied in the name of science, in all research: the subjective that is involved in choice of 'object'. This could be taken as a critique of structuralism: from what position are elements selected, and relations between them designated? Although Lévi-Strauss's (Bergsonian) answer to this question is that 'we' partake in the same structuring principles as those of the external world, there is no qualitative distinction between the internal of subjectivity and external reality, and thus there is nothing random about the identification of sets of relations (Lévi-Strauss 1985: 101–5; 1976: 67–8; von Sturmer 1987: 110–11; Rosso 1973: 27).

Barthes' decision to start with photographs that exist for him is connected with another related methodological principle: 'a desparate resistance to any reductive system' (Barthes 1984: 8), his dissatisfaction with the discourses with which he had worked, sociology, semiotics, psychoanalysis, and particularly any analysis that reduces an object to one of these. He is insistent on the specificity of objects, and the ways in which subjectivity is necessarily implicated. Thus, his methodology is one of particularity. It is on this issue of the particularity of subjectivity that Barthes departs from a Lévi-Straussian position.

In this, his last writing, Barthes seduces – again. There is pleasure in the reading. The openness, and the movement between the erotic and death, produce the pleasure of this text. Barthes does succeed in getting at the essence of photography, how it is experienced: the affect of photography, and of *this* text, is sadness, sorrow.

There are two parts to *Camera Lucida*, and it is in Part 2 that Barthes moves to the Winter Garden Photograph. Part 1 is ostensibly a systematic approach to the question 'What is Photography "in itself"?' (Barthes 1984: 3). But this text cannot be read in a linear way – Part 1 needs to be read in the light of Part 2. What initially fascinated and disturbed me about this book, was the apparently heretical semiotic position proposed in Part 1. Barthes is deliberately provocative with his asides at the semiological fashion of scorn for the real, and his claim to be a realist. In this latter respect he says that there is no discontinuity with his earlier essays on the photograph as an image without a code ('The Photographic Message', 'Rhetoric of the Image', 'The Third Meaning' (Barthes 1977: 15–68)). However, he does depart from these essays in his conceptualisation of the nature of photographic mediation, what is specific to photography's referent: 'Photography's Referent is not the same as the referent of other systems of representation' (Barthes 1984: 76). He begins by observing the 'stubbornness' of the referent; it 'adheres'. As the

Photograph always carries its referent with itself, the photographic signifier cannot be seen (Barthes 1984: 4–7). In attempts to be scientific he would always return to photographs he loved: 'Myself, I saw only the referent, the desired object, the beloved body' (Barthes 1984: 7). Speaking specifically of the spectator's photograph, he claims that the 'essential' is the chemical action of light (Barthes 1984: 10). This is confirmed by the experience of looking at the Winter Garden Photograph; it 'overwhelms' (Barthes 1984: 76). To say that the photograph is analogical does not distinguish it from any other representation: 'it is not a copy of reality' but 'an emanation of *past reality*' (Barthes 1984: 88). This is the noeme of photography.

Barthes (1984: 76) claims that the photographic referent is 'the *necessarily* real thing which has been placed before the lens'. In 'Rhetoric of the Image' he said much the same: the photograph's reality is 'that of *having been there*', 'this is how it was'. But there he claimed that the real unreality was that of the 'here-now'. The photograph was not in the present, but of the past (Barthes 1977: 44).

In *Camera Lucida* there is a significant shift: the 'that-has-been' is not a fixing in the past, but in a significant sense is in 'the present'. In these reflections the photograph is not so much iconic as indexical:

From the real body, which was there, proceed radiations which ultimately touch me, who am here: the duration of the transmission is insignificant; the photograph of the missing being, as Sontag says, will touch me like the delayed rays of a star (Barthes 1984: 80–1).

What is most interesting about this shift is the different assumptions about time: traces of the past in the 'present'. The photograph is only in the present, in what we might take to be a Bergsonian sense of the present, it is not in the past. The emanation of a past reality operates like an involuntary memory, as opposed to the voluntary memory of fixing a moment in the past. Furthermore, it is traces of a body, and the experience is not visual so much as tactile. What is crucial, then, in the indexical of the semiotics of photography, is that it temporalises.

The fascination with photography might be about the real, and a desire to make the absent, present: the promise of photography and the disappointment, the 'almost' of photography, as Barthes (1984: 66) puts it. It is the specificity of photographic mediation that produces the desire to know, to find the loved body (Barthes 1984: 99). But it also makes this impossible: the 'almost' of the referent produces the movement of desire, a relation to an other that eludes. For once a photograph 'worked' for Barthes; but not as a past that was a present. He found his mother in a photograph that did not look like her as he knew her. The one that does not 'look like her' gives him 'truth', authenticates (Barthes 1984: 89). Photographs that work by 'like-nesses' only 'look *like*' other photographs: copies of copies (Barthes 1984: 102). They suppress the body, both that of the subject and that of the spectator; they produce no affect, and block memory. The experience of authentication, on the other hand, is one of an involuntary memory.

Barthes speaks of a temporality in his desire for photographs. He does not like photographs that are motionless, that fix an object; his desire is for photographs that launch a desire beyond, that produce a metonymic impulse: make us add something *beyond what we see* (Barthes 1984: 45, 59). Photographs that set him off do so temporally, they exert an adventure, they animate him (Barthes 1984: 19–20), his whole body remembers (Barthes 1984: 45) – echoes of Proust and Bergson, memory and the moving body in duration.

In *Camera Lucida* a distinction is made between the studium and the punctum of a photograph. From his experience of looking Barthes derives a 'structural rule', the co-presence of two discontinuous elements: the studium is the cultural, the coded; and the punctum is that which breaks the studium, wounds, pricks, disturbs. His structural rule breaks with rules of structuralism: the punctum is accidental, uncoded and subjective. It is particular. The Winter Garden Photograph, for example, wounds only Barthes. He compares the punctum with involuntary memory. (See Proust (1966: 255) on the 'two ways' which have a 'significance which is for me alone'.) What is significant about the punctum is that it is temporal; it is the rupture, the discontinuous of time related to the operations of the unconscious. There is an obvious similarity with the *jouissance* of the text of bliss – the shock, disturbance – as opposed to the culturally comfortable of the text of pleasure (Barthes 1975: 14, 19). Just as in *The Pleasure of the Text* it was the body of bliss, the unspeakable (Barthes 1975: 21, 62, 66) that concerned Barthes, here it is affectivity, the 'irreducible' of affect (Barthes 1984: 21), the body moved. Again ' "nothing to say" ' (Barthes 1984: 93).

The reading of photographs through *Camera Lucida* is a process of verification of this structural rule. In Part 1 the interrogation is still from the viewpoint of pleasure, and the images can be seen as a series of substitutions, each with a partial object as punctum (Barthes 1984: 43) – feet, hands, fingers, teeth, arms. The final image is Mapplethorpe's 'Young Man with Extended Arm'. Barthes finds the openness of the boy's hand erotic: this is an example of a photograph that launches desire, it takes the spectator outside the frame, animating both the photo and the spectator. The boy's hand seizes the spectator. The punctum, then, is a 'kind of subtle beyond' (Barthes 1984: 59). It has a temporality, and not only moves the body of the spectator but transforms the photograph in that process. In a reading which is also a writing, the spectator *and* the photograph are put into motion, or we might say, duration.

With the move to the discovery of the Winter Garden Photograph, and from pleasure to love and death in Part 2, there is a shift in reading, and a movement towards the madness of affect. Nadar's 'The Artist's Mother' (or wife), a substitution for the Winter Garden Photograph (which is not reproduced), is 'one of the loveliest photographs in the world' (Barthes

1984: 70). This image forms part of a series through which he reflects on death, and love.

Nadar is followed by Kertesz's 'Ernest' (Paris, 1931): 'it is *possible* that Ernest is still alive today' (Barthes 1984: 84). Barthes has moved from a photograph of 'mother', his dead mother as child, to 'child', himself as child. About Ernest he says: 'I am the reference of every photograph . . . why is it that I am alive here and now?' (Barthes 1984: 84). It is specifically in connection with a photograph by Gardner, 'Portrait of Lewis Payne' (1865), that Barthes refers to the punctum of Time. This photograph is a combination of the erotic and death. The studium is that the boy is handsome; but now there is another punctum, not that of the detail, but Time. And the punctum of this photograph is 'he is going to die', 'this will be' and 'this has been', death in the future which is absolute past. 'In front of the photograph of my mother as a child, I tell myself: she is going to die: I shudder over a catastrophe which has already occurred' (Barthes 1984: 96). The boy is Barthes' object of desire, he puts himself in the place of the object who will die, has already died. But the effect of these photographs is not so much a death in life as the reverse, a life in death. They point to the duration of the body; the effects of a particular individual's death on his, Barthes' body – the *shudder*. Does duration hold out the possibility of transcendence?

Barthes speaks of his desire for the photographic look, to be looked at by someone in a photograph, a subject of the gaze. As a spectator who, in this case, is not subject of the gaze, he is not an object either. This look is a power that photography has that is forbidden by the fiction of cinema. The Look: 'looks you straight in the eye, but elides the vision', a gaze that avoids the fearfulness of the return of the gaze (Barthes 1984: 111). The final photograph is Kertesz's 'The Puppy' (Paris, 1928). This boy 'retains within himself his love and fear: that is the Look' (Barthes 1984: 113). Having gone out into the other who is dead, is going to die, Barthes returns to himself as child, as being for himself, love and fear turned in, in solitude? This is truth and madness (Barthes 1984: 113). The photographs in *Camera Lucida* are not simply illustrative of the analysis; as supplement to the written text, they mark a change in Barthes' relation to writing as he gives over to photography. The structure of the text parallels the movement from writing to photography. Writing, as an attempt to master madness or fear, is not now bodily enough for Barthes.

What, then, is the connection between mother and death in *Camera Lucida*? There is a reference to mother in Part 1 in connection with photographs of landscapes that awaken desire, that produce fantasies of his primal past, back to somewhere in himself, and fantasies of a utopian future: the certainty of having been there or going there (birth/death). It must be said that this looks like a desire for origins; and in this context he makes a reference to Freud on the maternal body in 'The "Uncanny"'. 'Such then would be the essence of the landscape (chosen by desire): *heimlich*, awakening in me the Mother (and never the disturbing Mother)' (Barthes

1984: 40). In this, he is implicitly denying the *unheimlich*, the uncanny. But I think the parenthesis could be read as: his mother is indeed disturbing, as is her death, and possibly his death. In Part 2 death is explicitly identified as disturbing, as punctum. The ambiguity in Barthes' desire is related to death. The certainty of the photograph contains within it the certainty of death, the defeat of Time: 'that is dead', 'that is going to die' (Barthes 1984: 117), and 'the imperious sign of my future death' (Barthes 1984: 97). The pathos of the photograph is: that is alive, is going to die, I am going to die. The photograph is the sign of both immortality and mortality; an individual dies, but there is also duration. Barthes claims that the photograph is absolute particularity, there is nothing transcendent in it, and yet his desire would seem to be for a photograph that will transcend his particularity.

Moving back through Time, Barthes found the Winter Garden Photograph and his mother-as-child. This was a movement he experienced in reality: he nursed her, she became his child, 'she had become my little girl, uniting for me with that essential child she was in her first photograph'. He becomes mother, experiencing her as 'my inner law', 'my feminine child'. And through this identification with his mother he 'resolves Death'. If he is mother, gives birth to his mother ('I engendered my mother'), he is also feminine child, 'mother-as-child' (Barthes 1984: 71–2). Is he, then, giving birth to himself as a way of resolving her absence? Once she was dead, he says, there was only his particularity left: his death would be undialectical. A possible way of reading this is that through an identification with her his particularity has already been transcended. He has put himself in the position of the feminine other and through her transcendental death he will have transcendence. There is something Hegelian about this, but I am not sure that it involves a negation of the other; there is a movement towards the other, but also perhaps, reversing Sartre and de Beauvoir, an idealisation of the feminine as transcendent. Furthermore, Barthes wants to retrieve his mother, bring the other back to desire, 'immediate desire'. This is the desire to which the Winter Garden Photograph speaks. And in a sense, through looking at this photograph, this desire is 'realised'.[3]

In making sense of Barthes' desire for immediacy in photography it is important to bear in mind the way in which the body figures throughout his writing, and certainly his later writing. 'The "grain" is the body in the voice as it sings, the hand as it writes, the limb as it performs' (Barthes 1977: 188). As with Irigaray's concern with touch, Barthes' desire cannot be read as one for unmediated presence. (Despite the claim that every photograph is a 'certificate of presence' (Barthes 1984: 87). It is also a testimony to absence – 'absence-as-presence' (Barthes 1984: 106).) He is not denying mediation, but rather reading photography in a way that breaks with the mediation–immediacy opposition. For example, he says: 'A sort of umbilical cord links the body of the photographed thing to my gaze: light, though impalpable, is here a carnal medium, a skin I share' (Barthes 1984: 81). If the umbilical cord (and Ariadne's thread) hints at the imaginary, an alternative reading is also possible. The attraction of photography is the form of mediation, not a desire to be done with mediation. Significantly, it is a mediation that is corporeal: carnal, a skin I share. Bodies touch without clear boundaries between them. The 'loved body is immortalised by the mediation of a precious metal, silver . . . ; to which we might add the notion that this metal, like all the metals of Alchemy, is alive' (Barthes 1984: 81). The body living in duration? The emphasis on light and rays as photographic mediation suggests a way of taking the analysis of time a step further. Perhaps it could be said that time, or duration, is mediation; but as it is lived, in the body, it is a form of mediation that disrupts the opposition between immediacy and mediation. Time is a bodily mediation in immediacy. And the converse of this is that meaning embodied is temporal.

Photography can be mad or tame. Barthes (1984: 119) chooses madness, madness which is 'intractable reality', affect, unspeakable: the 'photographic *ecstasy*'. This is the affect of involuntary memory, that cannot be put into representation. Involuntary memory is hysterical – 'the shudder' ('no sooner had the warm liquid, and the crumbs with it, touched my palate than a shudder ran through my whole body' (Proust 1966: 58)). Barthes' desire is not the negative desire of Hegel-Lacan, but a desire connected with the duration of photography. As Derrida (Derrida and Plissart 1989: 91) has said in connection with *Camera Lucida*, where the referent is framed in photography, 'the index of the completely other . . . nonetheless makes reference endlessly refer'. Photography 'gives the prerogative to the other, opens the infinite uncertainty of a relation to the completely other'. It is, then, a certain 'realness' of the photographic referent that produces deferral.

Benjamin's essay, 'A Short History of Photography', was written more than fifty years earlier than *Camera Lucida*. Not only are there echoes of Benjamin in Barthes, but this essay seems remarkably pertinent to current concerns in cultural theory. As Benjamin (1982: 7) so eloquently puts it:

> However skilful the photographer, however carefully he poses his model, the spectator feels an irresistible compulsion to look for the tiny spark of chance, of the here and now, with which reality has, as it were, seared the character in the picture; to find that imperceptible point at which, in the immediacy of that long-past moment, the future so persuasively inserts itself that, looking back, we may rediscover it. It is indeed a different nature that speaks to the camera from the one which addresses the eye . . .

Benjamin goes on to say that the major difference is that this is not a space worked through by consciousness, but rather one affected unconsciously. And here he coins his famous term 'the optical unconscious', which 'photography makes us aware of for the first time' (Benjamin 1982: 7). In this experience of looking there is something that escapes the framing of the photographer: an experience, Benjamin says, that has little to do with the eye. There are intimations of the significance of senses other than sight where photography is concerned – tactility, for example. This quotation hints at affectivity, and at a particular way of thinking the past, the 'immediacy of that long-past moment', in its relation to the future. Barthes' understanding of the temporal of photography as the moment of authenticity might be compared with Benjamin's 'spark of chance' that sears the picture making a 'long-past moment' immediate. In a reference to David Octavius Hill's 'Elizabeth Johnstone, the beautiful fishwife from Newhaven', Benjamin (1982: 7) says there is something that 'cannot be silenced, that impudently demands the name of the person who lived at that time and who, remaining real even now, will not yield herself up entirely into *art*'.

Benjamin expressed an ambivalence towards photography which bears comparison with Barthes' understanding of the two ways of photography. Barthes' (1984: 117–19) tame photography is that of the consumption of images, both photography as art, and photography generalised, made banal – the 'tyranny' of the photographic image in Western culture. His dislike of likenesses is clearly connected with this. To disrupt is to authenticate: mad photography obliges us to return to the very letter of Time, it reverses the course of things. Benjamin is critical of photography in so far as it partakes of and contributes to the development of a culture of commodification and fetishism. But, for Benjamin, there is also a critical potential in photography which relates to shock in its disruptive sense.[4] In particular, it is the optical unconscious that Benjamin regards as the critical moment of photography. As for Barthes, there is potential for authenticity in photography (Benjamin 1982: 25). For neither of them is authenticity understood in a nostalgic sense, but rather as a 'redemptive' experience in a world of commodification and quantification: it disrupts the 'sense of sameness of things in the world' (Benjamin 1982: 21). If photography is crucially implicated in this 'sense of sameness', and encourages voluntary memory (Benjamin 1973: 147), there is also the possibility of the invocation of involuntary memory which is disruptive to the sameness of the ever new. This is why Benjamin finds Freud's account of memory so attractive: there are ways in which mechanical reproduction, operating on the principle of consciousness and voluntary memory, undoes itself. Photography is a case in point.

Benjamin's concept of shock has a good deal in common with Barthes' punctum: both refer to a temporality of the unconscious that disturbs the culturally given. Both Benjamin and Barthes distinguish between different ways of photography in a way that is analogous to Bergson's method of multiplicity. And they both argue for the qualitative (authentic, affective) side of photography. To apply Bergson's method of multiplicity, the two ways of photography could be characterised as voluntary memory, representation, the studium; and involuntary memory, transformation, the punctum. The former is atemporal, the latter temporal. But, this applies generally to ways of meaning. What specifies the temporality of photography? In part, the provocation of questions of time and memory by the medium. And the specific way in which the 'realness' of the referent is mediated by time: bodies act on bodies ('the intractable reality' of affect, ecstasy) in such a way that they will never meet; a correspondence is, indeed, impossible. The referent is so close, but in this closeness infinitely deferred.

The critical, deconstructive concern with the metaphysics of presence has produced a certain vacation of the ground of experience. An emphasis on the mediations of signification, crucial to a critique of presence, has frequently led to a misplaced rejection of 'experience': meaning is counterposed to experience in a way that reinvents the representation–real distinction. What emerges from Barthes, Irigaray, Bergson and Benjamin is that experience need not be equated with presence. Once we think of mediations as constitutive, as having an immediacy in the body, 'experience', understood here as unconscious, marked by memory traces and bodily, becomes central to the *critique* of presence. To focus on mediations without recognising their constitutive character is again to presume the possibility of an unmediated presence: to be caught in the Hegelian dilemma. If signification is understood as a process of mediation in immediacy, Barthes' claim to being a realist does not seem semiotically heretical. 'The real' can never be a presence; but the materiality of meaning in the body is real. For Barthes, this real is hysteria.

7

PLACES IN TIME

The analyses in this chapter pursue the idea that different ways of being in place are connected with different ways of meaning. Implicitly I am questioning the view that a desire for 'a place', and attachments to places, are to be understood simply in terms of a nostalgic desire for home, the *heimlich*. What goes with this particular cultural studies argument is a valorisation of homelessness over home, with hints of an imperative to be 'on the move' as it were. But there are different ways of being in movement and thinking about movements through space, just as there are different ways of being in a place. A distinction between, or, in Bergson's terms, a dissociation of, stasis and movement can be made with respect to both. (It is a mistake to equate place with 'a signified' and movement with 'the play of the signifier'.) In this regard it is important to bear in mind that in Freud's account of the desire for a return to origins, the *heimlich* is marked by the unconscious, the *unheimlich*. My interest is in practices of space – 'place' or 'movement' – which are temporal, that is, consist in a writing that disturbs the order of discourse, the stasis of representation. And, in these terms, a rewriting of origins is not unthinkable either.

Walking: writing

New York was an inexhaustible space, a labyrinth of endless steps, and no matter how far he walked, no matter how well he came to know its neighborhoods and streets, it always left him with a feeling of being lost. Lost, not only in the city, but within himself as well. . . . Motion was of the essence, the act of putting one foot in front of the other and allowing himself to follow the drift of his own body (Auster 1985: 8–9)

The reader of the Text may be compared to someone at a loose end (someone slackened off from any imaginary); this passably empty subject strolls – it is what happened to the author of these lines, then it was that he had a vivid idea of the text – on the side of a valley, a oued flowing down below (*oued* is there to bear witness to a certain unfamiliarity); what he perceives is multiple, heterogeneous, coming from a disconnected, heterogeneous variety of substances and perspectives: lights, colours, vegetation, heat, air, slender explosions of noises, scant cries of birds, children's voices from over on the other side, passages, gestures, clothes of inhabitants near or far away. All these *incidents* are half-identifiable: they come from codes which are known but their combination is unique, founds the stroll in a difference repeatable only as difference (Barthes 1977: 159).

The stroll figures prominently in contemporary cultural theory as a metaphor for writing, and, specifically, writing the body. Different ways of walking are directly connected with different ways of meaning. Walking is a movement of the body in space, but following Bergson this movement can be thought in its spatial and temporal moments: immobility and mobility. When Barthes speaks of the stroll he is referring to metonymy, as is Cixous (1981: 53) when she uses the metaphor of wandering for a feminine text: the text of the unforeseeable. The movement of this textual reading-writing is, for both Barthes and Cixous, the movement of the body. Thus, it could be said that there is duration in the stroll, in wandering. To wander is to err from the straight and narrow of linearity, of the order. This way of walking is to be distinguished from the purposive walk which is concerned with an end, a goal: not seeing the detail, this walk would get to the end, the only place from which it is presumed the whole can be seen. The stroll, on the other hand, has no concern for a whole or an end; the unforeseeable excites.

While linearity, the teleology of an end in a beginning, works on the principle of repetition of the same (every walk is the same), the stroll is founded in repetition as difference. Barthes emphasises multiplicity, heterogeneity, qualitative differences in substances and senses, the unfamiliar in the familiar, and importantly, the particularity – the 'unique' – of combination of elements of codes. The irreducible, the particularity, of this has nothing to do with individuality (Barthes 1977: 159); it is, after all, an empty subject, 'slackened off' from the imaginary, and at a loose end, who strolls.

Barthes is talking about the openness of a text as opposed to a work which closes on the signified: the 'infinity' of the signifier in deferred action (Barthes 1977: 158). The work falls under the scope of an interpretation; the metonymy of the text invites the reading of the stroll, which, for Barthes, is a writing. Hence the distinction that Barthes (1977: 147) makes between deciphering which is interpretation, and disentangling. His conception of disentangling has a good deal in common with Bergson's method of multiplicity: the dissociation of composites is not an interpretation. For Barthes (1977: 159), multiplicity in meaning does not refer to several different meanings, a pluralism of signifieds, but the irreducibly plural of meaning – the weave of signifiers. The implication of this for cultural analysis is that, despite academic codes to the contrary, we should relinquish interpretation, the desire to find a meaning, even several meanings, and instead, engage in a *writing* of culture that is open, that invites further writing.

The stroll is generally associated with the urban, with the experience of the city in modernity and capitalism. In this respect the passage from Auster would seem to be more directly characteristic of contemporary cultural analysis than that of Barthes. In placing these quotations side by side, I want to question the distinctions city–country, urban–rural, and more generally, culture–nature. I will return to this issue in a moment. On the connection between the stroll and the experience of the city, Benjamin's account of the *flâneur* has come to hold considerable fascination for cultural theorists. And, indeed, the figure of the *flâneur* is sometimes taken as that of cultural analyst. Baudelaire's *flâneur* became the subject of modernity for Benjamin (although this place was also given, in different ways, to the prostitute and the ragpicker (Wohlfarth 1986)). Changes in the city – traffic, architecture, the manic behaviour and speed of the crowd – made the leisurely, turtle pace of the *flâneur* anachronistic (Benjamin 1973: 128–9). But, as with all of Benjamin's figures, there is an ambiguity in the *flâneur*. He is associated with a certain way of being in a society characterised by consumption, and from the arcades he moved to being at home in the department store (Benjamin 1973: 54), gazing at items of consumption, but not buying. In his stroll the *flâneur* notices the detail, 'botanising on the asphalt' (Benjamin 1973: 36–7), he is turned into a detective, 'catches things in flight' (Benjamin 1973: 41). The *flâneur* abandons himself in the crowd, intoxicated. In this respect, there is a 'negative' moment of strolling, for this abandonment is to share the situation of a commodity, and the *flâneur* is intoxicated by the dream-world of commodities (Benjamin 1973: 55). I say 'negative' with reservations, for part of the attraction of Benjamin's writing is that he does not adopt a form of argument that is for or against: his dialectical method is characterised by ambiguity rather than negativity. If the *flâneur* partakes of the world of commodities, he also subverts it.

A subversive moment is to be identified in the nature of the stroll. This way of walking is oppositional to the counting of time, Taylorism, the production process (Benjamin 1973: 129). His scrutinising, detective work, and dreaming set the *flâneur* apart from the rush-hour crowd, swept along by the time of capitalism. He dreams that 'he is like an artist' (Benjamin 1973: 41). But even in his practices of observation there is a double moment: 'he does not take his eyes off a miscreant' (Benjamin 1973: 41), he is a watcher who partakes of the movement of the city; but he also stands outside, observes from a window (Benjamin 1973: 130). The *flâneur* embodies a multiplicity of moments of capitalism or modernity: commodity, consumer (if not an actual buyer of commodities), and producer. The productive is potentially subversive – author, writer, observer.[1] What is most important here is that the temporality of the *flâneur*'s walk is subversive to the sense of time that is characteristic of modernity. In Benjamin, we find an exemplary analysis of different ways of walking, of being, in a city.

As with Barthes' distinction between the work and a text it could be said that some cities invite a writing of the stroll, others are closed, direct the walk, or make it impossible. Auster is suggesting that cities as texts mean in different ways. In *Invisible Cities*, very clearly 'about' both cities and meaning, Calvino (1979: 30) claims that some cities invoke desire, others erase it. But even relatively closed texts can be rewritten: the *flâneur* moved to the department store; the rush-hour crowd did not preclude the possibility of the stroll. The *flâneur*'s city was not that of the office worker. We might say that there is no *one* New York or Sydney or London; cities are multiple in differences in movement and the particularity of combination of codes. Following Bergson, there are ways of being in and moving in that correspond to different temporalities. (I am also alluding to the issue of different forms of transport, movement of bodies, and whether or not they allow for the possibility of duration.) Where the routine of the clock – purposiveness – imposes a sameness and simultaneity, the stroll of duration inscribes difference: rewrites the city. 'On his best walks, he was able to feel that he was nowhere . . . New York was the nowhere he had built around himself, and he realized that he had no intention of ever leaving it again' (Auster 1985: 9). Lost in the motion of the body: the production of a place to be in, but a place that is nowhere.

Barthes' stroll is in the country. There is a whole genealogy of 'country walks and writing'. But just as I am about to make reference to certain 'influences', I am warned by what Barthes says about intertextuality in the context of his discussion of the stroll. The text is necessarily woven with 'citations, references, echoes, cultural languages' (Barthes 1977: 160). However, in making reference to country walks, I want to make two points. First, the country is just as much coded as the city, which might seem obvious except that when 'the country' slides into 'nature' it becomes that which is not coded, in opposition to culture. Second, and more importantly, the city and the country cannot be held apart, fixed as an opposition: there is an interweaving of city and country codes, texts. If the city is commonly defined as archetypal of the experience of modernity, it is defined as such in relation to the country. While such definitions tend to align the country with the traditional and the pre-modern, I want to suggest that we think the city–country opposition in the now: the country is only defined as such within the context of modernity. One of the implications of this is that the experience of walking in the country need not necessarily be nostalgic. In setting alongside each other a country walk and a city walk, my concern is to bring to light the ways in which oppositional elements bear the traces of each other.

With respect to walking-writing my interest is in the complexity of the mixing of purposiveness and wandering, in both 'work' and 'pleasure'. There is in this no imperative to give up on the purposive dimension, but rather a concern to understand how it interrelates with the non-purposive. A transgressive moment lies perhaps not in a refusal of one side of the opposition but in a certain play with oppositions.

The walking-writing body is a body moved by affect, memories. If the stroll is solitary, this solitude is not that of the imaginary – the autonomous subject – but that of the subject that is lost, empty. This subject does not need to store up memories in the head, for the movement of the body itself invokes memories which are involuntary. Proust's walks are memories. For Bergson, the body in motion is the body of memory, and the 'source' of creativity (*élan vital*). In his *Reveries of the Solitary Walker*, Rousseau (1979 [1782]: 35) makes a distinction between recollection and creation, vital spirit, rather disingenuously saying that he is only capable of the former at this point in his life. The writing of the book, the walks, suggest otherwise.

> But if there is a state where the soul can find a resting-place secure enough to establish itself and concentrate its being there, with no need to remember the past or reach into the future, where time is nothing to it, where the present runs on indefinitely but this duration goes unnoticed, with no sign of the passing time . . . (Rousseau 1979: 88).

This, says Rousseau, would be the feeling of complete happiness, the simple feeling of existence. What is striking about this passage is a conception of duration and the body remembering which has nothing to do with conscious remembrance. Here also is an account of *being in* a place, a resting place, which is in duration. For Rousseau and Proust the memory which is walking is ecstasy; for Barthes the stroll is a reading which is *jouissance*. In 'A New Refutation of Time' Borges (1970: 261–2) cites a similar ecstatic experience, and he does so in the context of an argument that every moment is inseparable from its past:

> I managed, to the imperfect degree of possibility, to do what is called walking at random; I accepted, with no other conscious prejudice than that of avoiding the wider avenues or streets, the most obscure invitations of chance.

He is led on by an unfamiliar familiarity, and experiences a tenderness in the colour of a wall. In this involuntary memory, Borges has a sense of eternity.

However, Proust and Rousseau see a contradiction between the unreasoning pleasure of the walk, wandering – reflections of the sunlight, smells (Proust 1966: 245), the detail of the blade of grass (Rousseau 1979: 106–7) – and writing. But they both write it. And they both give the example of drifting in a boat as a moment of ecstasy (Proust 1966: 254, 250; Rousseau 1979: 88, 85–7). Rousseau (1979: 86–7) speaks of the noise of waves and movement of water as 'taking hold of my senses' invoking madness and passion. Waves and movement of water frequently figure in cultural theory as metaphors for writing the body and difference in repetition.[2] What is striking about the *Reveries* is affect, passion: Rousseau's claim to being moved by the senses, his desires (Rousseau 1979: 105, 115). If in Western conceptions of knowledge, reason and passion are regarded as mutually exclusive, Rousseau's passionate knowledge presents a disturbance to this distinction. Read together, these various texts of walking suggest a way of being in the world and writing that runs against homogeneity, abstraction, singularity: the wandering, empty subject writes the body, disrupting the order of discourse, the stasis of representation.

Touring time: English heritage

memory is a sort of anti-museum . . .
(de Certeau, 1984: 100)

Take A Journey Back In Time
(British Commercial Vehicle Museum, pamphlet)

This analysis of texts of English heritage focuses on the prevalent motif of travel: travel and storytelling, touring our past, or, as the British Commercial Vehicle Museum pamphlet has it, taking 'a trip down memory lane'. Such discourses are implicated in the production of public memory; in Benjamin's terms they are in the register of conscious discursive memory. The question to be asked of these texts of voluntary memory is, then: What do they open up or close off of the possibility of rewriting, the possibility of another moment – that of involuntary memory?

De Certeau is also concerned with the significance of personal memory to the rewriting of texts. Travel and walking are substitutes for legends – they are a sort of storytelling. While texts delimit a field, structure the relation between elements, these practices transform texts, 'open up space to something different' (de Certeau 1984: 106–7). They give a movement and temporality to the structure of text, dispersing it: travel works like memory, even if in 'a sort of reversal'. In this storytelling 'things *extra* and *other*', heterogeneous elements and details, insert themselves 'into the accepted framework', much like 'the tiny spark of chance' that Benjamin speaks of in connection with the photograph. Where, in de Certeau's view, museums fix and delimit, memory operates by dispersion, such that the memorable is also dispersed. These practices are ordinary everyday practices, practices of memory that cannot be put into representation, cannot be seen, fragmentary pasts that cannot be read by others. They produce 'anti-texts', in an operation much like that of involuntary memory.

It is interesting to compare de Certeau with Benjamin's account of storytelling in 'The Storyteller'. The decline in storytelling is associated with the debasement of experience in the modern world. As an oral form – unlike the novel and the forms of communication that emerged with capitalism – storytelling is 'public', the listener is in the company of the teller. It works through the involvement of the memories of both teller and listener; every listener is a potential reteller. And, significantly, it is performative: the whole body, and soul, tells the story. This is comparable to the contemporary understanding of writing as bodily performance, and the concern to diminish 'the distance between writing and reading' (Barthes 1977: 145–6, 162). While Benjamin (1969: 83–110) regarded storytelling as a craft, it is reasonable to presume in the light of his methodology, that storytelling in modernity, rather than being nostalgia might open up the possibility of a reclaiming of experience.

So, to English heritage in the North of England, specifically Yorkshire. 'English heritage' includes the institution English Heritage, but is taken to refer to discourses of nationality, pastness and memory more generally. One of the most noticeable features of these discourses is the lack of consistency within and between sites. History is not seamless: there are, in English heritage, disparate histories and different ways in which history is produced. The sort of history that does not figure much is the history of historians, and when a historical time is invoked it is usually obviously fictional. For example, dates or facts might be given, but in the context of what is clearly a story. However, whatever the particular strategy employed, the predominant effect of these discourses is a homogenisation of heterogeneity in the production of pastness. The past is commodified. But, in this regard, heritage discourses are also paradoxical: they frequently appeal to the qualitative, to personal memory; and yet a putting into discourse is a voluntary memory, a quantification and commodification.

The motif of travel is a constant theme in heritage in Yorkshire: what is it that the tourist audience, predominantly English, is being invited to tour, and how? 'Take a journey through 1,000 years of history.' This is the running head of a pamphlet called 'Inheritance Road', which is a classic of the genre of travel and history. The front page specifies length – 'A 140 mile long scenic heritage route', which 'links together one thousand years of English history' (Figures 1 and 2). Here we have a nice example of quantification, counting and a measurement of time: an equation, in fact, between 140 miles and 1,000 years. In Bergson's terms each point on the spatialised line of time is immobilised: each point on the road 'is a page of the story turned', fixed as a discrete moment. The road in this case, but sometimes a trail, is one of the main devices used to connect disparate sites and periods – the line quantifies, homogenises. (This does not preclude the possibility of it being given a dramatic structure.) We are invited to travel back in time, the way in which it is usually assumed memory works. For Bergson any attempt on the part of consciousness to go back, to represent a point in the past, is a cutting-out and an immobilisation: a repression of time and duration. How are we to travel back in time? The front cover of this particular pamphlet has an image of a couple in period costume, in an old car, motoring through scenic country (Figure 2). The accompanying images are of past forms of transport, one of the recurring ways in which we are invited to tour time. A going back into the past is signalled by forms of transport, representations of movement.

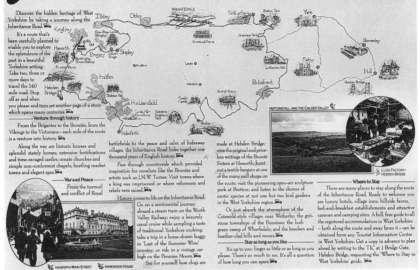

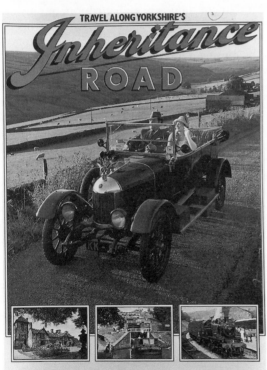

Fig. 1 'Take a journey' (Inheritance Road pamphlet)

Fig. 2 'Inheritance Road'

> Discover the hidden heritage of West Yorkshire by taking a journey
> along the Inheritance Road. It's a route that's been carefully planned to
> enable you to explore the splendours of the past in a beautiful Yorkshire
> setting ('Inheritance Road').

This opening invitation expresses a contradiction that also prevails in
heritage discourse: discovery versus planning. But what is to be discovered
turns out to be a repetition of the same: a return to origins of which the
planned is a representation. On the one hand, we are repeatedly told that 'you
will discover, you will be the first', that 'this is your history to be uncovered';
on the other hand, 'we have carefully planned it for you'. In general terms,
then, what runs through these pamphlets and sites is the idea of unmediated
experience, of the first, the original; history is simply there in all its immediacy
and presence to be (re)lived – the fullness of the past in the present. But a
heremeneutic exercise of uncovering seems to be required: it is hidden. And
this is where the 'we' of planning, knowledge, comes in: we need to tell you
what and how to experience your past. Immediacy is dependent on
mediation. The past persists, it lives, it is there to be discovered. And yet the
claim is frequently made that without 'us' – English Heritage, for example –
history would disappear: 'Without constant care and attention, our historic
inheritance would decay, collapse and be gone forever . . . we make history
come alive' (English Heritage pamphlet). English Heritage brings history to
life (Figure 4) – gives it life – by putting it into discourse.
    Note that in this pamphlet the we/our slides from the we of English
Heritage to the we and our of nation or community. But it is doubtful whether
any attempts at unifying a heterogeneous audience work. The slide into 'our'
is fairly apparent given the heaviness of the 'we' in English Heritage, and the
clear differentiation of we/you. Who exactly is speaking and who is being
addressed is not clear. The 'you' is generally non-specific, beyond, say,
'family'. In popular history discourse the unifying 'our' is more subtle than in
English Heritage, and the audience more specific. There is little talk of
Englishness; it is presumed. (This is a noticeable contrast with national
identity discourses in Australia; it would seem that 'Australians' need to be
constantly told what it is to be Australian.) Heritage is about the maintenance
of English values (white, middle-class); there are no competing histories here.
Popular history might be addressing the working class, but it is still very much
'English': difference is excluded.
    Experience, and associated notions of authenticity, are constant themes in
these pamphlets and promotion of sites. This is related to a distinct shift in
discourse from the stately home version – go and look at how the ruling class
lived – to the idea that this is 'our' history, not just to be looked at but
experienced, relived. The sites are sometimes the same (Fountains Abbey and
Studley Royal, for example). But a whole lot of new sites are opened up as
objects of tourism by this discourse, most noticeably in the North of England
where, with the decline of industry, disused mill buildings have become

museums and frequently 'living museums'. In such museums the tourist is not addressed as tourist, but as someone who lived this past. This is not the tourist experience of passing through, in transition, but rather one of belonging to, having a place. The workers are referred to as 'we' or 'our forefathers'. Picking up on History Workshop history, this is history from below.

Enter the world of 'the way we were' in 1900, and experience the way we lived, worked, played and died ... become a child again and experience the rigours of a strict Victorian education (Wigan Pier Museum).

The Calderdale Industrial Museum in Halifax is a good example of a living museum of 'our history', and includes sections on social history (written text, which is a bit unusual): information about the lives of working people, unions, Luddites, and so forth. The 'living' bit of the museum consists in sounds and smells of mining in a reconstruction of a mine; machinery running; the experience of clocking in and out of the museum. As one pamphlet puts it, 'clock in to experience the sights, sounds and smells of our industrial past'. This museum is located in an old pattern-making factory, and there is one display of machine tools. But would one want to say that this display of machine tools is any more or less authentic than the mine or the written text on the wall? Through these types of combination of displays, museums such as this one rather unsettle the authentic–inauthentic opposition.

Despite the supposed authenticity of the Calderdale Industrial Museum, the elements and approaches in displays are quite disparate; what unites them, weakly, is that in one way or another they relate to Halifax. The top entrance to the museum is in the Piece Hall, and the display which marks the transition from the 'real' of the marketplace to reconstruction of the museum is the pre-industrial era. The Piece Hall is presented as heritage; it is still a market place of sorts, but now a site for selling memorabilia, bric-à-brac, crafts – artefacts unspecifically associated with 'bygone days'. Thus there is little concern with the chronology of historical time, and, as the much used term 'bygone days' suggests, the past to be experienced is non-specific.

A pamphlet called 'Bygone Days' (Figure 3), advertising a number of West Yorkshire attractions, lists the following experiences: 'step back into the days of craftsmanship and innovation'; 'sample some of the delights and traditions of bygone ages'; 'combine a visit to two or three in order to experience the true atmosphere of those bygone days' (quantity clearly counts in this); 'experience those great days of steam'; 'enjoy the unforgettable sight, sound and smell of steam locomotives'; 'step back into the 17th century'; 'clock in to experience . . . .'. And, from an English heritage pamphlet: 'meet a legionary of the first century . . . listen to 17th century music . . . see monastic crafts . . . put on a period dress for a Victorian picnic . . . try pike drill . . . load a cannon'. We are offered 'hands on experience of a life gone by' and 'a flavour of the working lives of our forefathers' (Helmshore Textile Museums).

Fig. 3   'Bygone Days'

Fig. 4   'History alive'

Fig. 5   'Discover the Pleasures'

Experience is presumed to be unmediated and yet it is being mediated in a rather heavy-handed way; the form of address is quite directive: not only what to experience but how to experience. The front cover of an English Heritage pamphlet features more pamphlets including 'how to look at old buildings' and a camera (Figure 5). The directiveness of these pamphlets is hardly surprising given the non-specificity of the pastness to be experienced, the lack of any qualitative distinction. Discursive superimposition of the 'qualitative' simply quantifies – everything becomes interchangeable.

One particular device of mediation is the appeal to TV programs – here is an experience that *can* be relived. People are invited to insert themselves into a site by reference to television or film: 'take a trip in a horse-drawn buggy in "Last of the Summer Wine" country'; 'many items in the museum have been used in famous TV productions such as "Last of the Summer Wine", "In Loving Memory", "Rising Damp" and more recently "Watching"'; 'a superb station featured in the film "The Railway Children" '. The museum or landscape provides a *mise-en-scène* for the fiction of the past that you can be a character in. For example, in the 'Inheritance Road' pamphlet, the landscape provides this: 'explore the splendours of the past in a beautiful Yorkshire setting'. The past to be experienced is quite obviously fiction. Museums that are like film sets such as Bygone Days, Haworth, make no attempt at authenticity. Despite appeals to a desire for the presence of the past, the medium is hardly transparent. The appeal here is not so much the immediacy of the past perhaps, but the 'immediacy' of becoming an actor in what is usually experienced in the privacy of the lounge room, watching television. One can participate in the fiction.

There is considerable variation between and within sites in claims to authenticity. On the continuum preservation–restoration–reconstruction, it could be assumed that the preservation end would make the strongest claims to this, but there is not much talk of preservation; there is rather more of, and more coherence in, reconstruction. Reconstruction of the original is claimed to be the ground of authenticity; the Merseyside Maritime Museum, for example, '. . . includes a reconstruction . . . of an authentic Liverpool street in 1853', the specificity of the date lending weight to the notion of authenticity. The idea of reconstruction of the original clearly brings to light the mediation–immediacy opposition – the presence of the past is dependent on the mediation of reconstruction.

Even when there is talk about preservation, the distinctions between preservation, restoration, and reconstruction are somewhat blurred. In a National Trust video before the entrance to Fountains Abbey and Studley Royal, the narrator, Ian Carmichael, says 'we must preserve this heritage for our children and our grandchildren' (shots of families feeding ducks); meanwhile English Heritage seems to be rebuilding the ruins of the Abbey. The video explains that preservation requires recreation as the 'stone fabric' of the buildings has been 'battered by time'; and 'there's work to be done all year . . . brightening the beauty of bygone centuries' (music, Vivaldi's *The*

Four Seasons, to locate us in the time of the Renaissance, but not this place). History has to be embellished. 'Faithful restoration' is the most frequent means of implying authenticity: 'experience domestic life from the 1840s to the 1950s in the authentically restored 1830s cottages' (The Boat Museum, a living museum in 'England's North West'). (There is an amazing suggestion implicit here that for precisely a century there were no discontinuities in domestic life.) Although preservation, restoration and reconstruction involve different discursive strategies, when any of these is linked with authenticity there is something of a contradiction between the notion that the past is there forever, 'ours to be experienced', and the idea that the past is in danger of disappearing without 'us' to preserve it, and even bring it back to life. This is apparently resolved by the authenticity (accuracy) of representation of the original.

The exhortations to 'explore' and to 'discover' which run through these discourses hint at an originary experience, but the rediscovery requires directions. 'Join with us in some exciting discoveries'; 'we invite you to explore and enjoy the splendours of Yorkshire's monastic past'; 'a fascinating opportunity to discover for yourself the techniques used by monks . . .'; 'discover Bradford's fascinating industrial heritage'; 'rediscover the real age of motoring'; 'discover the pleasures of English Heritage'. Discovery implies that the tourist not only has choice but is the first to set foot on the terrain. Roads and trails make much of this: we are invited to discover, personally, a particular trajectory, albeit as a travelling back (backwards into the future); but, as it turns out, the narrative structure is already in place. The 'Inheritance Road' pamphlet offers the choice of going off the route, but always within the narrative structure of this road – this is a closed text.

The Captain Cook trail ('the heritage trail'; how many of these are there?) emphasises discovery through a condensation of Cook's discoveries and our discovery of the trajectory of his life, mapped out for us on the North Yorkshire landscape. We are invited to identify with Cook; we, too, can travel and discover. But in what sense is this a tour of discovery, if already mapped? The tourist is invited to explore the 'scenery' of the area on a 'Voyage of Discovery'. North Yorkshire is to be discovered as the place of discovery (Figures 6 and 7). It is explicitly said in one pamphlet that Captain Cook is a way of linking places in one area that are scenic and interesting – 'little has changed since the days when Captain Cook himself passed by', of course. Thus Captain Cook figures as a sort of third term to produce an abstraction of the landscape. Again, we are told that we do not have to stick to the given route, the route that we are meant to be discovering for ourselves: 'the route should be regarded as flexible and the visitor should take the opportunity to deviate from the prescribed route'. 'Should' seems rather heavy-handed for what is supposed to be an experience of discovery. The trail 'quite naturally' begins at Cook's origins, the Captain Cook museum which substitutes for 'the cottage', exported to Australia. It must be said, though, that there seem to be an awful lot of cottages that are 'Cook's cottage', and in

Fig. 6 'Captain Cook Country'

Fig. 7 Map of Cook Country

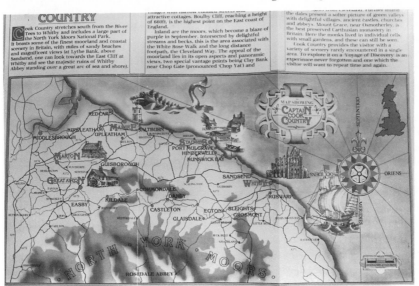

Australia we are told that Cook's cottage is in the gardens in Melbourne. But in Australia Cook is part of a different history, and story of origins. There is, in fact, a 'presence' of this in Whitby: on the headland there is a monument to Cook, and on the monument, a plaque presented by the people of Australia, on the occasion of Australia's first bicentenary – that of Cook's 'discovery' in 1770. As tourist promotion, Whitby celebrated 1988, Australia's second bicentenary. Australia figures quite prominently in the promotion of Whitby as a tourist site. So, if Australia were to designate sites in England as heritage would Whitby be among them?

The Captain Cook industry has recently expanded. In 1990 a three-year Captain Cook Country tourist campaign was launched, with the explorer himself arriving in a hot air balloon. Captain Cook's tours seem to have inspired a certain colonising process on the part of the Captain Cook Tourism Association:

> 'I can go into Brideshead and James Heriott country,' said Shirley Knight, a local courier, using the modern term for the Hambledon Hills and Yorkshire dales.
>
> 'And I can claim them for Captain Cook country too. Because who knows where Captain Cook may not have gone when he lived round here?' (*The Guardian*, 1 August 1990).

The same article reports a guest at the launch as asking: 'Might he have had an affair with any of the Brontës?'

Trails of discovery go through 'country'. The landscape becomes enculturated as, for example, 'Cook country', 'Brontë country', 'Last of the Summer Wine country'. The country paradigm thus includes the fictional; at Whitby, Dracula and the Dracula trail feature along with Cook in such a way that it becomes easy to forget a distinction between fact and fiction. (By association, then, is Dracula part of Australia's heritage?) Similarly, at Haworth, there is a blurring of the distinction between the Brontës' fiction and the Brontës as fiction, and both as real. Thus history is fictionalised, and the country is fictionalised as a setting for stories and characters. Contrary to the moralistic response that this is not real history, might it be that the play with the fact–fiction opposition is disruptive to the notion of real history, hinting at the mythic of all history? Furthermore, despite 'the country' and 'the trail', it cannot necessarily be assumed that different historical figures function discursively in the same way – Cook and the Brontës, for example. For me one of the pleasures of Haworth, Brontë country aside, is the play with fact and fiction: walking the moors, it is possible to identify with both Emily and Heathcliffe. Emily's rather literal translations (Top Withins–Wuthering Heights, to cite the most obvious) invite this. In this landscape, marked by a fiction that tells of passions, perhaps a space is opened up for the transformation of stories (de Certeau 1984; Morris 1988b: 37).

One site after another is spoken of as telling a story: the museum, the trail, the gallery, tell the story: for example, 'this unique museum which tells the story of horses at work'. If, as de Certeau suggests, there is a contradiction between the museum and storytelling, this is apparently resolved by 'living museum', 'our story', 'our living past'. The tourist is invited to do more than just look at from a distance, regard moments of the past filed away, dead, in the museum. There is, none the less, some tension between the functioning of the museum in a delimitation of a field, and what is being appealed to: a past that lives, memory. In texts of travel and storytelling the movement invoked is that of the straight line, which immobilises; we are not talking wandering here. As in Bergson's account, the straight line homogenises, by, for example, reducing everything to heritage (the Inheritance Road, the heritage trail). Or, more precisely, the concept 'heritage' allows the drawing of a straight line. The prevalent sentence construction 'from . . . to . . .', which is a means of linking disparate bits of history, is an aspect of this homogenisation. Sometimes there is a direct connection between this discursive form and the road or trail: 'From the turmoil and conflict of Royal battlefields to the peace and calm of hideaway villages, the Inheritance Road links together one thousand years of history'. The time of history is quantified and spatialised via the road, the sentence. So one wonders what space there is for any retelling, for personal memory.

Pastness is discursively produced through a series of oppositions between the present and the past, which nevertheless fail to be held apart as oppositions. At the most general level this is manifest in the following: the tourist is invited to step back into the past, to relive it, but the form of this reliving is consumption. In Bergson's approach there is no contradiction between these, as any notion of going back is a representation and hence quantification. Properly speaking, the past cannot be relived, even if it 'lives' in the present.

Let me give some examples of the paradoxical in the production of pastness, which serve to highlight the ways in which 'the past' is represented in relation to, in terms of, 'the present'. Roads, and frequently trails, are to be driven: the tourist is invited to travel back in time, in the car, to a time when travel was more leisurely, before the modern car. Many sites promise the experience of former modes of transport: 'go on a sentimental journey aboard a steam train . . . canal cruise . . . horse-drawn buggy . . . vintage car'. The irony in this sentimental return to the leisurely past is that it requires the car: you must engage in the very problem that you are invited to escape. 'The parking problem', and resolution of it through 'ample parking', are common features of heritage sites.

Invitations to repeat, to remember, frequently slide between the memory of the tour and that of the past. For example, with reference to a repetition of Cook's story: 'to explore it on a "voyage of discovery" is an experience never forgotten and one which the visitor will want to repeat time and time again'. And, in the pamphlet 'Bygone Days', you are invited to 'leave the bustle and strain of everyday life behind and step back into the days of craftsmanship and innovation'; a series of sites are described, followed by 'an experience you won't forget', 'didn't we have a lovely time' (Figure 3). Apparently the experience of the past, but also the experience of the visit.

The past is fun. The predominant message is that history is fun, pleasure and entertainment. Indeed the audience is frequently exhorted to have fun. This is not serious history and there is scant reference to education. At Bradford Industrial Museum, a party of schoolchildren and teachers dressed in non-specific period costume, engaging in Victorian discipline, looked as if they were using the excuse of education to get out of the classroom. And yet this particular museum makes no claims to recreating experiences; it preserves industrial heritage, rather than being a living museum, and apart from the ubiquitous mill and tea shops it is not promoted as fun. This school party had turned it into 'living history' and fun; they were performing. There are differences between sites but, generally speaking, history is to be consumed as leisure. The connection between the past and pleasure is made by the invocation of a past that is pleasurable, easy, leisurely.

This past is produced through a series of related oppositions: craft–mass production, quality–quantity, leisure–work. And there are some obvious paradoxes in this: craft and quality are commodified in the commodification of history. This is closely associated with other forms of commodification – mill shops, tea shops, bric-à-brac – which appear in every historical site, selling the same items, with scant reference to the specificity of the site. These are frequently listed as part of what is to be discovered: 'discover its art, craft and antique shops' (the Piece Hall, next to the Calderdale Industrial Museum). The tourist can hunt for bargains in mill shops, have cream teas in Victorian surroundings, and so on. History is a repository of artefacts to be consumed. The hunting for bargains, whose association with the past can be quite tenuous, becomes a metaphor for the consumption of history, the old.

What emerges from this is a close connection between fun and commodification; the experience of fun is located within a culture of commodification. Associated with this is the pleasure of accumulation – the number of sites visited, frequently measured in souvenirs, which are identical apart from the designation of the site. There is no specificity in this culture of tourism. And the pleasure is a comfortable, coded pleasure, which in turn relates to the 'tame' of the past. Not only is the past commodified, but it is also a past that does not disturb. It is without violence or oppression, difference or discontinuity.

Although the 'histories' of these discourses do not neatly correspond to Nietzsche's classifications of modes of history in *Untimely Meditations*, some of his critical descriptions seem very apt: for example, 'everything old and past that enters one's field of vision at all is in the end blandly taken to be equally worthy of reverence' (Nietzsche 1982: 74). One wonders about 'reverence' though, given the emphasis on fun. On the other hand, there is something of the blind rage for collecting, 'raking together everything that has ever existed'. Both Nietzsche and Benjamin were critical of a living in the past, a 'wish to relive an era' (Benjamin 1969: 258). The approaches to history to which they objected are certainly evident in heritage discourses: 'we are all suffering from a consuming fever of history', and 'the oversaturation of an age with history' (Nietzsche 1982: 60, 83). However, it is not a question of being for or against history or the past. Nietzsche and Benjamin were critical of specific uses of history, particularly notions of progress: the nostalgic past projected into the future. (There is certainly evidence of this in English heritage: the return to our glorious past in the future.) As opposed to the backward-looking nature of progress, their concern, like Bergson's, was with a movement forward, a becoming. For Benjamin (1969: 256) temporalised history offered the possibility of redemption: 'the past carries with it a temporal index by which it is referred to redemption'.

Now it would probably be going too far to suggest that there is such a redemptive moment in English heritage, that is, the registering of an experience not yet claimed by economic rationality or fixed by historicism. Indeed, there is something to the common claim that these discourses, far from being merely benign, are reactionary. There is no doubt about their singularity with respect to Englishness, and, thus, their racism; nor about the nostalgia which can be located within the context of both the decline of the empire and Britain's relation to both 'Western' and 'Eastern' Europe. Holding on to a glorious past has been very much on the political agenda. But there is ambiguity, and, as Bergson would have it, these discourses can be thought in terms of multiplicity – thus bringing us back to the multiplicity of memory.

In English heritage we are not only invited to remember, we are told what and how to remember. This process of putting memory into discourse corresponds to Bergson's conscious imaging of the past, and Benjamin's understanding of voluntary memory. For the latter, mechanical reproduction made possible the mass production of such a memory. One of the initial appeals of mechanical reproduction was that it made accessible what had previously been the property of the few. In heritage discourse there is a nostalgia for the authenticity of craft production, the memory of which is itself being mass produced. While memory is being mass produced the notion of memory as individual or personal is constantly appealed to. And it is not only memory associated with sight: sound and smell recur as the essence of the memory we are supposed to have. In short, there is an appeal to affectivity and qualitative difference of the senses. Even a drifting is appealed to: 'allow yourself to drift into an altogether different way of life' (Shibden Hall and Folk Museum, Halifax).

The constant references to former modes of transport and, for example, the sound and smell of trains, clearly touch upon something of the experience of the technology of modern forms of transport: the blocking of the senses in the capsules of travel, and the immobility that characterises movement through space in the aeroplane, car, and modern train (de Certeau 1984: 111). De Certeau (1984: 112) says that the train station is mobility in comparison to the immobility of the rationalised panoptic cell of the train. So, while the talk of former modes of travel and the reconstruction of railway stations might be read as nostalgia, it might be that there is simultaneously another moment in this: not a nostalgic desire but a positive desire – to feel, touch, smell, move. (The Keighley and Worth Valley Railway is exclusively used for leisure and tourism, but has become part of local life, a site of ritualistic events. Might this be living history?) 'Living history' can be thought about in terms of the different ways in which the past lives. Again, in discourse there is a going back, an appeal to the reliving of a past, and hence an operation that fixes. But it could be that this has the effect of deferral: if the referent of the past moment eludes, what of the possibility of a movement induced by the evocation of other memories? Perhaps what people 'look for' when on voyages of discovery is the spark of chance that sears, the mark of time. This would be a past in a 'present' that lives, moves.

It has been suggested that these texts of travel and memory follow a straight line, immobilise. However, de Certeau's (1984: 115) emphatic claim that 'Every story is a travel story – a spatial practice' invites us to think of at least the possibility of a double moment in these texts. A spatial practice is a reading which is a transformation. As opposed to the order of the location of elements in 'place' or a written text, spatial practice temporalises, mobilises elements (de Certeau 1984: 117). Specifically on the story and narrative, de Certeau (1984: 129) claims that, unlike the map, the boundary setting of such texts puts emphasis on 'movements in space', limits are marked out, but they are 'transportable'. There is no stability in the stopping place.

Texts of English heritage are certainly 'about' travel and stories, and in some ways appeal to storytelling and movement. On the other hand, the boundary setting and instructions on how to read a site, or travel, are overbearing. But then who is to say what is made of these texts in practices of travel-story, and whether people follow the route or wander? (See Morris 1988b: 36–44.) In 'the shuttle' between texts that place, and between these and personal trajectories, might not spatial stories be written and the memorable be dispersed? The museum, the trail, the pamphlet are structured spaces, texts (the trail being perhaps more open than the museum or the pamphlet); but it is possible that the constructed order of these is 'punched and torn open' by the extra and other – the ways of the unconscious. And in a strange way they almost invite it.

Sense of place: Bondi

Bondi is a site of national identity: Australia is the beach, and this is *the* beach. Or is it? Here I will look at how Bondi is produced as a national symbol, and the popular myths and images that figure so frequently in the constitution of Bondi as *the* beach. Let me say that it is a mistake to assume that Bondi works as such a symbol, that there is anything unifying about it or that attachments to it are attachments to an abstract unity, the nation. For example, it is a contested site; in public discourse there are disputes over the real Bondi, the authentic, and who it belongs to and who belongs to it. But if competing claims on Bondi invoke a national symbol, equating Bondi with Australia, they do so strategically; and, far from having unifying effects, they bring differences and different Bondis to light. My contention is that there is no one Bondi: as an identity, it comes undone. Furthermore, it will be argued that there is something in the experience of this beach that escapes discursive attempts to fix it. This argument turns on the question of place, for, unlike other symbols of Australian national identity, Bondi is constituted as a place. 'Place', however, can mean differently, and a distinction will be drawn between a pinning down of place in representation, and a way of being in place that is meaning embodied in movement, in deferral. Disputes are about place. The desire for identity (not necessarily national) and presence is one side of this, with contestations of the meaning of Bondi. But place also makes Bondi, as a presence, impossible.

This analysis is, then, a dissociation of 'place', of the different ways of meaning of place, and the tension between these. On the one hand, a nostalgic desire for origins is apparent in discourses around Bondi, and this is associated with the production of Bondi as a specular site. Nostalgia is particularly evident in processes of commodification and the marketing of Bondi as a place, which consists principally in the constitution of Bondi as the object of the tourist gaze. On the other hand, I want to suggest that there is a way of 'being in' that refuses an objectifying gaze, and inscribes a different desire. This desire is not primarily specular, but relates to touch. And, in the affectivity of involuntary memory, as opposed to the voluntary memory of nostalgic discourse, it is perhaps possible to discern what Benjamin referred to as a redemptive moment that is disruptive to the world of commodification.

The blurb placed next to the 1930s travel poster in the *Bondi* book (Figure 8) says:

> Bondi has always reflected what's happening in Australia at large. Somehow it combines everything that is Australian in one small area. It has all the elements of the outdoors life combined with what is at heart a very suburban environment. It sounds like it should be a contradiction, but it isn't (Drew *et al.* 1984: 27)

This book, sold by newsagents, is a collection of myths, public memories, anecdotes, experiential accounts and images. It contains the same oft-repeated stories found in a range of different sources and frequently reproduced in feature articles in the popular press; it is characteristic of the production of Bondi. The travel advertisement, which also appears in different contexts, is an image of Australia with Bondi written across the bottom of it: Bondi stands for Australia. This image is paradigmatic of the Bondi photo/image, signifying the *combination* 'everything that is Australian'. Such images present an imaginary resolution to contradictory elements

Fig. 8 P. Trompf (artist), travel poster

in Australian national identity, or the paradox of defining ourselves on the side of nature from the position of the urban. What is generally regarded as an opposition becomes a combination or continuum in the case of Bondi.

So how does the nature–culture opposition operate in discourses of national identity, and how does Bondi figure in these? In some ways nature substitutes for a past. (There might be something liberating about the lack of past to be constituted as Australian heritage, but I do not want to press this point.) Constructing a mythical national history, or locating origins, is highly problematic: what past is to be drawn on for an imagined 'immemorial past' of nation (Anderson 1983: 14–16)? With the rejection of Britain we turn to nature for what makes us distinctive. (Note that the 'we' here is 'Australia'.) Travel brochures tell us that Australia is 'the oldest continent of all', the primordial – Aborigines and animals, a living museum. It is a timeless land (or land of dream-time, dream-time tours), which persists irrespective of culture or civilisation. The more enlightened version of this incorporation of Aboriginal culture is 'the oldest continuous civilisation on earth', 'continuous' being a means of defining this civilisation on the nature side of the opposition. 'We' are ephemeral. Our transcendence is in nature. The contradictions involved in white Australia's national identity and particularly constructions of the bush, landscape, desert, centre, have been pointed out by many commentators (Hamilton 1984); they constitute part of the problem, the need to search for an identity.

A highly urbanised society with a population concentrated on the eastern seaboard looks inwards, for the 'real us'. Our relation to nature as other is one of ambivalence: desire structured around fear. The landscape is beautiful but threatening. The centre is empty – the dead red (dreaded) centre. This is a strange emptiness, filled as it is with otherness. Stories tell us that it is a harsh uncaring nature that should remain untouched, we do not belong: explorers came to terrible ends; tourists go on shooting sprees, or get eaten by crocodiles; people disappear in the bush (the 'Picnic at Hanging Rock' myth); dingoes, mothers and babies, and so on. The relation to the landscape can be understood as a relation to the mother/other as disturbing. Manning Clark, for example, speaks of the 'emptiness', the 'nothingness', the 'void', 'the one thing we have in common is the land of Australia – our common mother as it were' (*Good Weekend*, 1 August 1987); in short, the feminine as lack.

As a symbol of national identity Bondi also aligns on the side of nature, but differently. Here, nature is to be cultivated and engaged with rather than sanctified, visited and left. There is no ambivalence about the beach; it is an everyday affair, an other that can be incorporated. We can be natural at the beach, put ourselves in the place of nature. And this is a familiar place: the uncanny of the maternal body is displaced onto the centre, a centre which speaks of our lack of centre. Bondi is a site of repeated return – return visits, and the waves repeating themselves over and over. And it is lived in. If familiar, there is, none the less, something of the primordial in the nature of Bondi: an endless possibility of a new origins with each return to the place and, particularly, the sea – the source of life. There is, then, a tension between the view that nature can be incorporated here, and an attraction to nature as an other that defies incorporation. And in this resides the possibility of refiguring a relation to nature as other in a positive structure of desire.

What differentiates Bondi, makes it the profane to the sacred of the centre, is the combination of the urban with nature; this is how it is produced as place. (Bondi is located in the most densely populated area of the largest Australian city.)

> Syringes in the sand, contraceptives in the surf and, new bane of metal detectors, spent cartridges littered like droppings, junkies in the toilet, Bondi is undeniably urban. But the sea is the sea, and Bondi shines like a pearl from its sometimes seedy shell. Being a city beach is its charm, what makes it so hard to give up (Steward 1984: 28).

The urban produces attachments, 'an addiction' to a site of nature. The paradigmatic Bondi image aims to invoke this through a combination of nature and culture which aspires to resolve the oppositional relation between these elements.

Images of Bondi are ubiquitous, and there are striking structural similarities among the images that are recycled in publications and in public spaces – the Council Chambers, the Pavilion, restaurants and cafés – and on walls in private spaces. What predominates, and is invariably included in selections of Bondi photographs, is 'the old photograph'. Anecdotally, the 1870s photograph of Bondi as uncontaminated nature produces a response of 'look how it was and how quickly it changed'. This is invited by the usual positioning of this image in a 'historical' series that represents a narrative from nature to culture. The photograph that follows this one is from 1880s, with people on the beach: the same 'nature', and people fully clothed – the elements still remain distinct. Then the 1920s, cars and buildings, the original trees gone, crowds on the beach in 'beachwear', and an urban public life established at the beach: culture and nature combined (Figures 9–12). I will come back to the question of how these images (particularly the quite numerous images from the 1920s and 1930s) are used to promote Bondi as a fashionable place, but here I want to note the comfortable pleasure of them, and the smoothness of the nature–culture combination: here we have everything.

It is deceptive, however. There is little agreement about what constitutes the culture or nature of Bondi, or their respective valuations. On the one hand, culture controls and mediates nature which is potentially out of control. On the other, culture damages the beauty of nature: undesirable elements of culture make Bondi unlovely. There are natural dangers at the beach, but controlling these is positively valued. Surf and shark disasters are prominent in Bondi mythology, the struggle with nature, and the overcoming. As the story goes, sharks have been beaten (*Daily Telegraph*, 14 January, 1950; *National Times*, 6–12 April, 1980) and 'fear of the surf was lost between 1930 and the 1950s' (*Follow Me*, August 1984). Lifesavers, they who do battle with the waves, are referred to as national heroes. The mythic event in this history is Black Sunday in 1938, when 'freak' waves dragged hundreds of people out to sea. This is spoken about in terms of 'people fighting for their lives', 'fear maddened surfers' (*The Sun*, 3 August, 1964; *Mirror*, 8 March, 1972), 'chaos', 'deaths', 'a battlefield', 'lives saved', 'the greatest labour of love in the world' (Drew *et al.* 1984: 45, 53; White 1981: 155). Recent newspaper reports have claimed that it is tourists who have to be saved now – it is not their place, they go out and do not return. The struggle with the surf continues, but the common claim today is that sewage has replaced sharks as the primary danger, or disaster, in the sea. If culture sets limits on the disorder of nature it also brings its own disorder. 'You brave more than the waves at beautiful Bondi . . . !', 'you run the risk of being offended by thieves, perverts, drink and drug users, hoodlums – and the occasional indecent costume' (*The Sun*, 14 February, 1975). In some discourses, then, the only order is the natural order.

Sewage has come to predominate in all talk about Bondi: bad nature is contaminating good beach culture. A whole way of life – on the beach in summer (Australians prefer to forget winter) – is supposedly under threat. Over the last couple of years there has been a public outcry over sewage at all beaches, with the focus on Bondi as *the* beach. Hardly a day goes by without a media report; there has been a major review of public service departments and policy; and protests, including a huge rock concert at Bondi on Good Friday, 1989. A front-page headline in September 1989 ran '$4.5bn plan to fix Sydney sewers' (*Sydney Morning Herald*, 11 September, 1989). A government that is making massive cuts in all areas, except the police, proudly announces big spending on sewers. The sewage issue provides the opportunity for more storytelling around Bondi. The sewers, particularly the tunnels under the sea, hold a certain fascination. Sewage brings to the surface doubts about our origins, about the source of contamination. (The latter is hinted at in the headline: 'A bung in every bottom, and our sewage crisis is solved at last' (*Sydney Morning Herald*, 22 November, 1989).) How, now, can one emerge from the sea anew?

'Bondi the beautiful' is a frequently reproduced 1920s postcard. 'Bondi the unbeautiful', 'But Bondi you are no beauty' (*Daily Mirror*, 25 November, 1968) are references to this postcard. Bondi is described as 'seedy', 'tatty', 'vulgar', 'tawdry', 'bad taste', 'shabby', 'run-down'. The unbeautiful ranges across and condenses, architecture, condoms, fish-and-chips wrappers, pollution and undesirable people. In some discourses there is a reversal of valuation on the unlovely: 'people don't understand the aesthetics of sleaze. The sleaze of Bondi is beautiful' (*Mode Magazine*, July 1985). In current disputes about what Bondi should be, with reference to the authentic, this question of aesthetics revolves particularly around architecture (Sanders 1982).

Whatever the classification of nature, there is something in Bondi's being nature that makes it unchangeable: 'the beach remains unchanged' (*The*

Fig. 9   Bondi, 1870s

Fig. 10   Bondi, 1880s

Fig. 11   Bondi, 1920s

Fig. 12   Bondi, 1931

Weekend Australian, 14–15 March, 1987), 'despite what man has done to it, the beach remains inviolate' (Drew *et al.* 1984: 10), 'polluted, despoiled . . . untarnished' (*National Times*, 30 March–5 April, 1980), 'Bondi is a beautiful jewel in an ugly setting' (*Daily Mirror*, 25 November, 1968). Definitions of Bondi slide: the 'real' Bondi is 'the beach', but there are also 'beach', 'sea', 'sand', 'rocks' which have been despoiled. Despite attempts at fixing nature to provide a clear and certain reference point for the valuation of culture, its meaning shifts. Paradoxically, nature is both affected by culture and outside culture.

Nature also functions in productions of the egalitarian myth in relation to Bondi.

> Bondi symbolises Australia. The long golden sweep of Bondi Beach is one of the most famous in the world. Thousands of people flock there in summer, united in the democracy of sun and sea worship. For there's no class distinction at Bondi. Even Prince Charles swims there (Drew *et al.* 1984: back cover).

Nature levels us (we can be counted), the sea is an equaliser. John Pilger, on the BBC (Radio 4, October 1989), claimed that our democracy is not to be located in the founding fathers but in taking our clothes off on Bondi. 'There's no class distinction at Bondi' shifts the basis of egalitarianism from 'we all work' to 'we all have the same fun' (which rather contradicts the dominant discourse on egalitarianism; although, as we shall see, 'fun' is crucial to the commodification of Bondi). At Bondi freedom and democracy are not only linked with pleasure, but a pleasure that is not a reward for or complement to work. 'The sea is free':

> Why toil to get rich to do exactly the same thing that you are doing now, not rich? Why get all hot and bothered over More Production when the thing you want is produced by the Pacific cost free? It is a philosophy that drives the American efficiency expert into a mental home (Drew *et al.* 1984: 39).

Egalitarianism is given by the sea, the sun, a natural democracy, but also a hedonistic democracy. On the one hand, there is a disruption to the opposition between work and play, which is exemplified by the quest for the perfect wave or the perfect body pursued with all the purposiveness of the work ethic. On the other hand, the discourse of equality in pleasure is a denial of differences and different experiences of Bondi. For example, what is frequently represented as the uniqueness of Bondi is the heterogeneity, the diversity of cultures, classes, sexualities, ages: 'a microcosm of a nation'. Everyone is happy here together, social harmony is possible. Discourses such as this aim to incorporate otherness and difference to the same.

There is something puzzling about the nature–culture opposition that is highlighted in discourses of national identity in Australia, where identity is defined in relation to nature. In terms of what has been said previously about identity and binary oppositions, we might expect this opposition to be written as culture–nature, with a negation of nature (the feminine), in a return to culture. But of course it is not; there is an ambiguity about this particular opposition, with nature coming first, which is connected with temporal assumptions: nature comes before culture. And in these particular discourses nature is not simply defined negatively in relation to culture: 'that is not me', but rather there is an identification with nature.

The relation to nature is central to stories of origins. And origins are a constant theme in Bondi discourses: Bondi as origin ('the birthplace of our national image', *Daily Mirror*, 6 February, 1981; 'the birthplace of organised life-saving', *Sun*, 3 August, 1964); the origins of Bondi; and personal origins. Stories of origins come of a desire for presence and repetition of the same; they figure in representations of Bondi that would fix it as a national symbol or place – the real, the authentic. But each retelling or re-enactment of a story is, in a sense, a transformation. I want to suggest the possibility of a rewriting of origins, in connection with a different way of meaning of place.

Bondi (Drew *et al.* 1984: 28) quotes a surfer from the 1920s on the myth of the origin of surfing:

> Yes it was about fifty years ago on a bright summer's day that a party of we boys stood on the Bondi beach, watching the blacks, who were camped at Ben Buckler, enjoying the ocean waves, with their wives and children . . . And how we made them laugh when we would join in a corroboree with them. Said one of the boys, 'If the sharks don't touch them what about us?' So you may say that was the start of surfing at Bondi Beach.

The original surfing at Bondi is repeated with each re-entry into the water, facing the dangers of sharks or their substitutes. Unlike the myths of the bush which tell of the possibility of disappearance, no return from somewhere we do not belong, this is a successful pioneering story: we can return from the sea alive, we do belong.

The repeated story of the first swimming at Bondi could be located within a general mythology of the sea as origins, the source of life: before land there was sea; from the sea we come and to the sea we will return; and myths that involve being eaten by a whale or shark and returning alive. We can read *Moby Dick* in Hegelian terms as the life-and-death struggle with an other who is both feared and revered. Ahab is driven by this desire in relation to one whale: who will eat whom? In his extraordinary, and quite sensuous descriptions of whales, Melville suggests not only that this is an other deserving of recognition, but also that in its unknowable otherness it perhaps surpasses humans. Barnes' *A History of the World in 10½ Chapters* retells stories of the sea and origins, starting with Noah's ark. Why is it, Barnes (1989: 178) asks, that the story of Jonah and the whale still has such a grip on us? What we remember of the story is the whale, not the allegorical point (which, incidentally, is confirmed by Melville's (1967 [1851]: 304–8) retelling of the story in *Moby Dick*). Reminiscent of Freud's account of the uncanny, Barnes (1989: 178) makes reference to the fear of live burial, returning to the womb:

> Like Jonah, we are all storm-tossed by the seas of life, undergo apparent death and certain burial, but then attain a blinding resurrection as the car-ferry doors swing open and we are delivered back into the light and into a recognition of God's love. Is this why the myth swims through our memory?

He tells of stories of repetitions of Jonah's experience, saying that he believes these myths: they are real.

> For the point is this: not that myth refers us back to some original event which has been fancifully transcribed as it passed through the collective memory; but that it refers us forward to something that will happen, that must happen. Myth will become reality, however sceptical we might be (Barnes 1989: 181).

This is the point that I have made about myths and stories (Oedipus and Hegel's master–slave story, for example): they are always at work; the reliving and retelling are not copies of an original. Re-enactments are not a going back: myths refer us forward.

To return to Bondi: the 'start of surfing' points to the figuring of Aborigines, constituted as part of nature, in stories of origins. In that story 'we' learn from nature how to mediate nature or 'they' mediate it for us: they are not harmed by sharks, we will not be harmed. There is a recurring fantasy of 'going native', a repetition of origins with reference to Aborigines. We put ourselves in the place of the other, appropriate it: 'in the sand where tribes of Aborigines hunted ducks 200 years ago' (McGregor 1984: 9). Thus Aboriginal history is made to coincide with white history. 'Going native', of course, relates to the constant theme of nakedness in Bondi mythology; they went naked, so will we – a continuity of past and present imagined from the present. And, indeed, it is our fantasies that assign Aborigines to nature. There is some mystique about the naming of Bondi and the origin of Bondi as an Aboriginal word, which provides the opportunity for endless speculation about the real source (Drew *et al.* 1984: 10; *Daily Mirror*, 8 March, 1972; *Telegraph*, 14 January, 1950; *National Times*, 30 March–5 April, 1980). Often in the same context 'the rock' at Ben Buckler is referred to as something mysterious and primordial – how did it get there? Was it thrown up from the sea in a storm? Did it fall from the sky? In a reference to the 1920s postcard 'The Playground of the Pacific', a headline went 'Bondi was once playground for Aboriginals' (*Daily Mirror*, 8 March, 1972). Thus Bondi is produced as a site of hedonism and pleasure via a mythic past of hedonistic, fun-loving, fearless Aborigines. (In the surfing story above, note a similar means of producing Bondi as the family beach.)

The origins of surfing story usually implies that Bondi is the origin of surfing, certainly the home of surfing now. In all popular publications it is claimed that Bondi is the origin of surf lifesaving and had the first lifesaving club in the world in 1906 – a claim which is disputed by nearby Brontë beach. Bondi also claims to be the Australian, if not the world, original of sunbathing, and the undressed body. There is a recycled history of nakedness, the flouting of swimwear regulations and prohibitions against daylight swimming: 'pioneers who broke the ice' (*Sun*, 11 October, 1958), 'the frontier of the body controversy' (*Follow Me*, August 1984). Pioneering at Bondi involves going into the sea and/or a state of undress.

As the body is central to productions of Bondi, I want to turn now to the body and Bondi as a way into thinking about other ways of meaning of place and a rewriting of origins. Bondi is supposedly the place where we can find ourselves, and this finding of self comes of being nearly naked, connected with sand and sea. Experiential accounts make frequent reference to being enveloped in the 'crescent of sand', 'merging', as in this extract from Michael Blakemore's film, *A Personal History of the Australian Surf* (Drew *et al.* 1984: 20):

> Digging in it, lying in it, cheek against it, the length of one's shivering body warmed by it. What is it about an ocean beach that so marvellously pacifies a child's discontents? . . . kids don't need to be told what to do on the beach. They know it already.

'They know it already' does bring to mind a place we know with certainty we have been before – an origin to which we will return (Freud 1985c: 368). Talk of merging and so on would seem to be appealing to identifications of the imaginary: a self that is unified in a relation of immediacy with nature. The pleasure of many Bondi photographs derives from the invocation of immediate sensuousness, immersion in sea or sand. This is so of the front-page photograph of the *Bondi* book (Figure 13), and Max Dupain's famous photograph, 'Sunbaker' (Figure 14). Dutton (1985: 140) has claimed that this is 'the archetypal image of the Australian at the beach – flat on his or her belly, sleeping, or at least dozing, shining with suntan oil, sliding into oblivion'.

The relation of immediacy of the body with 'nature' need not, however, be thought of in terms of a desire for either nature as presence, or self-presence. The desire to put one's feet or body in the sand, to be in the water, can be understood as meaning embodied – feel, touch, fluid – and possibly not speakable. If visual images invoke such a desire they are not enough. Perhaps they work precisely by demanding more: a desire related to senses other than sight. (It is myths and images of 'nature' rather than 'nation' that have this effect: mobility as opposed to immobility (see Morris 1988b:37).) In this regard there is a deferral of the referent, and something of a giving of the prerogative to the other as opposed to the appropriation of nature as other in a return to self. This is a desire to lose self in a blurring of boundaries between the body and sea, sand ('the curve' of the beach), and other bodies in the mass

Fig. 13 O. Strewe (photographer), front cover, *Bondi*

Fig. 14 M. Dupain (photographer), 'Sunbaker', 1937

of people: a bodily attachment. The 'beyond' is perhaps not that of another place (beyond the north headland; the aeroplanes that fly in and out over Bondi), but the elsewhere of this place, here and now. The apparent familiarity of Bondi somehow makes it all the more elusive.

Taking inspiration from Calvino's 'Blood, Sea' in *t Zero*, I want to propose a play with origins. Implicitly a critique of Freud's account of a return to origins in death, a stasis, and the association of the maternal body with death, 'Blood, Sea' is a recollection of a primordial experience, when life had not yet emerged from the sea and the human body was bathed by 'the primordial wave', which is not the false return to origins in death (Calvino 1976: 39). As with all Calvino's writing, this is about different ways of meaning and writing. A false return to origins inscribes a desire for meaning, it is static, without motion, a repetition of the same. This desire for meaning superimposes on the primordial, 'our free and real swimming' (Calvino 1976: 46). The recollection is taking place in the course of a car journey. While the sea is movement, inside and outside the body, the movement of the car and that of the journey are false movements. The line of cars is motionless, the car moves as if it were still, there is only a repetition of the same; road signs, white stripes; and passing cars is like a passing of fixed, immobile objects (Calvino 1976: 44). This is the superimposition of representation. When we lived in the sea there were colours, our surface was in contact with, touched, different substances; we undulated with no sense of direction, 'drawn by an obscure current' (Calvino 1976: 41). If now we are swum, then we were swum in a different way: 'without any intervention of my will', a current 'enfolded me and carried me this way and that, a gentle and soft fluid', and a lightness. There were no walls, no fixed boundaries, a fluidity of movement between the outside and the inside (Calvino 1976: 41). Now the outside is dry, everything is interchangeable, without qualitative distinction; and meaning is sought by a false return, the 'silliness' of 'risk of blood' – speeding and overtaking cars. Which is neither sea nor blood (Calvino 1976: 46). Thus origins are rewritten in terms of an embodiment of meaning, nearness and metonymy: a fixing of meaning is impossible with fluidity. This is not about consciousness, but the body drifting, writing itself. So, might there be a way of being in the beach – a drifting of the body, qualitative differences of the senses, involuntary memory – which refuses the quantification of commodification, and the superimposition of representations of Bondi? And is there something of a desire for the primordial in our relation to nature as other: a positive desire for the absolutely other?

Bondi is differentiated from other beaches by the combination of the urban and nature; this is not a deserted beach, it is crowded. (The summer Bondi is 'Bondi', which would be disputed by 'locals'.) The body is not a solitary body but one among a diversity of bodies in an urban crowd. (Newspaper reports always give numbers in describing the Bondi crowd, thus, through quantification, repressing or discounting heterogeneity.) This is not a crowd characterised by speed and manic behaviour; and, if there are elements of purposiveness they are mixed with a wandering. An exception to this is the annual city to surf run – mad purposiveness that has an end in mass drunkenness. On the other hand, the crowd of the festival of winds in September 1989 was one that invited the pleasure of drifting. There is, of course, a differentiation of activities marked, for example, by Campbell Parade, the lawn, the Pavilion, the promenade, the beach. (On the festival of winds day there was a good deal of crossing of boundaries going on, the usual points of differentiation did not seem to be operative.) The crowd is differentiated by codes of activity in different spaces. On the beach bodies are lined up against bodies; on some days there is hardly any walking space. 'Only on the beach are so many so close with so little on' (Stewart 1984: 48). It is this Bondi, particularly the south end of the beach, that is regarded as a site of voyeurism – go to Bondi to look at, look at looking at, be looked at; but this is not necessarily the threatening gaze.

Bondi is also a place where people eat and drink, to such an extent that it is frequently commented on, certainly by people not familiar with it. Campbell Parade is the focus of these activities. Clearly this has a significance in terms of plans to develop the tourist industry, to which I will return in a moment. But, there is another side to it. Eating and drinking can also be understood as an extension of the sensuality and physicality of the place, and the beach. Rules about the sequence or combination of elements, for example, lying in the sun, swimming, and eating and drinking, seem to be flexible. Even in terms of the dress system, for all the talk about undress, there is considerable variation on the beach, and someone walking on the beach 'fully clothed' may risk passing unnoticed, unless perhaps wearing shoes. One gets the impression that people follow their own particular trajectory, even if it is ritualistic. So, there are recognisable codes, but varied particularity in the combination of codes, practices of this place. And in this wandering who is to say what is nature and what culture?

I have found another Calvino story suggestive for thinking about the connections between eating and being in a place. One of the last books he wrote was a series of short stories, each on a different sense. One of these, 'Under the Jaguar Sun', is about taste: a couple of lovers are travelling in Mexico in search of the perfect meal of red chillies; making love is deferred. The only point of travel in these days when anything visible can be seen on television is to smell, and eat of another culture; indeed eat, incorporate the culture: 'making it pass between the lips and down the esophagus' (Calvino 1988: 12). (It is in this story that the tour of the site of rituals of human sacrifice and cannibalism is to be found.) However tourist discourse operates, this suggests a desire in tourism that is not about sight, but relates to other senses. Whether this is a desire for incorporation, or a desire to be incorporated by, is an open question. But the combination of eating and being in the sea at Bondi perhaps points to a sensual experience that escapes tourist discourse.

There is a history of attempts to turn Bondi into a proper tourist site, to commodify pleasure, leisure. But turning this symbol of national identity into a commodity has met with considerable opposition, and it has come from those speaking from a position of 'living in', claiming to represent that position. These disputes are about attachments, but not to nation as much as to place. The tourist industry and governments want to market Bondi as a place; there are other claims on it. To put a place on the market is to erase qualitative distinction and memory. Whatever the specific terms of disputes may have been, they can perhaps be understood along these lines.

Since the 1920s there have been plans to develop Bondi as 'a great tourist attraction' and 'struggles' (incorporated as part of a history of struggle) over such developments. Without going into details, I will draw out some of the key features of the most recent of these, which took place in 1986–7, but which could not be regarded as the end of the story. In that instance various campaign groups speaking on behalf of 'the locals' won: a plan for 'international tourist facilities' was dropped, and the pro-development local government lost the 1987 elections. The major competing discourses in this dispute were: 'Bondi is a national symbol because it is recognised overseas; hence it must be developed as a tourist site in order to remain such a symbol' and 'A national symbol cannot be commercialised, it belongs to us: nationalism is above commerce'. Thus nation is appealed to in order to produce different Bondis.

In a proposal put up by a developer to 'revitalise' the Pavilion, it was claimed that Bondi was now 'a poor reflection of our national identity', that it required restoration.[3] The developer, Ian Hayson (Merlin International), was offering to do this restoration with the development of international tourist facilities – boutiques, restaurants, cafés, beachwear shops. Strategically linking capitalism and the work ethic with pleasure, he claimed that incentives for fun were needed. People need amusements, swimming is not enough: 'the sun and the sea will be complemented by outstanding tourist facilities'. Nature is not sufficient; tourists cannot 'experience' this as national identity, but with the 'rebirth' of the Pavilion they 'will take home a strong and positive memory of beautiful Bondi'. Thus he was going to be the source of a new origins, rebirthing the Pavilion and, by extension, national identity. It seems that a natural site of national identity has to be produced as memorable. Here again is the paradox: the mass production of memory (a voluntary memory) and the notion of experience as personal.

Hayson was offering to 'create' 'the perfect leisure, pleasure and retail mix' which 'is a reflection of our national character'. However, his Bondi was not envisaged as a no-place international consumption space (unlike Darling Harbour, in which he was also involved); Bondi-ness was to be combined with the international tourist code. What was to be marketed was a sense of place: 'Bondi festivals', 'Bondi's history', 'Bondi locals' were all to be included in the entertainment package. The commodification of the locals as objects of the tourist gaze is not peculiar to this developer; it is central to all plans for developing the tourist industry at Bondi. And it produces some interesting contradictions: what is frequently regarded as a blatant display of refusal of the work ethic – hedonism, doing nothing, surfing, lying on the beach – becomes an attractive proposition in selling Bondi as a place.

Opposition to the plan came from those claiming to belong to Bondi, to live in 'the local community'. (Despite this unity there were considerable disagreements, in public, among 'locals'.) Their argument was that as a site of national identity Bondi cannot belong to private commercial interests, it belongs to Australia. The local community is Bondi, Bondi is Australia, it belongs to us. There is a rather obvious slide in the 'we' of Bondi to the 'we' of Australia in this. 'Bondi doesn't belong to the Markhams or Hayson, but to Sydney and Australia.'[4] And 'if the principle is carried through there's no reason why at some stage we won't see toll gates on Bondi Beach' (*Eastern Herald*, 30 July, 1987). (There are, in fact, toll gates for those who drive to the beach.) No one can own nature, no one can own Bondi; here, what is naturally Bondi includes the Pavilion.

Hayson's response to this opposition was: 'Bondi belongs to Sydney, but it also belongs to the world' (an international development company). He made a bid to incorporate the 'belonging to' position: 'If a tourist facility appeals to the locals it is more likely to attract tourists. When you're overseas you immediately say "where do the locals go?"' (*Eastern Herald*, 25 June, 1987). Thus a sense of place was to be constructed, not for those who live there, but for those who come to see, to consume.

One of the effects of tourist discourse such as this is to detach people from place; and it could be claimed more generally that this is an effect of attempts to put attachment into discourse, representation: the production of voluntary memory that disembodies and immobilises. Some objections to making Bondi a specular site can be understood in this context: first, as a response to attempts by governments and industry to constitute locals as an object of the gaze; and second, the place as something to be looked at. In connection with the latter, disputes have focused on Campbell Parade. With one exception, campaigns against high-rise, 'shadows on the beach, Surfers' Paradise' culture, have been successful. I take this to be about the beach as a place to be in. The high-rise conditions of looking would erase the possibility of 'being in' the sun. At Surfers' the beach is overshadowed by high-rise; it is not the focal point of activities. But it is not just the transformation of the beach that is at issue: there are disputes over Campbell Parade itself, particularly the basis of valuation of the architecture. Again appeals are made to the authentic: 'Bondi has always been seedy, and hence should remain so' or 'Bondi was once a fashionable destination, and hence should be restored'. Locals want it to remain as it is on the grounds of personal attachment. There have been numerous competing schemes for preservation, restoration, reconstruction, redevelopment, which range from colour co-ordination and façadism to razing to the ground. If what is currently there is deemed to have no intrinsic value this constitutes a basis for pulling down and producing a new origins (something that happens a lot in Sydney). However, what seems to have greatest currency at the moment, the past designated as the original, is 'the fashionable 1920s and 1930s'. There is a nostalgic return, in government and tourist discourse, to an urban, public life, as evoked in the 'old' photographs and advertising images. These images are pleasurable, they touch on what is currently fashionable; plenty of 'the locals' would not disagree, particularly those who have been vocal in opposition to development (referred to in the press as artists, filmmakers, trendies; the locals of the Bondi icebergs or diggers – the older Australian working class – would presumably have different priorities).

In discourses of tourism the authentic is not nature but the cosmopolitan; the fashionable is, of course, what can be commodified. In a recognition of the popularity of the art deco architecture, and its commercial potential, the buildings remain standing; and painting of yellow and blue seems to have begun. Sometimes only the façade remains. A government planning and environment report emphasised that what counted in preservation was the look from the front. One prominent building that housed a coffee shop that was a focal point for locals has been completely gutted; only the outside wall stands, rather precariously. It is to be filled with real estate agents, beachwear shops and new restaurants. A trivial example perhaps, but not to those for whom the gelateria was an everyday place. To preserve the look of buildings is not the point from this perspective, it is what practices a place makes possible, or closes off. The recent local government restoration of the Pavilion, nicely blue and yellow (mirroring 'nature'), is another, less commercial, case. Somehow with the arrangement of seats and paving around it, the walk has become more directed, encroaching upon the space of the stroll. The ridiculous 'landscaping' at the south end, where there had been a much used playground (a different group of users from that of the gelateria, as indeed the gelato bar is used by different 'locals' again), was completely avoided for months, and is now only minimally inhabited, even on crowded days. Its emptiness, along with that of various tourist ventures on Campbell Parade, stand as examples of the tension between the production of a place to look at and a place to be in.

Haunted places are the only ones people can live in – and this inverts the schema of the *Panopticon* (de Certeau 1984: 108).

In this analysis I have been concerned to dissociate place in terms of different ways of meaning, identifying, on the one hand, attempts to fix or delimit Bondi as a place, which are particularly associated with commodification and tourist discourse, and, on the other, a being-there, a bodily attachment which is transformation of place. Even in the quoted retelling of tales, always in the form of a personal story about a Bondi myth ('how I remember it' from Bondi 'originals'), there is a hint of the haunted. In this regard de Certeau's comments, above, on the ways in which personal memories tie us to places seem pertinent. There is a living in a place that refuses the objectifying gaze; and what cannot be seen cannot be spoken either: 'This is a sort of knowledge that remains silent' (de Certeau 1984: 108). In the case of Bondi, there is a lot of inflated talk. None the less, one gets the impression that this might be the other side of what de Certeau refers to as the 'under-expressed' of 'well-being': 'Surf til death' is a graffiti that has survived on the wall at the south end of the beach for some time – a public inscription perhaps and pretty ordinary, but every time I see it I find it mysterious. Places are 'fragmentary', 'inward-turning histories', 'enigmatic'; they cannot be read by others, but are about 'the pain or pleasure of the body' (de Certeau 1984: 108). Is there something of this pain and pleasure of the body in the experience of Bondi that is not in discourse, and is possibly unspeakable?

De Certeau (1984: 109) speaks of the originary experience of the being-there of spatial practices, 'in ways of moving into something different': the differentiation from the mother's body (which could also be read as a critique of Lacan's account of the symbolic order and the phallus as mark of differentiation). This is rather like Calvino's story of 'real' origins – an originary differentiation and movement. For de Certeau (1984: 109) every spatial practice is a repetition of this experience which inaugurated the 'possibility of space . . . of the subject'. This repetition is very different from a nostalgic desire for the imaginary, repetition of the same; it breaks with any notion of the original and the copy. And the space is a 'not everything'. The possibility of a movement that is temporal, transformation, is inaugurated. 'To practise space is thus to repeat the joyful and silent experience of childhood; it is, in a place, to be other and to move toward the other' (de Certeau 1984: 110). To claim that there is a way of being in Bondi that inscribes this relation of a desire might seem romantic. But this is how I like to think of Bondi, a place where I live.

In the light of this analysis of Bondi, let me make some remarks about the analysis of English heritage. Obviously I write about each of these from very different positions. But it is not simply the fact of being Australian that differentiates my relationship to each of these 'objects'. In fact, my desire in England has been to become part of a place – Haworth. It now strikes me that it is appropriate, having started with discourses of nation and identity (one of which turns on the past, the other on nature), instead to compare places that I desire. Somehow, the subjective, directly connected with the place of the self, is what can be 'spoken' about. In Haworth, my desire has indeed been to know the place, to be able to read the codes of, for example, public footpaths and bridle ways; to have a competence with respect to this landscape, as I do in body surfing at Bondi; to be a local and party to local stories. In a sense this is a desire to 'know' what cannot be seen.

Now I am aware of parallels between Bondi and Haworth: the superimposition of homogenising tourist codes, and the possibilities of something that escapes, eludes these. In each case this experience relates to a complexity in the relation between nature and culture, and a culture marked by a certain wildness, the unknowable of nature. In Bondi this is connected with sensuality, in Haworth dark passions. But in neither instance would one have nature appropriated to culture. The desire is for nature as other, the movement towards and deferral of the primordial.

But throughout this book I have stressed the double moment of desire and meaning. In part, my desire is for mastery, to know places; and in reading Bondi and Haworth together I am necessarily engaging in a superimposition, an imposing of my rituals and desires. There is no easy way out of this dilemma; there is an obvious paradox in speaking about the unspeakable. Are we back in the register of representation? There is a similar problem with Irigaray's and Cixous' concern to 'represent' the unconscious: once in discourse, otherness is no longer other. Nevertheless, in walking and riding the moors the thought has often crossed my mind that this personal and subjective experience also has a universality about it. And that this universal is the desire to give over to affect, passion: the body mediated by nature as other, in such a way that we might lose ourselves in duration, despite purposive compulsions.[5]

With respect to different ways of meaning, it is not a matter of either/or. For example, to reject the purposive walk in favour of the stroll, or to deny any pleasure in purposiveness, would amount to a negation. Multiplicity, which is associated with a positive desire, consists in a mixing of and (a working at) a play between both 'sides'. In this process there is a potential for the transformation of purposiveness, and a transgression of systems structured by binary opposition.

CONCLUSION

The issues about meaning and knowledge that have been addressed in this book are not random or fanciful. The questions that French theory has put on the intellectual agenda are central questions of the present era; they cannot be avoided (except, of course, through repression). This bears on Foucault's insistence on the acknowledgement of the conditions that motivate conceptualisation, and his concern with the interconnections between knowledge, politics and ethics. Over the last twenty years or so there has been a crisis in authorisation: Who can speak for the other? From what position and on what basis? What has been called into question is the justification of representation with reference to a logic of society, or from a position of a political doctrine or movement. Foucault himself identifies a series of struggles around Same and Other, and the demand 'to be different', as central to the operations of power in the present era. What is of particular importance in this is the acknowledgement that the (self)Same–Other relation structures knowledge. In other words, Hegel is at work in our knowledge practices. This calls, then, for a process of constant critical checking, a critique of 'the present', and, importantly, self-critique. Sameness cannot simply be refused, and most certainly not through an identification with the other, which reinvents the same.

Let me give a specific example. Feminism (or at least, a certain feminism) has become institutionalised in the academy and, in some places, in sections of the state. Speaking on behalf of 'women' has been justified by the claim that 'we' are the other. This involves a reification of women, and a failure to acknowledge that the speaking 'we' is necessarily implicated in a structure of self–other relations. To constitute women, or indeed any other group, as the bearers of what is good and radical is to reinvent a politics of sameness. At the same time, though, feminism has been one of the major influences in raising precisely these critical questions about power and knowledge. What this points to is the constant tension between the desire for representation and the process of critique, and the importance of the notion of permanent critique to an ethics of theorising.

Sociology textbooks invariably conclude with a chapter on social change, drawing out the conclusions for change from the previous representation of the social. The rationale of the discipline is commonly understood to be the capacity to identify the sources of change. The structure of the textbook maps the assumption that sociologists represent 'the real' from which is derived 'the possible' – social change. The principle of meaning of 'the real and the possible' is one of resemblance: a repetition of the same. As an alternative to this, Bergson's conception of the movement from virtual to actual has been proposed, based on the principle of difference in repetition. Both the virtual and the actual are real, but as they are constituted in movement, the real is itself in a process of deferral. In this account there is not 'a social order' that might be changed: movement – 'change' – is of the essence of 'life'. While the formulation 'the social and social change' assumes a sameness, the movement from virtual to actual is understood as an ongoing process characterised by positive differentiation, and without an end. A knowledge practice that partakes of this process is to be distinguished from knowledge understood as representation, which presumes to stand outside and mirror the whole or total, and from this position of knowing, to effect change.

These different formulations of the question of 'change' presuppose different approaches to 'the social'. One of the central arguments in this book has been that the social world might be thought of in terms of multiplicity. For example, rather than the binary structure of social order–disorder and 'the social'–social change, it has been suggested that we think of the social world as consisting of a multiplicity of orders that are not reducible to one another. In this view, one of the orders is indeed that characterised by a binary structure of oppositions. This has been referred to as the order of negativity and sameness. Another order is that of multiplicity and qualitative difference. If not reducible, these orders are defined, none the less, in relation to each other. A crucial question, then, is: What is the nature of this relation?

I have emphasised the coexistence of different orders, or different ways of meaning – what I take to be a methodology of multiplicity. But still it must be asked: Is there a hierarchy of orders? If there is a relation between the orders, is it a hierarchical one? Feminist work has been particularly important in this regard, drawing attention to the hierarchisation in binary oppositions, and the dominance of the singular and the same. In this view, subordination consists in a repression of the multiple and plural. But it is not as if the multiple has any prior existence; it is constituted, albeit in repression, in the constitution of the same–other relation of sociality or the symbolic order. The singular order of sameness is dependent on a repression of multiplicity, and is, in a sense, productive of multiplicity. The world of commodification, capitalism, makes possible something more, something else; there is a double moment in commodification – the quantitative and the qualitative. Bergson and the French feminists (and, in a sense, Benjamin) emphasise that it is not a question of either/or, but rather 'both, simultaneously'. If they are 'for' the positive and plural, this way of meaning nevertheless comes out of, is a response to, the negative and singular of the Hegelian tradition, a tradition that one cannot simply be free of by proposing a 'new order' of the multiple. This point has been made, in particular, with respect to the desire for mastery. While we are implicated in such a desire, there is also the possibility of a different desire in knowledge, which turns on the idea that something escapes, exceeds the negative order.

What escapes is an otherness that cannot be appropriated to the same. This is an idea that, one way or another, runs through the 'theories' that have been addressed in this book, those of Irigaray, Cixous, Bergson, Derrida, Barthes, Foucault and Freud. Through reading these theorists together, it has been argued that the site of this otherness is the unconscious, and the body. The precondition of knowledge and the symbolic order is the unconscious, and power-knowledge works through the body. It is precisely these operations that make the bodily unconscious potentially transgressive of the order of discourse. It is no accident, then, that the unconscious and the body are exclusions in discourses that give themselves the status of knowledge or science.

My interest has been in theories which focus on the principles of meaning of the unconscious and the ways in which meaning is embodied. These aspects of signification processes come together in memory, and the idea that 'your body remembers': memory is both bodily and unconscious. Memory, and particularly 'memory trace', also point to a temporality. For example, the moving body is the body of memory. Thus, it has been argued, the components of an other way of meaning, indeed a materialist conception of meaning, are the body, the unconscious and time. These are central to an understanding of signification processes as transformation.

The idea of transformation displaces that of social change, just as it is counterposed to meaning as representation. What is so compelling about 'transformation' is that it suggests change, in the sense of movement, in the very *process* of signification. Derrida's 'concept' of *différance* makes structure inseparable from movement. He does not refute the basic structuralist claim that binary oppositions are the predominant principle of meaning; rather his concern is to demonstrate the ways in which the two sides of an opposition cannot be fixed in separation, despite the desire for such a fixing in the Western philosophical tradition. In this regard, the term 'post-structuralist' sits oddly with deconstructive principles: for Derrida it is not a matter of being *post*-structuralist, but rather bringing to light the play of differences in structure. The transformation of binary oppositions is a writing practice in the now. The Saussurian opposition between synchrony and diachrony is of particular significance in this respect. Once meaning is understood, materially, in terms of practice, the synchronic of structure can no longer be held apart from the temporality of signification processes. And the time of meaning points to the possibility of 'change'.

Foucault and Derrida insist, despite their different formulations, that transformations are partial. There is no waiting for a final moment of truth and total transformation. Rather, a process of making shifts in rules of relations between elements in systems and between systems is ongoing. This is an altogether more positive and materialist understanding of the nature of change from that to be found in radical social science. We are written, our bodies are discursively produced; but we also write, in all practices, not only practices of knowledge. And in this writing, or practice of codes of the culture, there is a possibility of rewriting – rewriting ourselves. Transformation, or writing the body, implies that 'change' is a change in way of meaning *and* in way of *being* – a becoming. These are inseparable in a materialist understanding of signification. A writing practice is potentially transformative of human beings 'here and now'.

For the French feminists, otherness is specified as 'feminine', the repressed of the symbolic order; and transformation is understood as a reinscription of sexual difference. The feminine is simultaneously the negative of the masculine in a singular order, and the repressed multiplicity that presents a disturbance to that order. The structure of binary opposition is sexual; the order is phallocentric. Feminists in this tradition are insistent that we not reinvent this order by making woman either the subject or object of knowledge. In the light of this concern it is important that their writings not be read as valorising the feminine as that which counters the masculine order. For this would indeed be a reinvention of the same. The object of feminist deconstruction is totalising discourse. Identifying the feminine as the repressed on which presence is dependent, is a strategic move. There is no goal of making the feminine a presence, or countering totalising discourse with a 'feminist revolution'. (In connection with the previous remarks about feminism I am suggesting, of course, that there is no unity 'feminism', although it is fair to say that a totalising impulse characterises some feminisms.)

Given the tendencies, in some feminist discourse, to valorise the feminine, I have emphasised sexual indeterminacy. It has been suggested that we might identify moments of sexual indeterminacy in discourses as various as Hegel, Freud, Foucault, Bergson and Barthes. For example, that the master–slave story does not neatly map the masculine–feminine distinction is something positive about Hegel's story. It invites an investigation of the complexity in relations, including the sexual dimension of these, that is closed off if it is assumed that master–slave is masculine–feminine: we can rewrite Hegel's story. In the case of Freud, despite his explicit concern to define masculinity and femininity, his own discourse contributes to an undoing of such fixings.

Some feminists have been critical of Foucault for his apparent failure to adequately address sexual hierarchisation. There is obviously something in this in that Foucault does leap to the multiple without sufficient emphasis on hierarchisation. On the other hand, his concern with multiplicity, and indeed the specificity of otherness that is not reducible to, or even structurally homologous with, masculine–feminine, could be regarded as a move beyond the fixity of sexual differentiation. Phallocentricism might seem all-pervasive, but if we take the idea of specificity seriously, might it not be the case that sexual subordination intersects with other forms of subordination in such a way that openings are presented for shifting relations? This is how Foucault's concern with the multiple positioning of the subject might be read. Not only are we not simply positioned as masculine or feminine – it depends on the context of relations – but we are positioned in all sorts of other ways as well. In this complexity of positioning there is room for movement.

Bergson's philosophy allows for a non-fixity of positions and the inscription of bodily difference. His concept of multiplicity is, in a sense, beyond sexual differentiation. And it has been suggested that Barthes' writing 'inscribes' a sexual ambiguity: different desires coexist – the masculine and the feminine – in such a way that disrupts the order of the same.

In terms of a methodology of multiplicity, one of the key strategies has been to read stories against and with each other. Any specific instance can be read in relation to a number of stories, without being reduced to a single story. By setting up a dialogue, which includes everyday stories, it is possible to rewrite stories, the narratives of the culture. Stories frequently take the form of stories of origins, but it has been argued that they are most fruitfully read as 'originary' in the sense of generative in the now. This relates to Freud's argument about the temporality of psychical processes and the effectivity of the past in the present. Thus a rewriting of stories, in part, consists in bringing this temporality to light – a rewriting of 'origins'. Despite the structure of stories, they are not in the past; they refer us forward.

In turn, this bears on my concern with particularity: any (writing) practice is particular (what Derrida refers to as 'originary', and Barthes as 'unique') in its combination of codes. Narratives of the subject do not simply impose on us; there is a particularity in practices. Thus, the idea of multiplicity is closely connected with the particular: the subject is positioned in a multiplicity of stories. It is for this reason that specificity of analyses has been emphasised over 'theory'. We cannot simply read a specific instance off a general theory (which includes feminist theory). Benjamin's concern with uniqueness and the particularity of experience is also compatible with this methodological approach. In the tradition of French theory, the process of analysis is itself understood as a writing or transformation. Freud's case studies have been cited as exemplary of this form of analysis.

Stories have been emphasised as a means of displacing the oppositions between fact and fiction, and theory and fiction, and the distinction that is made in sociological discourse between theory and the empirical. Thus, I have investigated the implications of thinking of theorising as fictionalising, in the broad sense of a writing practice, and in the narrower sense of storytelling. It has been suggested that theories and analyses that take the form of stories have an openness about them that invites rewriting. Furthermore, in this form

of writing the position of the writing subject is more likely to be acknowledged, and so, too, is the fact that we are necessarily in language. Such
discourse contributes to an undoing of pretensions to science, truth and
knowledge.

Of course the choice of 'theorists' is not random. For example, Hegel and
Freud are regarded as particularly important, both for what they tell us about
the nature of Western culture and thought, and for providing bases for an
undoing of the order of discourse, which includes their own discourse. In
both cases, the desire in their knowledge can be brought to light in the terms
of their own discourse.

Taking up a methodology of multiplicity in specific cultural or social
analyses is one means of writing in a more open way than is allowed for by the
rules of academic (specifically social science) discourse. Such a methodology
not only refuses reductionism but also disrupts a desire for interpretation. It
allows for the possibility of acknowledging such a desire while simultaneously opening up other desires. Again what is to be emphasised here is
that it is not a matter of replacing one form of sociality – the Hegelian
self–other relation – with an alternative sociality. To think in multiplicity is to
refuse such formulations.

What is being raised here is the question of evaluations. A crisis in
evaluative models is closely connected with a crisis in authorisation. Without
the 'safety rail' of 'the real' or the certitude of a political doctrine, how are
knowledges, discourses, to be evaluated? Certain principles of evaluation
have been proposed in this book – most generally, the criterion of openness of
texts. Of the 'theorists' addressed, it has been suggested that Barthes is
exemplary in this regard. Barthes is open, both about himself and in his
writing strategy. He is seductive, incites further writings. He succeeds in
transmitting pleasure, in producing a culture of pleasure. There is a double
moment in this culture of pleasure: the desire for mastery, and a *jouissance*. In
talking about himself, Barthes does not remain within himself: he gives the
prerogative to the other. However difficult it might be, I am suggesting that
we take this as a 'model' of cultural analysis.

Along with openness of texts, disturbing pleasure has been proposed as a
basis of evaluation – that which disrupts the givenness of the social world in
the positive form of pleasure, rather than fear which produces negation and
closure. Implicit here is a reference to Freud's account of the pleasure
principle as the breaker of the peace, for which we might read the comfortable
coded of culture. Furthermore, the pleasure principle is associated with life
and is constituted in deferral: a disturbing pleasure is that which never
arrives, but moves us forward in infinity. It is precisely the disturbing nature
of this that provokes negation and closure – a death. Faced with this
alternative, the risks of infinity, with hints of madness (Barthes), are far
preferable to the safety (and, possibly, bad faith) of closure.

Disturbing pleasure is directly connected with affect: the body moved by
involuntary memory. In turn, this relates to different conceptions of

knowledge and truth. The unconscious, the body and the subjective have been emphasised in a critique of knowledge understood as speculative and rational, and as the product of a consciousness that might know the whole. But this is not an argument against knowledge; nor is it an argument against consciousness so much as a critique of a conception of consciousness as disembodied. My concern has been to argue that the body provides the basis for a different conception of knowledge: we know with our bodies. In this regard, the authentic of experience might be reclaimed; if there is any truth, it is the truth of the body.

NOTES

1 Sociological fictions

1 For an excellent critique of Jameson see Weber (1987: 49–52).
2 For more positive receptions in the social sciences see Weedon (1987), who argues that post-structuralism is fruitful for feminist social scientists, but provides literary texts as examples; and Barrett (1988), who claims that feminists today cannot ignore what she inaptly refers to as 'post-modern' philosophy. Despite this, Barrett (1988: v–xxxiv) continues to employ a sociological language of conceptual adequacy, explanation, and structure/agency.
3 The French sociologist, Bourdieu (1977: 1–29) has also developed a theory of knowledge as practice, drawing on Marx's conception of practice, and thus suggesting a rather different genealogy of Marxism from that which prevails in sociology. And, in his critique of the conception of philosophy as mirror, Rorty (1979: 171) argues for a philosophy understood as conversation and social practice.

2 The sociological mirror

1 Probably the most influential sociologist in this tradition in Australia is Connell. See, for example, Connell *et al.* (1982). For his critical reflections on the Birmingham School, particularly their use of the concept of culture, see Connell (1983: 222–30).
2 See also Foucault's (1977: 53–67) reference to Borges on the labyrinth and the endless process of mirroring which is language in 'Language to Infinity'.
3 Of these three social theorists, Simmel is the one who does sometimes make his way into sociological discourse, but he tends to be read in relation to Marx and Weber: what his account of money owes to Marx, and his professional relation to Weber. Frisby (1981: 26–9), on the other hand, draws attention to the philosophical influences – including that of Bergson – and the trajectory of Simmel's work from sociology towards philosophy.

4 For a critical analysis of my own research practices, see Game (1989). Critical comments on research are based on my research experience.

5 McRobbie's (1980; 1982) work raises this issue in connection with the choices of objects made by men in cultural studies, and the fantasies involved in identifications with masculine subcultures.

3 The subject

1 It is commonly assumed that liberal political philosophy presupposes an individual prior to the social or political order. However, it is possible to read Hobbes, for example, in a rather different way: far from pre-existing the contract, the 'subject' of 'liberty' is produced by, or is an effect of, the social contract. In this regard he can fruitfully be read with Foucault. Hobbes, like Foucault, emphasises bodies and bodies in motion. See for example Hobbes (1962 [1651]: 159–68).

2 Although Foucault is critical of any notion of a total process of rationalisation, his understanding of specific rationalities is comparable to Weber's (1974: 196–244) account of rational-legal forms of authority and disciplinary modes, including the secrecy of knowledge.

3 For an excellent account of Foucault on power, and 'The Subject and Power' in particular, see Patton (1989).

4 See Eco (1977: 24–6) on reading Marx's account of the exchange of commodities as a semiotic phenomenon. See also Foucault (1970: 166–213, 221–6).

5 In this context of a discussion about power operating positively through the body, attention might be drawn to Marx's concept of labour *power*. Although Marxists tend to assume that power is a negative phenomenon, labour power, which is bodily, 'human flesh and blood' (Marx 1969 [1847]: 74), is clearly, for Marx, a positive force.

6 See, for example, Calvino (1988): a story of tourists' desire literally to eat a culture; their tour of taste includes a visit to a place of human sacrifice and cannibalism. On incorporation and the displacement from eating to visual incorporation see Laplanche (1985: 20). The idea of incorporating the other is also central to Hegel's story of the development of self-consciousness and the move from nature to culture (to be discussed in Chapter 4).

7 Specifically in connection with Oedipus, the not-man – woman and animal – of the Sphinx comes to mind here. She is positioned outside the city – the law – of man, but brings chaos and death to men. It was in Oedipus that 'the creature met her match'; her power was destroyed with his answers to the riddle (Sophocles 1974: 24). If, in a masculine order the feminine is associated with death, and an overcoming of death requires the death or negation of the feminine, there is nevertheless an irony to this story as Oedipus is the instigator of the Sphinx's death. It is he, after all, who brings chaos, and ends up being supported by his daughter, Antigone, having foretold his *own* failure in solving the riddle (Borges 1974: 134–5). See also Cixous (1981: 49); and de Lauretis (1984: 156–7) on rewriting this story.

8 See Benjamin's (1986: 86–9) rereading of Freud's account of daughter–father relations as a positive identification with the subject of desire. This casts a somewhat different light on women's complicity in the order.

9 In a footnote in *Civilisation and its Discontents*, Freud (1985a [1930]: 295ff.) claimed that with the development of civilisation smell was repressed and replaced

by sight as the dominant sense. See also Benjamin (1969: 214) on the significance of smell as the 'bottom-most stratum of involuntary memory', in his essay 'The Image of Proust'.

10 See Jacobus's (1986: 137–93) refiguring of the mother through the significance of the Sistine Madonna.

11 For an excellent critique of Sartre and Lacan on this point see Bryson (1988).

4   Power

1 All Hegel references are to paragraph numbers in *The Phenomenology of Spirit*.

2 See Lloyd (1983) for a clear exposition of this; also Gadamer (1971: 54–74).

3 I am following Lacan's spelling of 'other' with either capital 'O' or lower case 'o'. He generally uses the latter to refer to the experience of inter-subjective relations, while the former refers to Otherness in a more general sense – the repressed of culture. I have retained specific philosopher's spellings in discussions of their work.

4 See also Barthes (1985: 249) who claims that *Fort! Da!* is 'the best legend which accounts for the birth of language'. Lacan emphasises the child's use of *fort* and *da* from the discursive environment; Barthes focuses rather on the miming as sign, which is significant as it emphasises the embodiment of meaning. Furthermore, he draws attention to the significance of listening in both *Fort! Da!* and the psychoanalytic relation: the body in the voice, in the ear. Listening is a theatre on the stage of 'power and desire' (Barthes 1985: 260).

5 See Bataille (1986: 11–25) on desire as a desire for death. In *Erotism* Bataille pushes Hegel to the limit. 'If philosophy were to shift its ground from work and taboo' to transgression – death and eroticism – it would no longer be philosophy.' This would amount to a transgression of language, philosophical language (Bataille 1986: 273–6).

6 On Hegel and Antigone see Irigaray (1985b: 214–26).

7 There is a striking parallel between the feminist conception of the feminine as simultaneously singular and multiple and Borges' story about Shakespeare, 'Everything and Nothing', in which he says:

   The voice of the Lord answered from a whirlwind: 'Neither am I anyone; I have dreamt the world as you dreamt your work, my Shakespeare, and among the forms in my dreams are you, who like myself are many and no one' (Borges 1970: 285).

5   Time

1 Surprisingly little attention is paid to Bergson today, despite the influence of his ideas on various traditions of thought, including the critical theory of the Frankfurt School (Jay 1973:48–53) and French philosophy. There are echoes of his thought in contemporary French philosophy and cultural theory, for example in Foucault, Barthes, Derrida, Cixous and Irigaray. But a debt to Bergson is rarely acknowledged, which might simply suggest that he is assumed as part of a philosophical tradition. Levinas (1987 [1947]: 128), who draws considerably on Bergson in *Time and the Other*, describes him as 'so unjustly forgotten today'. Lévi-Strauss, although ambivalent about Bergson, does acknowledge a debt to him. However, Bergson is not generally recognised as one of the major influences on the thought of Lévi-Strauss. One contemporary French theorist who is 'excited' by Bergson is

196   UNDOING THE SOCIAL

Deleuze. In *Bergsonism* (1988 [1966]), he argues for the significance of philosophical intuition and multiplicity to contemporary philosophy; and more recently he has written two volumes on film which draw on Bergson's conception of duration. It might also be noted that in 'A New Refutation of Time', Borges (1970: 252) suggests that to write about time after Bergson – in 1947 – is anachronistic.

2 If the method of dissociation that Bergson applies to time were to be applied to space, I suspect that the result would be similar to Derrida's disruption of the space–time opposition. Merleau-Ponty makes a similar point, claiming that Bergson's condemnation of space is not necessary to arrive at authentic time. It is only necessary 'if we consider space as objectified in advance' and ignore 'a primordial spatiality' (Merleau-Ponty 1962: 415). However, this does not stand as a refutation of the claim that spatialisation and objectification do, as a rule, go hand in hand.

3 Feminists concerned with 'women's time' tend to invert Hegel's account of the time of knowledge without questioning the temporal assumptions involved in the way that, for example, Bergson and Irigaray do. Whether acknowledged or not, de Beauvoir's sexualisation of Hegel would seem to be crucial to these formulations. Her argument is that woman is, in her reproductive capacity, 'destined for the repetition of Life' (de Beauvoir 1972: 96). In this adaptation of Hegel, life is understood as a repetition of the same. For Bergson, of course, life is characterised by difference in repetition. We need not read this as a debate about the 'reality' of evolution and reproduction of the species, but rather as different conceptions of meaning processes, made with reference to 'life'. In questioning Hegel and de Beauvoir, some feminists have simply reversed the valuation on the repetition of life: changing a negative valuation to a positive one. This is particularly clear in conceptions of women's time as cyclical: if not, strictly speaking, linear, it is nevertheless a spatialised conception of time, and one that implies a repetition of the same (Kristeva 1986: 187–213; Forman 1989). Nothing of the temporal assumptions shifts in these accounts of 'women's time', only the valuation.

4 This is comparable with Foucault's project of countering the order of same–different with a history of the Other. Implicit in this is a conception of a multiplicity of orders.

5 See also Deleuze (1988: 122) on Bergson and Proust: the major difference is that whereas for Proust the past can be experienced, for Bergson the pure past is not in the domain of the lived.

6 It should be noted that Benjamin's (1969: 261–3) notion of the now time also has the dialectical form of the double moment of modernity. For a discussion of the double meaning of 'now' see Ricoeur (1989: 97–8). In this book I use 'now' to refer to the lived moment that cannot be a presence in the present.

6   Mediation and immediacy

1 [] denotes containment within a particular answer or sequence. The complete text is not reproduced, but as little as possible is excluded from sequences. Emphasis, particularly of repetitions, is mine.

2 See Hiatt (1975) for a discussion of interpretations of the motif of swallowing and regurgitation in Australian Aboriginal myths in terms of male fantasies of giving birth, and the idea that 'swallowing symbolises reunion with the mother while regurgitating signifies rebirth by males' (Hiatt 1975: 143). Following Freud and

Lévi-Strauss, it could be suggested that there is something universal about this fantasy, which does not obviate the need for analyses of specific cultural forms.

3 Barthes claims that *Camera Lucida* is a text of mourning. Cixous (1981: 54) has argued that mourning is a masculine 'refusal to admit that something of your self might be lost in the lost object'. It means resigning oneself to loss so as not to lose. This is an obvious reference to Freud's (1984 [1917]: 253) account of the work of mourning as a shoring up of the ego in the face of loss in 'Mourning and Melancholia'. Cixous (1981: 54) claims that woman does not resign herself to loss but '*takes up the challenge of loss* in order to go on living'. Barthes (1984: 90) says that his grief cannot be transformed into mourning. He admits that something of himself (as feminine?) is lost with the loss of his mother and the feminine child. The paradox of the photograph: I am connected with that being, but it is lost, absolutely. But there is a resignation towards death: 'At the end of this first death, my own death is inscribed; between the two, nothing more than waiting . . . nothing more to say' (Barthes 1984: 93). Waiting: the interval, the mark of time that inscribes the relation to the other, which cannot be put into discourse.

4 I am necessarily condensing complex discussions in Benjamin and the current debate around his ideas. For an excellent account of these issues with particular reference to film and photography, see Hansen (1987).

7 Places in time

1 For a good account of the *flâneur* embodying a transformation of perception, and *flâneur* as writer, see Buck-Morss (1986). She argues that there is nothing nostalgic about Benjamin's approach to the *flâneur*. See also Foucault (1984: 40) on the *flâneur* as storehouse of memories.

2 In connection with Rousseau's pleasure in botanising, it is interesting to note Benjamin's (1973: 36) mixing of city and country codes in his description of the *flâneur*, 'botanizing on the asphalt'.

3 The Hayson Plan was called 'Growth . . . Change . . . Decline . . . Rebirth! A New Lease of Life. Bondi Pavilion', June 1987. Quotes from Hayson are taken from this document, which is not publicly available. He was frequently quoted in the press at the time, emphasising his personal agency in this cyclical rebirthing process. He made much of his status as Australian – a proper parenting – to fend off criticisms that his company had foreign capital in it.

4 'The Markhams' is a reference to the pro-developer mayor at that time, and her husband. Mrs Markham lost in the next election as a consequence of this campaign.

5 Throughout *The Waves* [1931], Woolf makes an association between waves and horses. See also Malouf (1983: 30–4).

BIBLIOGRAPHY

Anderson, B. (1983) *Imagined Communities*, London, Verso.

Auster, P. (1985) *City of Glass*, Penguin.

Barnes, J. (1989) *A History of the World in 10½ Chapters*, London, Jonathan Cape.

Barrett, M. (1988) *Women's Oppression Today: The Marxist/Feminist Encounter*, revised edn, London, Verso.

Barthes, R. (1975) *The Pleasure of the Text* (trans. R. Miller), New York, Hill and Wang.

Barthes, R. (1977) *Image-Music-Text* (trans. S. Heath), Glasgow, Collins-Fontana.

Barthes, R. (1984) *Camera Lucida*, London, Fontana.

Barthes, R. (1985) 'Listening' in *The Responsibility of Forms* (trans. R. Howard), New York, Hill and Wang.

Barthes, R. (1986) *The Rustle of Language* (trans. R. Howard), Oxford, Basil Blackwell.

Bataille, G. (1986) [1957] *Erotism: Death and Sensuality* (trans. M. Dalwood), San Francisco, City Lights.

Baudrillard, J. (1975) *The Mirror of Production* (trans. M. Poster), St Louis, Telos Press.

Beechey, V. and Donald, J. (eds) (1985) *Subjectivity and Social Relations*, Milton Keynes, Open University Press.

Benjamin, J. (1984) 'Master and Slave: The Fantasy of Erotic Domination' in A. Snitow, C. Stansell and S. Thompson (eds) *Desire: The Politics of Sexuality*, London, Virago.

Benjamin, J. (1986) 'A Desire of One's Own: Psychoanalytic Feminism and Intersubjective Space' in T. de Lauretis (ed.), *Feminist Studies: Critical Studies*, Bloomington, Indiana University Press.

Benjamin, W. (1969) *Illuminations* (trans. H. Zohn), New York, Schocken Books.

Benjamin, W. (1973) *Charles Baudelaire: A Lyric Poet in the Era of High Capitalism* (trans H. Zohn), London, NLB.

Benjamin, W. (1982) [1931] 'A Short History of Photography', *Screen*, vol. 13, no. 1, pp. 5–26.

Benveniste, E. (1971) *Problems in General Linguistics* (trans. M. E. Meek), Miami, University of Miami Press.

Bergson, H. (1950a) [1889] *Time and Free Will* (trans. F. L. Pogson) London, George Allen & Unwin.

Bergson, H. (1950b) [1896] *Matter and Memory* (trans. N. M. Paul and W. Scott Palmer), London, George Allen & Unwin.

Bergson, H. (1913) [1907] *Creative Evolution* (trans. A. Mitchell), London, Macmillan.

Bernheimer, C. and Kahane, C. (eds) (1985) *In Dora's Case: Freud-Hysteria-Feminism*, New York, Columbia University Press.

Beynon, H. (1975) *Working for Ford*, East Ardsley, Wakefield, UK, EP Publishing.

Borges, J. L. (1970) *Labyrinths*, Harmondsworth, Penguin.

Borges, J. L. (1974) *The Book of Imaginary Beings*, Harmondsworth, Penguin.

Bourdieu, P. (1977) *Outline of a Theory of Practice* (trans. R. Nice), Cambridge, Cambridge University Press.

Bryson, N. (1988) 'The Gaze in the Expanded Field of Vision' in H. Foster (ed.), *Vision and Visuality*, Dia Art Foundation Discussions in Contemporary Culture, Number 2, Seattle, Bay Press, pp. 87–114.

Buck-Morss, S. (1986) 'The Flâneur, the Sandwichman and the Whore: The Politics of Loitering', *New German Critique*, no. 39, Fall, pp. 99–140.

Butler, J. P. (1987) *Subjects of Desire: Hegelian Reflections in Twentieth-Century France*, New York, Columbia University Press.

Calvino, I. (1976) *t Zero*, New York and London, Harcourt Brace Jovanovich.

Calvino, I. (1979) *Invisible Cities*, London, Picador.

Calvino, I. (1987) *The Literature Machine: Essays*, London, Secker and Warburg.

Calvino, I. (1988) *Under The Jaguar Sun* (trans. W. Weaver), New York and London, Harcourt Brace Jovanovich.

Centre for Contemporary Cultural Studies (1978) *On Ideology*, London, Hutchinson.

Cixous, H. (1979) 'Portrait of Dora' in S. Benmussa (ed.), *Benmussa Directs* (trans. A. Barrows), London, John Calder.

Cixous, H. (1981) 'Castration or Decapitation', *Signs*, vol. 7, no. 1, Autumn, pp. 36–51.

Cixous, H. (1986) 'Sorties: Out and Out: Attacks/Ways Out/Forays' in H. Cixous and C. Clément, *The Newly Born Woman*, Manchester, Manchester University Press.

Cixous, H. and Clément, C. (1986) *The Newly Born Woman* (trans. B. Wing), Manchester, Manchester University Press.

Clément, C. (1983) *The Lives and Legends of Jacques Lacan* (trans. A. Goldhammer), New York, Columbia University Press.

Clifford, J. (1983) 'On Ethnographic Authority', *Representations*, vol. 1, no. 2, pp. 69–73.

Clifford, J. (1986) 'Introduction: Partial Truths' in J. Clifford and G. Marcus, *Writing Culture: The Politics and Poetics of Ethnography*, Berkeley, Los Angeles and London, University of California Press.

Connell, R. W. (1983) *Which Way is Up?: Essays on Sex, Class and Culture*, Sydney, George Allen & Unwin.

Connell, R. W., Ashendon, D., Kessler, S. and Dowsett, G. (1982) *Making the Difference*, Sydney, George Allen & Unwin.

Corrigan, P. (1988) 'The Body of Intellectuals/the Intellectual's Body (Remarks for Roland)', *The Sociological Review*, vol. 36, no. 2, May, pp. 368–80.

Crapanzano, V. (1977) 'On the Writing of Ethnography', *Dialectical Anthropology*, vol. 2, no. 1, pp. 69–73.

Creed, B. (1990) '*Alien* and the Monstrous-Feminine' in A. Kuhn (ed.), *Alien Zone: Cultural Theory and Contemporary Science Fiction Cinema*, London, Verso.

Culler, J. (1976) *Saussure*, Glasgow, Collins-Fontana.

de Beauvoir, S. (1972) [1949] *The Second Sex* (trans. H. M. Parshley), Harmondsworth, Penguin.

de Certeau, M. (1984) *The Practice of Everyday Life* (trans. S. F. Rendall), University of California Press.

de Lauretis, T. (1984) *Alice Doesn't: Feminism, Semiotics, Cinema*, London and Basingstoke, Macmillan.

de Lauretis, T. (1987) *Technologies of Gender: Essays on Theory, Film, and Fiction*, Bloomington and Indianapolis, Indiana University Press.

Deleuze, G. (1988) [1966] *Bergsonism* (trans. H. Tomlinson and B. Habberjam), New York, Zone Books.

Derrida, J. (1976) *Of Grammatology* (trans. G. C. Spivak), Baltimore and London, Johns Hopkins University Press.

Derrida, J. (1978) *Writing and Difference* (trans. A. Bass), Chicago, University of Chicago Press.

Derrida, J. (1982) *Margins of Philosophy* (trans. A. Bass), Brighton, Harvester Press.

Derrida, J. (1987) *Positions* (trans. A. Bass), London, Athlone Press.

Derrida, J. and Plissart, M.-F. (1989) 'Right of Inspection' *Art and Text*, no. 32, Autumn, pp. 20–97.

Doane, M. A. (1982) 'Film and the Masquerade – Theorising the Female Spectator' *Screen*, vol. 23, nos 3–4, pp. 74–88.

Drew, R., Kingsmill, J., Stewart, M., Whitlam, M., McGregor, C. and Holmes, C. (1984) *Bondi*, Surry Hills, James Frazer.

Dutton, G. (1985) *Sun, Sea, Surf and Sand – The Myth of The Beach*, Melbourne, Oxford University Press.

Eco, U. (1977) *A Theory of Semiotics*, London and Basingstoke, Macmillan Press.

Fiske, J., Hodge, B. and Turner G. (1987) *Myths of Oz: Reading Australian Popular Culture*, Sydney, Allen & Unwin.

Forman, F. J. (ed) (1989) *Taking Our Time: Feminist Perspectives on Temporality*, Oxford, Pergamon.

Foucault, M. (1970) *The Order of Things*, London, Tavistock.

Foucault, M. (1977) *Language, Counter-Memory, Practice* (trans. D. F. Bouchard and S. Simon), New York, Basil Blackwell.

Foucault, M. (1980) *Power/Knowledge* (edited by C. Gordon), Brighton, Harvester Press.

Foucault, M. (1981) *The History of Sexuality*, Volume 1, Harmondsworth, Penguin.

Foucault, M. (1982) 'The Subject and Power' in H. L. Dreyfus and P. Rabinow, *Michel Foucault: Beyond Structuralism and Hermeneutics*, Chicago, University of Chicago Press.

Foucault, M. (1984) *The Foucault Reader* (edited by P. Rabinow), New York, Pantheon Books.

Foucault, M. (1985) *The Use of Pleasure*, Volume 2 of *The History of Sexuality*, New York, Pantheon.

Freud, S. (1973a) [1916] 'Dreams' in *Introductory Lectures on Psychoanalysis*, Pelican Freud Library, Vol. 1, Harmondsworth, Penguin.

Freud, S. (1973a) [1917] 'General Theory of the Neuroses' in *Introductory Lectures on Psychoanalysis*, Pelican Freud Library, Vol. 1, Harmondsworth, Penguin.

Freud, S. (1973b) [1933] 'Femininity' in *New Introductory Lectures on Psychoanalysis*, Pelican Freud Library, Vol. 2, Harmondsworth, Penguin.

Freud, S. (1976) [1900] *The Interpretation of Dreams*, Pelican Freud Library, Vol. 4, Harmondsworth, Penguin.

Freud, S. (1977a) [1905] 'Three Essays on the Theory of Sexuality' in *On Sexuality*, Pelican Freud Library, Vol. 7, Harmondsworth, Penguin.

Freud, S. (1977a) [1925] 'Some Psychical Consequences of the Anatomical Distinction between the Sexes' in *On Sexuality*, Pelican Freud Library, Vol. 7, Harmondsworth, Penguin.

Freud, S. (1977b) [1905] 'Dora' in *Case Histories I*, Pelican Freud Library, Vol. 8, Harmondsworth, Penguin.

Freud, S. (1977b) [1909] 'Little Hans' in *Case Histories I*, Pelican Freud Library, Vol. 8, Harmondsworth, Penguin.

Freud, S. (1979) [1909] 'The "Rat Man" ' in *Case Histories II*, Pelican Freud Library, Vol. 9, Harmondsworth, Penguin.

Freud, S. (1984) [1915] 'The Unconscious' in *On Metapsychology: The Theory of Psychoanalysis*, Pelican Freud Library, Vol. 11, Harmondsworth, Penguin.

Freud, S. (1984) [1917] 'Mourning and Melancholia' in *On Metapsychology: The Theory of Psychoanalysis*, Pelican Freud Library, Vol. 11, Harmondsworth, Penguin.

Freud, S. (1984) [1920] 'Beyond the Pleasure Principle' in *On Metapsychology: The Theory of Psychoanalysis*, Pelican Freud Library, Vol. 11, Harmondsworth, Penguin.

Freud, S. (1984) [1925a] 'A Note upon the "Mystic Writing Pad" ' in *On Metapsychology: The Theory of Psychoanalysis*, Pelican Freud Library, Vol. 11, Harmondsworth, Penguin.

Freud, S. (1984) [1925b] 'Negation' in *On Metapsychology: The Theory of Psychoanalysis*, Pelican Freud Library, Vol. 11, Harmondsworth, Penguin.

Freud, S. (1985a) [1930] *Civilisation and its Discontents* in *Civilisation, Society, and Religion*, Pelican Freud Library, Vol. 12, Harmondsworth, Penguin.

Freud, S. (1985b) [1913] *Totem and Taboo* in *The Origins of Religion*, Pelican Freud Library, Vol. 13, Harmondsworth, Penguin.

Freud, S. (1985c) [1919] 'The "Uncanny" ' in *Art and Literature*, Pelican Freud Library, Vol. 14, Harmondsworth, Penguin.

Frisby, D. (1981) *Sociological Impressionism: A Reassessment of Georg Simmel's Social Theory*, London, Heinemann.

Frisby, D. (1985) *Fragments of Modernity*, Cambridge, Polity Press.

Frow, J. (1983) 'Annus Mirabilis: Synchrony and Diachrony', in F. Barker, P. Hulme, M. Iversen and D. Loxley (eds), *The Politics of Theory*, Colchester, University of Essex.

Gadamer, H. G. (1971) *Hegel's Dialectic*, New Haven, Yale University Press.

Gallop, J. (1982) *Feminism and Psychoanalysis: The Daughter's Seduction*, London, Macmillan Press.

Gallop, J. (1985) *Reading Lacan*, Ithaca and London, Cornell University Press.

Gallop, J. (1988) *Thinking through the Body*, New York, Columbia University Press.

Game, A. and Pringle, R. (1983) *Gender at Work*, Sydney, George Allen & Unwin.

Game, A. (1989) 'Research and Writing: Secretaries and Bosses', *Journal of Pragmatics*, vol. 13, pp. 343–61.

Gatens, M. (1983) 'A Critique of the Sex/Gender Distinction' in J. Allen and P. Patton (eds), *Beyond Marxism?: Interventions after Marx*, Sydney, Intervention.

Giddens, A. (1982a) *Profiles and Critiques in Social Theory*, London and Basingstoke, Macmillan Press.

Giddens, A. (1982b) *Sociology: A Brief but Critical Introduction*, London and Basingstoke, Macmillan Press.

Giddens, A. (1987) *Social Theory and Modern Sociology*, Cambridge, Polity Press.

Grosz, E. (1987) 'Notes towards a Corporeal Feminism', *Australian Feminist Studies*, no. 5, Summer, pp. 1–16.

Hall, S. (1986) 'Popular Culture and the State' in J. Donald and S. Hall (eds) *Politics and Ideology*, Milton Keynes, Open University Press.

Hall, S. and Jefferson, T. (eds) (1976) *Resistance through Rituals: Youth Subcultures in Post-war Britain*, London, Hutchinson, in association with the Centre for Contemporary Cultural Studies.

Hamilton, A. (1984) 'Spoonfeeding the Lizards: Culture and Conflict in Central Australia', *Meanjin*, vol. 43, no. 3, pp. 363–78.

Hansen, M. (1987) 'Benjamin, Cinema and Experience: "The Blue Flower in the Land of Technology"', *New German Critique*, no. 40, Winter, pp. 179–224.

Heath, S. (1982) *The Sexual Fix*, London and Basingstoke, Macmillan Press.

Hegel, G. W. F. (1977) [1807] *Phenomenology of Spirit* (trans. A. V. Miller), Oxford, Clarendon Press.

Henriques, J., Hollway, W., Urwin, C., Venn, C. and Walkerdine, V. (eds) (1984) *Changing the Subject: Psychology, Social Regulation and Subjectivity*, London, Methuen.

Hiatt, L. R. (1975) 'Swallowing and Regurgitation in Australian Myth and Rite' in L. R. Hiatt (ed.), *Australian Aboriginal Mythology*, Canberra, Australian Institute of Aboriginal Studies.

Hobbes, T. (1962) [1651] *Leviathan*, London, Collier-Macmillan.

Hollway, W. (1984) 'Gender Difference and the Production of Subjectivity' in J. Henriques, W. Holloway, C. Urwin, C. Venn and V. Walkerdine (eds) *Changing the Subject*, London, Methuen.

ICA (1984) *Desire*, London, Institute of Contemporary Arts.

Irigaray, L. (1981) 'And the One Doesn't Stir Without the Other', *Signs*, vol. 7, no. 1, Autumn, pp. 56–67.

Irigaray, L. (1985a) *This Sex Which Is Not One* (trans. C. Porter with C. Burke), Ithaca, Cornell University Press. Essays quoted from this book:
'The Power of Discourse and the Subordination of the Feminine.'
'The "Mechanics" of Fluids.'
'This Sex Which is Not One.'
'Women on the Market.'
'Commodities among Themselves.'
'When Our Lips Speak Together.'

Irigaray, L. (1985b) *Speculum of the Other Woman* (trans. G. Gill), Ithaca, Cornell University Press.

Jacobus, M. (1986) *Reading Woman: Essays in Feminist Cricitism*, London, Methuen.

Jameson, F. (1981) *The Political Unconscious: Narrative as a Socially Symbolic Act*, Ithaca, Cornell University Press.

Jay, M. (1973) *The Dialectical Imagination: A History of the Frankfurt School and the Institute of Social Research 1923–1950*, London, Heinemann.

Kirby, V. (1989a) 'Re-writing: Postmodernism and Ethnography', *Mankind*, vol. 19, no. 1, April, pp. 36–45.

Kirby, V. (1989b) 'Corporeographies', *Inscriptions: Journal for the Critique of Colonial Discourse*, vol. 5, pp. 103–19.

Kofman, S. (1985) *The Enigma of Woman: Woman in Freud's Writings* (trans. C. Porter), Ithaca and London, Cornell University Press.

Kristeva, J. (1986) 'Women's Time' in T. Moi (ed.), *The Kristeva Reader*, New York, Columbia University Press.

Kristeva, J. (1987) 'The Pain of Sorrow in the Modern World: The Works of Marguerite Duras', *PMLA*, vol. 102, no. 2, March, pp. 138–52.

Krupnick, M. (1987) 'Introduction' in M. Krupnick (ed.), *Displacement: Derrida and After*, Bloomington, Indiana University Press.

Lacan, J. (1977) *Écrits: A Selection* (trans. A. Sheridan), London, Tavistock.

Lacan, J. (1979) *The Four Fundamental Concepts of Psychoanalysis* (trans. A. Sheridan), Harmondsworth, Penguin.

Lacan, J. (1982) 'The Meaning of the Phallus' in J. Mitchell and J. Rose (eds), *Feminine Sexuality*, London and Basingstoke, Macmillan Press.

Laplanche, J. (1985) *Life and Death in Psychoanalysis*, Baltimore, Johns Hopkins University Press.

Laplanche, J. and Pontalis, J. B. (1973) *The Language of Psychoanalysis*, London, Hogarth Press.

Lawson, H. (1985) *Reflexivity: The Post-Modern Predicament*, London, Hutchinson.

Levinas, E. (1979) [1961] *Totality and Infinity: An Essay on Exteriority* (trans. A. Lingis), The Hague, Martinus Nijhoff.

Levinas, E. (1987) [1947] *Time and the Other* (trans. R. A. Cohen), Pittsburgh, Duquesne University Press.

Lévi-Strauss, C. (1968) *Structural Anthropology* (trans. C. Jacobson and B. G. Schoepf), Harmondsworth, Penguin.

Lévi-Strauss, C. (1969) [1949] *The Elementary Structures of Kinship* (trans. J. Bell, J. von Sturmer and R. Needham), Boston, Beacon Press.

Lévi-Strauss, C. (1976) *Tristes Tropiques* (trans. J. and D. Weightman), Harmondsworth, Penguin.

Lévi-Strauss, C. (1985) 'Structuralism and Ecology' in *The View from Afar* (trans. J. Neugroschel and P. Hoss), Oxford, Basil Blackwell.

Lloyd, G. (1983) 'Masters, Slaves and Others', *Radical Philosophy*, no. 34, Summer, pp. 2–8.

Lloyd, G. (1984) *The Man of Reason: 'Male' and 'Female' in Western Philosophy*, London, Methuen.

Luke, A. and McHoul, A. (1989) 'Discourse as Language and Politics: An Introduction to the Philology of Political Culture in Australia', *Journal of Pragmatics*, vol. 13, pp. 323–32.

McGregor, C. (1984) 'Bondi Revisited' in Drew *et al. Bondi*, Surry Hills, James Frazer.

McRobbie, A. (1980) 'Settling Accounts with Subcultures: A Feminist Critique', *Screen Education*, no. 34, Spring, pp. 37–49.

McRobbie, A. (1982) 'The Politics of Feminist Research: Between Talk, Text and Action', *Feminist Review*, no. 12, October, pp. 46–57.

Malouf, D. (1983) *Fly Away Peter*, Ringwood, Victoria, Penguin.

Mannheim, K. (1960) [1936] *Ideology and Utopia*, London, Routledge and Kegan Paul.

Marcus, S. (1985) 'Freud and Dora: Story, History, Case History' in C. Bernheimer and C. Kahane (eds), *In Dora's Case: Freud-Hysteria-Feminism*, New York, Columbia University Press.

Marx, K. (1969) [1847] 'Wage Labour and Capital' in K. Marx and E. Engels, *Selected Works*, New York, International Publishers.

Melville, H. (1967) [1851] *Moby Dick*, New York, Norton.

Merleau-Ponty, M. (1962) *Phenomenology of Perception* (trans. C. Smith), London and Henley, Routledge and Kegan Paul.

Mitchell, J. and Rose, J. (eds) (1982) *Feminine Sexuality: Jacques Lacan and the École Freudienne*, London and Basingstoke, Macmillan Press.

Morris, M. (1988a) 'Things to Do with Shopping Centres' in S. Sheridan (ed.), *Grafts: Feminist Cultural Criticism*, London, Verso.

Morris, M. (1988b) 'At Henry Parkes Motel', *Cultural Studies*, vol. 2, no. 1, January, pp. 1–16, 29–47.

Nietzsche, F. (1982) *Untimely Meditations* (trans. R. J. Hollingdale), Cambridge University Press.

Oakley, A. (1981) 'Interviewing Women: A Contradiction in Terms' in H. Roberts (ed.), *Doing Feminist Research*, London, Routledge and Kegan Paul.

Oakes, G. (ed.) (1984) *Georg Simmel: On Women, Sexuality, and Love*, New Haven and London, Yale University Press.

Patton, P. (1989) 'Taylor and Foucault on Power and Freedom', *Political Studies*, vol. XXXVII, pp. 260–76.

Proust, M. (1966) [1922] *Swann's Way*, Part One, London, Chatto and Windus.

Ricoeur, P. (1989) 'Mimesis, Reference and Refiguration in *Time and Narrative*' in *Scripsi*, Ringwood (Victoria), Penguin, pp. 91–102.

Rorty, R. (1979) *Philosophy and the Mirror of Nature*, Princeton, Princeton University Press.

Rosso, I. (1973) 'The Unconscious in the Anthropology of Claude Lévi-Strauss', *American Anthropologist*, vol. 75, no. 1, Fall, pp. 20–48.

Rousseau, J.-J. (1979) [1782] *Reveries of the Solitary Walker* (trans. P. France), Harmondsworth, Penguin.

Runciman, W. G. (1983) *A Treatise on Social Theory*, Cambridge, Cambridge University Press.

Sanders, N. (1982) 'Bondi the Beautiful: The Impossibility of an Aesthetic', *Media Papers*, no. 16, Sydney, Humanities and Social Sciences, NSWIT.

Sartre, J.-P. (1969) [1943] *Being and Nothingness* (trans. H. E. Barnes), London, Methuen.

Saussure de, F. (1966) *Course in General Linguistics* (edited by C. Bally and A. Sechehaye), New York, McGraw-Hill.

Sheridan, S. (1988) 'Introduction' in S. Sheridan (ed.), *Grafts: Feminist Cultural Criticism*, London, Verso.

Silverman, K. (1983) *The Subject of Semiotics*, New York and Oxford, Oxford University Press.

Simmel, G. (1982) [1900] *The Philosophy of Money* (trans. T. Bottomore and D. Frisby), London, Routledge and Kegan Paul.

Simmel, G. (1984) [1923] 'The Relative and the Absolute in the Problem of the Sexes' in G. Oakes (ed.), *Georg Simmel: On Women, Sexuality, and Love*, New Haven and London, Yale University Press.

Sophocles (1974) *The Theban Plays* (trans. E. F. Watling) Harmondsworth, Penguin.

Spivak, G. C. (1987) 'Displacement and the Discourse of Woman' in M. Krupnick (ed.), *Displacement: Derrida and After*, Bloomington, Indiana University Press.

Spivak, G. C. (1988) *In Other Worlds*, New York and London, Routledge.

Stanley, L. and Wise, S. (1983) *Breaking Out: Feminist Consciousness and Feminist Research*, London, Routledge and Kegan Paul.

Stewart, M. (1984) 'Beachstruck on Bondi' in Drew *et al.*, *Bondi*, Surry Hills, James Frazer.

Strathern, M. (1987) 'Out of Context: The Persuasive Fictions of Anthropology', *Current Anthropology*, vol. 28, no. 3, June, pp. 251–81.

Taussig, M. (1988) 'The Nervous System. Part 1: Homesickness and Dada', unpublished paper, New York, Dept of Performance Studies, NYU.

von Sturmer, J. (1987) 'Claude Lévi-Strauss' in D. J. Austin-Broos (ed.), *Creating Culture: Profiles in the Study of Culture*, Sydney, Allen & Unwin.

von Sturmer, J. (1989) 'Aborigines, Representation, Necrophilia', *Art and Text*, no. 32, Autumn, pp. 127–39.

Weber, M. (1974) 'Bureaucracy' in H. H. Gerth and C. W. Mills (eds), *From Max Weber: Essays in Sociology*, London, Routledge and Kegan Paul.

Weber, S. (1987) *Institution and Interpretation*, Minneapolis, University of Minnesota Press.

Weedon, C. (1987) *Feminist Practice and Poststructuralist Theory*, Oxford, Basil Blackwell.

White, H. (1978) *Tropics of Discourse: Essays in Cultural Criticism*, Baltimore, Johns Hopkins University Press.

White, H. (1979) 'Michel Foucault' in J. Sturrock (ed.), *Structuralism and Since: From Lévi-Strauss to Derrida*, Oxford, Oxford University Press.

White, R. (1981) *Inventing Australia*, Sydney, Allen & Unwin.

Wohlfarth, I. (1986) 'Et Cetera? The Historian as Chiffonnier', *New German Critique*, no. 39, Fall, pp. 143–68.

Wolin, R. (1982) *Walter Benjamin: An Aesthetic of Redemption*, New York, Columbia University Press.

Woolf, V. (1977) [1931] *The Waves*, London, Grafton.

INDEX

'Little Hans', 118
Lloyd, G., 78–9
Luke, A., 28

Marcus, S. 58–9
Marx, K., 21, 47, 61–4, 74
Marxism, 5, 12, 21–24 *passim*, 34, 42
masculine, 9, 14, 39, 46, 62–3, 74, 78–9, 121–30 *passim*
    see also hierarchisation: sexual
masquerade, 53, 123
master-slave, 8, 42, 45, 65–79 *passim*, 81, 115–29 *passim*, 131–7 *passim*, 176, 189
mastery, 7, 8–9, 14, 31, 66, 72, 75, 80, 83, 130–1, 185, 191
McHoul, A., 28
mechanical reproduction, techniques of, 110–11, 146, 165
mediation
    feminine as, 62–3, 79, 85, 119–21, 131–4
    and immediacy, 30, 31, 64, 69, 71, 85, 91, 109, 115, 134, 136, 139, 144–5, 146–7, 156, 159
    in knowledge, 66–73 *passim*, 85
    photographic, 138, 140–1, 145, 146–7
    in research, 30–2, 127
memory, 91–2, 96–8, 103–11
    preservation of, 97–8, 104
    voluntary and involuntary, 92, 106–11, 137–9, 141–2, 145–7, 152, 153–4, 165, 167, 179, 182, 191
memory trace, 92, 94, 98, 104–6, 109, 147, 188
Merleau-Ponty, M., 110
metonymy, 56, 86, 88, 90–1, 142, 149, 179
mirror, 9, 20–1, 23, 27, 42, 57, 61–4 *passim*, 68–72 *passim*, 74, 75, 86–7, 89, 119, 121, 129, 131, 134
    see also double, the
mirror phase, 56–7, 75, 87, 129, 131, 135, 137
Mitchell, J., 49, 52, 55
Moby Dick, 175–6
modernity, 23, 25, 64, 110–11, 139, 150, 151, 154
Morris, M., 29, 162, 166, 177
multiplicity, 46–7, 52, 57, 59, 66, 80, 82–4, 86, 89, 91–6, 108–11, 116, 128, 137–8, 146, 149, 150, 165, 185, 187, 190–1
museum, 153, 157–66 *passim*, 169

nation, 156, 166–9, 181–2, 184
nature–culture opposition, 33–4, 63, 150–3, 169–80, 184–5
Nietzsche, F., 26, 164–5
normalisation, 41–4 *passim*

nostalgia, 25, 129–31, 136, 138, 146, 148, 151, 154, 165–6, 167, 183

Oakley, A., 30
Oedipus, 50–7, 82–3, 176
order, 13, 17, 47, 48, 52, 55, 61–2, 64, 74, 77, 84, 89, 92–3, 149, 184, 187
original and copy, 22, 51, 88, 98, 129, 184
originary, *see* origins
origins, 24, 25, 51, 55, 56, 67, 75, 81, 98, 102–3, 109, 129–31, 136, 143, 148, 156, 159, 160, 169, 171, 179, 181, 183, 190
    stories of, 47, 51, 162, 175–9, 184, 190
overdetermination, 104

particularity, 40, 45, 46–8 *passim*, 57, 140, 142, 149, 151, 190
past, 94, 96–8, 101, 104, 107–8, 137, 141, 143, 146, 154, 156, 159, 163–6
Patton, P., 45
perception, 91, 96–7, 105–6
phallologocentric
    definition of, 14
    see also hierarchisation: sexual
place, 148, 152, 167, 169, 177, 179–81, 183–4
pleasure, 18–19, 46, 50, 73, 78, 80, 83, 86, 89, 100, 138–9, 142, 151–2, 164, 181, 184–5, 191
    see also jouissance
politics, 36, 43–5
    feminist, 77, 186–7
    of theorising and research, 24, 30–2, 35–6, 43–5, 186–7
Pontalis, J., 48, 105
power
    counter, 47, 65, 89
    and desire in work of French feminists, 79–89 *passim*
    and desire in work of Hegel, 8–10, 66–73 *passim*
    and knowledge, 13, 34–5
    and knowledge in work of Foucault, 9, 35, 40–7 *passim*, 89
    and knowledge in work of Hegel, 8–10, 66–73 *passim*, 100–102, 129
    sociological conceptions of, 21, 34–5
presence, 13–16 *passim*, 26, 49, 53, 63–4, 72–3, 80, 84–5, 91–8 *passim*, 100–1, 104–5, 108, 139, 144, 147, 156, 159, 175, 177, 189
presence–absence opposition, 49, 52, 55, 75–6, 84–5, 87, 141, 144
present, 94, 96–8, 100, 104, 108, 141
primal father, *see* primal feast
primal feast, 50–1, 62, 125–6